2001

3 0301 00209828 9

Issues in Business Ethics

VOLUME 9

The titles published in this series are listed at the end of this volume.

WORKING ACROSS CULTURES

Working Across Cultures

Ethical Perspectives for Intercultural Management

edited by

HEIKO LANGE

Deutsche Lufthansa AG,
Frankfurt, Germany

ALBERT LÖHR

University of Erlangen-Nürnberg,
Germany

and

HORST STEINMANN

University of Erlangen-Nürnberg,
Germany

KLUWER ACADEMIC PUBLISHERS

DORDRECHT / BOSTON / LONDON

A C.I.P. Catalogue record for this book is available from the Library of Congress.

ISBN 0-7923-4700-5

Published by Kluwer Academic Publishers,
P.O. Box 17, 3300 AA Dordrecht, The Netherlands.

Sold and distributed in the U.S.A. and Canada
by Kluwer Academic Publishers,
101 Philip Drive, Norwell, MA 02061, U.S.A.

In all other countries, sold and distributed
by Kluwer Academic Publishers,
P.O. Box 322, 3300 AH Dordrecht, The Netherlands.

Printed on acid-free paper

Printed in the Netherlands

Contents

Acknowledgements

This volume provides a selection of plenary speeches and workshop papers presented at the 9th Annual Conference of the European Business Ethics Network (EBEN), which took place from 18-20 September 1996 at the Lufthansa Training Center in Seeheim, Germany. Roughly 200 people from 30 countries came together at this place in the heart of Europe for a stimulating, actually multi-cultural discussion on the conference theme: *"Working Across Cultures. Ethical Perspectives for Dilemmas of Diversity"*.

Right from the beginning the EBEN 1996 conference project has been developed as a joint venture between two hosting organizations, Deutsches Netzwerk Wirtschaftsethik (DNWE), the national network of EBEN in Germany, and a distinguished partner from the international business world, Deutsche Lufthansa AG. What started just as an attempt to organize an EBEN conference in the spirit of the primary goal of the association, namely to further the dialogue betweeen the academic perspective and the business view on business ethics, turned out as a remarkable success for the international buiness ethics movement. The co-hosting concept proved an enormous catalytical function for the communication between participants from theory and practice.

Now, at the end of this project, we would like to express our gratitude to all people who contributed to the conference and this publication of topical papers. Above all, we want to give a warm thank you to all the authors who have been spending their time and energy to share their knowledge and ideas with us. Notably, many of them had to prepare a paper in a language which is not their mother tongue, making it even more significant that they contributed dependably in time. Thank you so much, again, for your dedicated cooperation.

Regarding the conference, the organizers are obliged to so many helping hands, intellectual and financial support, and spontaneous cooperation, that it is actually impossible to provide comprehensive words of thanks. Regardless of position and name, we would like to cordially thank everybody who was involved for doing a great job on the organization, and for supporting the event in so many effective ways. We can only hope that nobody is feeling treated inadequate when we are mentioning only some people in particular here.

In this sense, it is our pleasure to address some hearty thanks to the colleagues on the Programme Committee, who brought in excellent ideas and prominent speakers, and who were so extremely effective in acquiring and reviewing papers: Sheena Carmichael (London), Fabio Corno (Milano), Arild Lillebo (Oslo), Thomas Sattelberger (Frankfurt/Main), Fred Seidel (Lyon), and Jacek Sojka (Poznan). Although not being formal members of the Committee, two heads of associations which stay in a very friendly relation with EBEN, deserve our special appreciation for the acquisition of contributions: Peter Eigen, Chairman of Transparency International, who was extremely supportive in the organization of the focus on international corruption; and Tom Dunfee from The Wharton School, who kindly organized a track of workshop presentations as a special sponsoring of the EBEN 1996 conference by the Society for Business Ethics.

With respect to the hard work of the conference organization, which kept some people busy for almost one and a half years, we are particularly indebted to Siegfried Blasche (Philosophische Gesellschaft Bad Homburg) and his secretary, Uta Reiling, who did so much dedicated work especially on the operative level. Further, we owe our gratitudes to many members of the Lufthansa staff who were engaged in the conference organization, above all Stefan Wendlandt and Hans-Jörg Fitger, and the excellent crew of the Lufthansa Training Center in Seeheim under the direction of Axel Goerges, who proved to be an ideal host for a multi-cultural event.

As for the preparartion of this publication, another couple of people deserve our additional thanks for the much too often nerving work of type-writing (Erika Gruß), translating (Susan Pope), and computing (Thomas Olbrich). Also, some friendly specialists of reading the proofs and manuscripts are kindly asked to accept a warm thank you for their helpful comments, among them especially Bill McKinley (University of Wisconsin).

As representatives of the host institutions of the EBEN 1996 Conference we are very pleased to present this volume the audience.

Frankfurt/Main & Nürnberg, July 1997 Heiko Lange
Albert Löhr
Horst Steinmann

PART I

Introduction and General Overview

Welcome Address

Jürgen Weber

Reading my newspaper the other day, I came across a provocative thought by a professor on the subject of globalisation. He wrote: "Globalisation and the decline of ancient Rome have one thing in common – both were unavoidable."

Ominous as his statement may sound, the historian is probably right: The decline of Rome gave way to a new world order. And many of us feel that the "opening up of the world" which we have witnessed in the wake of the liberalisation of world trade, the collapse of communism, the creation of the World Trade Organisation, and the harmonisation of life styles and the change of values that comes along with it is also creating a different world order.

At the same time it is raising a host of questions which you intend to tackle at this conference. One might ask for instance:
- Will the different sets of values lead to clashes or will they create a new "Weltgeist" – a culture of tolerance and greater humanity?
- What effects will cross cultural co-operation have on the attitudes of the people involved?

Lufthansa has followed a policy of creating global strategic alliances. And we have been very successful at this. It is our answer to the challenges of liberalisation and globalisation in the airline industry. Alliances weld together many different ethnic and company cultures and people, – in our case Americans, Thais, South Africans, Latinos and Europeans.

What will be the common denominator of all our doing, what attitudes can take us into danger zones? I am glad to say that we have developed - more by intuition than by resolution – a principle which has been recognised since by many economists as the essential basis of any good alliance: The principle of mutual benefit, commitment and trust and the resilience to resist every attempt to dominate.

H. Lange et al., Working Across Cultures, 3–5.
© 1998 *Kluwer Academic Publishers. Printed in the Netherlands.*

I can only agree with the findings of a Harvard professor, who stated after having investigated the secret of good alliances: "The relations amongst partners, their cultural, organisational and human dimensions are much more demanding than the pure commercial aspect of an alliance."

Another thought on the subject of globalisation: The prominent features of the enhanced world economy certainly are mobility, open markets and – above all – competition. In competitive situations, however, ethics are always put to the test. To be or not to be becomes a question which easily blurs the borderline between fair and unfair practices and could corrupt morals and mind. That is the great danger I see in our times of fundamental change.

Balance is what we need. We at Lufthansa have recently mounted a new communications campaign called *"Balance"* to reflect on what we are doing, and weigh up what we are saying.
– Are we really doing all that we can? or
– Are we truly communicating all that we are doing? For ethics and communications are closely connected, we believe.

A second step was a workshop for senior management entitled "Ethics and leadership in difficult times". The response was enthusiatic. And we are considering whether to make such a seminar a regular feature in our management development calendar of events. This pilot project probably will be the seed of a promising plant to flourish in day-to-day company life.

Ethics become the pivot on which the beam of a balance rests. If one of the scales is becoming too weighty you have to adjust either by putting a counterbalance on the other pan or you extend one arm of the beam to achieve more leverage.

And that is my wish for your conference – that you may define the exact leverage required to ensure a balance of humanity, finding solutions to some – if not all – of the dilemmas which you have defined. Lufthansa is happy to be associated with the European Business Ethics Network, and we are hoping that this event will be the first salvo in what we trust will become a series of similar discussions in this country. Dr. Lange, our Chief Executive Personnel, will certainly aim for that in his capacity as the chairman of the curatorium of the German network.

I am confident that you will be inspired by our Seeheim location. I am almost tempted to say: Like globalisation, that is unavoidable. Many a conference has found the atmosphere at our training center to be stimulating and prolific. And I trust, so will you.

The Ethical Dimension of Cross-cultural Business Activities

Albert Löhr & Horst Steinmann

1. The Ethical Challenge of Cross-cultural Business

Globally active businesses are becoming increasingly aware of the ethical dimension of their activities in different cultures. In a world where cultures are still characterised by very different norms and values, while business relations are moving closer and closer together, the problem of a reasonable way to deal with cultural differences is not simply academic, but reveals itself as a practical challenge.

What does this challenge mean exactly? It is clear that, above all, we have to address the question about rules of conduct for cross-national business relations with respect to the historical *diversity* of cultural norms and values. How can we cope with the fact that very different moral norms and values meet in international competition? Should one agree to the old saying: "When in Rome, do as the Romans do?" Or should one stick to certain company principles in every case, freely modified: "When at McDonald's, do as McDonald's does"?

This fundamental conflict between *adapting to local conditions* or *following a unified policy* is known to be constitutive for every problem of international management and has been dealt with in theory and practice as a classical problem (Fayerweather 1969; Prahalad/Doz 1987). However, while this classic debate has been focusing almost exclusively on corporate strategy, the explicitly *ethical* dimension of dealing with the tension of "local-central" orientation has become more important in the recent past (Kumar 1991). In our context, this conflict between local adaptation and global unifying can be interpreted in the light of a classical philosophical tension in arguments, namely between ethical "*relativism*" and "*universalism*" (for a detailed discussion, see also Steinmann/Scherer 1997). Therefore, the debate on international business ethics has to tackle this fundamental conflict,

7

H. Lange et al., Working Across Cultures, 7–19.
© *1998 Kluwer Academic Publishers. Printed in the Netherlands.*

and has to develop reasonable solutions for theoretical and practical orientation. With respect to the importance and difficulties of this challenge, one must not wonder that recent publications on international business ethics are often seen as milestones of the business ethics movement (Th. Donaldson 1989, DeGeorge 1993).

As for the foundation of business ethics, it is all a question of an interculturally binding reasoning of moral norms. Those who proceed on the assumption that a foundation is possible will naturally propose certain global standards, and will want to ensure adherence to these standards through a set of measures. In this sense, one can particularly inquire about the chances of reason in a plurality of cultures (besides the work of Gethmann on this problem, we would like to suggest reading the philosophical groundwork of Kambartel 1989), and one can discuss institutional means to promote the idea of reason. On the other hand, those who dispute the reasoning of moral norms – and this is a position that is highly acclaimed in the so-called enlightened plurality of opinions today – will consistently take all local features for granted and will claim that one simply must adapt to these local conditions. But, with what or against what should one side if no standard at all can be reasonably distinguished?

Given this dilemma, the discussion of certain business ethics issues apparently becomes a question of belief. For example, *corruption* and *corruptibility* are seen as quite acceptable by certain circles, who argue that these practices belong to the culture of certain regions which one must adapt to in order to survive in international competition (e.g. Lay 1995). The opposing position – represented in this volume by prominent authors – assumes that corruption is basically an unacceptable distortion of the (moral) principles of open market competition and must therefore be combatted by effective means. Moreover, corruption is not at all an integral cultural element of less developed countries, but a problem that was brought into these countries by international business practices (see Ginwala in this volume).

Also, with the current *transformation processes* of corporations and economies, there is a controversy about the reasonable way of dealing with the normative foundations of business. Let us take as an example the process of the European integration, whose fundamental cultural dimension can be seen in many company mergers. On the one hand, represented by economic hard-liners and purists, there is the assumption that socio-cultural integration will automatically take place as the result of economic integration („*culture follows economy*"). On the other hand, some claim that peaceful business in a common market is only possible on the basis of comprehensive social integration, because we first of all have to learn about the diversity of historically grown cultural norms and values („*economy follows culture*"). We must, therefore, invest a lot of energy in mental change processes in order to create the cultural preconditions for successful business activities (see Lange in this volume). Of course, such considerations on changing deeply rooted cultural orientations carry enormous ethical implications: which norms, which values can and should be changed, or undergo a transformation, in the name of global competition?

With regard to such different opinions about business ethics, the crucial question posed here is: which view should one adopt if one is looking for ethically justified perspectives for business in multicultural environments? Those who seriously pose this question – having realised that corruption, for example, has a *moral dimension* which goes far beyond the traditional *strategy perspective* which aims at economic optimisation only – cannot be satisfied with the usual answer that one should just adapt one's convictions to the particular situation in global competition, and that one should act according to those standards which prove to be advantageous. Given that the question about reasonable norms and values is seriously asking for *morally acceptable* behaviour, we would need, instead, an idea of reasoning that is strictly independent of economic calculation, and that leads to convincing results which *oblige* to act accordingly. This is, however, only possible by committing oneself in those situations as well where deviating from the morally correct norm would bring predictable advantages, or meeting the norm seems to be disadvantageous. Otherwise, values and norms would be sacrificed without hesitation on the altar of utility, or, to put it another way, would be subject to the constraints of economic rationality.

Claiming for an ethical commitment to certain moral standards cannot and should not lead to the idea of business ethics as a cause of making loss. On the contrary, an integral part of the challenge of ethically responsible international management actually is to make a profit. What is required is simply that cultural norms and values should not be *instrumentalised* for the sake of making profits, and that certain principles are to be adhered to when doing business *for their own sake*. When in the end adhering to what is morally acceptable is also economically profitable, then we can speak eventually of success-ful management. Viewed in this way, business ethics should certainly be part of economic performance. However, a serious concept of busi-ness ethics demands that reasonable ethical norms and values are to be adhered to even when it seems economically disadvantageous to do so.

2. Ethical Perspectives for Cross-cultural Business

Nevertheless, although accepting the *necessity* of business ethics, managers will also ask about the *possibility* of business ethics, since they are practically facing the problem of dealing responsibly with cultural standards in an ever expanding global competition. We can, of course, only offer a few fundamental considerations on this issue. These considerations should promote the idea that a proper under-standing of working across cultures should avoid the traditional perspective of *imperial implementation* of certain cultures, but should instead lead to the concept of a *multicultural co-operation* of different norms and values.

In order to follow this suggestion one must refer to the difference between the *culture-free* and the *culture-bound* understanding of eco-nomic processes (Oberg 1963). Until now the process of internation-alisation has often been understood as a simple enabling of a border-less stream of goods and money which has an economic logic inde-pendent of all socio-cultural differences. Following this notion, global business activities create a *culture-free* economic maelstrom, where only those normative standards can survive, if any, that prove them-selves to be economically advantageous. All other norms and values would be eroded in the process of globalisation, since they cannot stay robust in permanent competition.

At least empirical experience suggests, however, a persistently *culture-bound quality of economic processes*. We would even go one step further and claim that the "social embeddedness of economic action" (Granovetter 1985) is of a *systematic* nature. In particular, there is an unavoidable interaction between the historically developed and deeply rooted norms and values of a culture, and the specific "way of working" of its economic institutions. This cultural embeddedness

of economic action is also a central precondition for the specific competition in a market economy, and it determines to a great extent
society's moral acceptance of the entire system of competition.

As long as there are these persistent differences in the cultural
foundations of competition, the idea of competition itself is not homo-
geneous in all market economies, but develops as specific "*cultures of
competition*". But, in view of this colourful diversity of cultural
embeddedness of economic action, how will international competition
be affected? Does it mean a threat or rather a chance? To put it another
way: can comparative advantages be linked to the specific characteristics of a culture, or will these special cultural features be smoothed out
in the course of time?

The current debate in Germany is dominated by the perspective of
a threat to the national economic culture, summarized in the arguments about the *"Standort Deutschland"* ("Germany as a location for
business"; for an overview see a study of the Prognos Consult GmbH
1996). There is concern, certainly not unfounded, that the societal consensus about the expediency of economic competition could break
down if the specific culture of the "social market economy", and all its
social achievements, is questioned on the stage of international competition. The fear is, that the different cultural standards could lead to
an international „race to the bottom", down to a conformity to the
more „cost-effective" norms and values of other cultures. All those
who are too inflexible to adapt to these cost-effective standards would
be wiped out in competition.

Germany is not alone in Europe in harbouring these fears. Worries
about social decline and loss of cultural identity are present everywhere. When one looks at the endless list of ethical problems that
occur in this context, one tends to share this pessimistic view and
resign: where can exporting jobs to other countries, avoidance of environmental standards, flight of capital, and rationalisation of human
relations, lead to, apart from an erosion of the supposed high moral
standards in the European economy? Is global competition in the end
only another expression for the tendency to break national models of
consensus concerning questions of value? How to prevent a situation
where the *"decreasing marginal morality"* (absinkende Grenzmoral)
in society, as Götz Briefs (1957) once put it, will always lead to a

competitive advantage? Which transnational institutions could assure certain ethical minimum standards in this tumultuous global market?

Those who ask and argue in this way will certainly tend to interpret the ethical debate on "working across cultures" as a *story of losses*. At best, they will refer to the fact that cultural norms and values are very deeply rooted. Consequently defending strategies have been developed against the economic pressure for cultural change. In this sense, some recent voices have predicted a return to the idea of protectionism, due to the apparently insurmountable difficulties of international integration. They come to the conclusion that national or regional standards will lead to culturally motivated fields of conflict in the future, and possibly battles over cultural integrity will arise, which may even lead to a new kind of wars (Huntington 1996).

Given these fears, there is an urgent need for developing positive perspectives for working across cultures and coping with the ethical consequences. In this sense we would like to propose the key idea of *culture-bound economic systems*, with a particular spectrum of performance in each case. The norms and values of a culture – especially the moral ones – must be taken into consideration in order to develop competitive economic institutions, and they must play a key role in the decisions of corporations because they are a unique resource that is strategically valuable for world-wide competition. Only this reference to the normative embeddedness of economic action will help to further the development of a specific and globally competitive "economic culture". Every region, every country, every economic system must, therefore, try to develop a concept of competition that corresponds to its culture, i.e. the normative fundament of the society, in order to create a unique "fit" between culture and economy.

Of course, these culturally bound economic systems must also experience a certain degree of change in order to adapt to changing historical conditions. However, they should be able to start this change then from their own cultural foundation, based on their own experience and learning, instead of being forced to approximate a certain uniform culture which is defined by some global „value leaders". There is, therefore, no set solution, e.g. the American or Japanese way of doing business, just as there is no simple implementation of success models. At the most there are models which are similar, as for instance in Western European countries.

This idea of culture-bound economies corresponds in principle to the debate on strong corporate cultures, which argues that strong cultures could be an important resource if one develops an appropriate strategic position for them (Deal/Kennedy 1982). If there were not the potential for every regional or national culture to develop competitive advantage based on its own unique culture, it would be pointless to seek a normative consensus about competition within each society. One must consider here that cultural identity and ethical standards are in fact threatened in the so-called developed countries of the Western world, or at least are experiencing dramatic changes. But, the problem of the cultural embeddedness of economic action is also relevant for those who have been the so-called less developed countries until now. They are facing dramatic challenges of traditional norms and values as well, and above all they have to develop a competitive profile in order to become attractive as a partner for the global market (Porter 1990). From their perspective, the possibility of developing competitive institutions based on their very own cultural standards must be understood as an argument to participate in the adventure of open international business relations without categorical submission under global standards. Since less developed nations cannot overtake established competitive cultures on their highly developed paths, each nation must find its own way.

The theory that the concept of market economy is open for diverse combinations of cultural values must be put forward against the idea of a standard competition model, since the latter increases the risk of eroding social and moral standards. In principle, and this is the central point we want to emphasize here, this would mean that there is also room for the development of *ethical models* of socio-cultural identity, which form a competitive basis for business in the global arena. The efforts of business ethics must be aimed at developing such models and their practical perspectives, especially with respect to the arrangement of institutions to protect ethically sound models from moral hazards.[1] For this purpose, the collection of papers in this book has a catalyst function for understanding different perspectives of

---

[1]   The recent experiences with the U.S. Sentencing Commission Guidelines could be very helpful to develop comparable ideas for institutional support of business ethics initiatives. Cf. U.S. Sentencing Commission (1996), Steinmann/Olbrich (1995), Wieland (1993).

business ethics, but not the role of offering ready-made solutions for this problem.

3. The Collection of Articles in This Book

The papers in this volume offer a representative overview of the plenary lectures and workshop discussions which took place at the 9th annual conference of the European Business Ethics Network (EBEN). The conference theme, *"Working Across Cultures. Ethical Solutions for Dilemmas of Diversity"*, generated lively discussions among the participants in both the plenary sessions and the workshop part of the conference. Unfortunately, the stimulating atmosphere of the conference cannot be revealed just by the documentation of some written papers. Thus, to get the reader involved like the conference participants themselves have been, we would like to invite all of you who think that this collection opens new perspectives on busines ethics, to become an active member of EBEN, and to attend future conferences of the network.

As for this documentation, it should be mentioned that the style of papers varies according to the different presentation purposes.[2] Since one of the primary goals of EBEN is to provide a forum for the debate among academics and business people, readers will find both types of contributions: traditional academic papers as well as speeches, conceptual thinking, and statements from managers who are engaged in business ethics. Of course one should be aware of the fact that there are pragmatists on the one side, and reprensentatives from the ivory tower on the other side, who usually say that it is impossible to bridge the gap between theory and business. But, we think, and would actually like to insist, that the collection of papers presented here, like the experience of the EBEN 1996 conference, is an excellent proof for the success of our common endeavour called business ethics. We think it definitely makes sense to work across the academic, business, and political culture to discuss perspectives for the challenging fields of business ethics. However, it should also be clear that the reflections presented here are, in general, not yet representing a status of final

---

[2]   Also with regard to the formal aspect, we only made some slight adjustments on the different styles of quotation.

answers to the many questions. Business ethics is still an emerging field which is taking shape gradually.

According to the conference arrangement, the following collection of articles is divided into four systematic groups: the opening discussion which embraces all core issues, the two focuses of international corruption and the process of corporate transformation, and finally a selection of trans-cultural problems of business ethics. We will limit ourselves in the following to just a few remarks on the papers in order to emphasise their central points.

In view of current events at Shell (the sinking of the oil platform Brent Spar, environmental problems in oil extraction in Nigeria, and the killing of Ken-Saro Wiwa in Nigeria), the *opening speech* by *Peter Duncan,* CEO of Shell Germany, was of particular importance for the general understanding of the conference theme. This was clearly demonstrated by the lively discussion at the end of his presentation. In his contribution, Peter Duncan portrays the situation of Shell as a dilemma the company has faced again and again when it has been involved in conflicts with its stakeholders. The difficult challenge of handling all the competing claims in such dilemmas with ethical responsibility, while also not forgetting the economic purpose of a multinational corporation, was a central theme in Peter Duncan's speech. Although some self-critical comments are mentioned in passing, e.g. the way Shell conducted dialogue with the public, Peter Duncan insisted that the economic task of the multinational corporation must be at the centre of all considerations, mainly because a significant contribution is made by Shell to the prosperity of every nation in which the company is active.

During the lively discussion of Peter Duncan's speech, which also included some remarkable comments of *Jürgen Weber* on the situation of the Deutsche Lufthansa AG as a multinational corporation, various aspects of Shell's dilemma were discussed in more detail. Given the background of the public dispute about the Shell case, numerous critical comments came up from the floor. The transcript of this discussion has been extended here with a comprehensive statement by *Nicola Pless* and *Thomas Maak* from the University of St. Gallen.

The first thematic focus of the conference was *international corruption. Peter Eigen,* Chairman of Transparency International, a non-governmental organization which is fighting against corruption world-wide, will introduce this problem more substantially so that only a few remarks should be made from our side in order to give a basic orientation about the contributions. The significant speech by the Speaker of the South African Parliament, *Hon. Dr. Frene Ginwala,* leads above all to the understanding that international corruption is not a phenomenon that can be blamed on certain countries – just as the blame for corrupt practices is often placed on the developing countries from the point of view of the industrial nations. She stated that corruption is not at all a genuine phenomenon of certain cultures which forces industrial companies to bribe in order to run a business. Corruption is rather furthered by the behaviour of international companies themselves and the features of certain national laws (like the fact that international bribe money is tax-deductible) in developed countries. Ultimately, what she demanded is that the national states develop and establish a standard procedure for fighting international corruption.

The contributions of *Ugo Draetta* and *Mark Pieth* presented the efforts that have already been made in this area. Both are members of various important international committees on fighting corruption. Draetta provided a report of the current situation of the efforts which have been made so far within the framework of the European Union. Pieth enlarged the perspective to include the position of the OECD and the efforts of the G-7 States. Both contributions included suggestions and consequences for future action, in particular concerning the question of translating supranational suggestions into national laws.

The considerations of *Klaus M. Leisinger* offer an important complement to these contributions. He deals with the problem of international corruption from the perspective of the multinational corporation, and, therefore, points out the problem of management that must deal with the tension of economic imperatives and the demands of business ethics. The final contribution from *Karl Theodor Paschke,* the most senior German executive at the UN, concerns the question of what difficulties arise when fighting corruption within the United Nations as a genuine multicultural and world-wide organisation. His observations also provide a report of the experiences of establishing an internal control system at the UN.

The second large thematic focus was the importance of values and ethical considerations during processes of *corporate transformation.*

Both contributions from Lange and Dahlberg deal with this problem from the point of view of business management, while the other two papers summarise empirical research results on the social effects of transforming values within the framework of management.

In his contribution, *Heiko Lange* refers to the long and difficult processes of mental change at Lufthansa, a former state-owned company which had to be developed for international competition in a multi-cultural environment. *Bjoern Dahlberg's* paper provides particular insight into the Scandinavian culture of conflict resolution, as exemplified in the process of merging two companies where very different values met. Also, the relations with the business environment are discussed. *Gerrit Popkes and Kati Rieger* deal with a question that is usually of special interest for an international audience, i.e. the effects of the transformation process in East Germany. Their interviews with managers in the New German Länder provide interesting glimpses into the functionality and stability of values in the context of the new demands of a market economy. Finally, *Thomas Kieselbach* deals with the problem of company transformation from the empirical perspective on psychological justice, and asks what contribution management can make toward coping with the feelings of injustice experienced by employees who are told to be redundant.

In the final section on *"Reflections on cross-cultural issues in Business Ethics"*, papers have been gathered from various academic disciplines. The first contribution of this section is from *Carl Friedrich Gethmann*, who provides his philosophical considerations on the question of universalism versus relativism. He develops the idea that our social environment, the so-called life-world *("Lebenswelt")*, must be understood as the basis for the development of intercultural ethics.

For the two following two contributions from the ESC Lyon and the University of Georgia, the intercultural perspective is prominent. *Fred Seidel, Hans-Joerg Schlierer, and Ian Tovey* provide a report on the different cultural contexts of the discussion on business ethics in France, Great Britain, and Germany. The differences between the three countries, as seen by the authors, are developed and expressed in terms of central realisations. Following this explanation of differences, the contribution of *Warren French and Bernd Mühlfriedel* then deals with the question how discoursive processes should be designed in intercultural relations in order to overcome or neutralise national prejudices.

Their suggestion consists of teaching a guided approach to negotiations between two cultures in order to improve business relations.

Peter Koslowski in his reflection on the concept of the so-called "historical school" of economics then shows very precisely that the necessity of linking economic theory with the cultural bases of national economies was already evident in former (German) economic theories. His conclusion is that economic processes cannot be explained neutrally with the analytical tools of modern economic theories. Apparently this argument fits very well into our thesis about the relevance of cultural norms and values as pre-conditions for the particular functioning of national or regional economies. The basic idea of an embeddedness of economic processes in cultural contexts is also dealt with in the contribution from *Luk Bouckaert,* who demonstrates with the issue of interest that also economic core elements have different meanings in different cultures.

The final contribution to this volume is from *Eduardo Brioschi,* who discusses the chances for successful self-regulation of advertising in Europe. On the basis of central principles such as those developed by the international Chamber of Commerce, the author examines which of these principles have been taken into account in national rules on regulating advertising, and how these have been implemented in the concrete fields of advertising.

References

Briefs, G. (1957): Grenzmoral in der pluralistischen Gesellschaft, in: von Beckerath, E. / Meyer, F. / Müller-Armack, A. (Hrsg.): *Wirtschaftsfragen der freien Welt.* Zum 60. Geburtstag von Bundeswirtschaftsminister Ludwig Erhard, Frankfurt/M. 1957, S. 97-108.

Deal, T.B. / Kennedy, A.A. (1982): *Corporate Cultures. The rites and rituals of corporate life,* Reading/Mass. 1982.

DeGeorge, R. (1993): *Competing With Integrity in International Business,* New York 1993.

Donaldson, Th. (1989): *The Ethics of International Business,* New York 1989.

Fayerweather, J. (1969): *International Business Management: A Conceptual Framework,* New York 1969.

Granovetter, M. (1985): Economic Action and Social Structure: The Problem of Embeddedness, in: *American Journal of Sociology*, 91, pp. 481-510.

Huntington, S.P.: *The Clash of Civilizations and the Remaking of World Order*, New York 1996.

Kambartel, F. (1989): *Philosophie der humanen Welt*, Frankfurt/M. 1989.

Lay, R. (1995): Einem Stern folgen, in: Das Sonntagsblatt vom 17. Feb. 1995, S. 18.

Oberg, W. (1963): Cross-cultural Perspectives on Management Principles, in: *Academy of Management Journal*, 6, pp. 141-152.

Porter, M.E. (1990): *The Competitive Advantage of Nations*, New York 1990.

Prahalad, C. / Doz, Y. (1987): *The Multinational Mission. Balancing local demands and global vision*, New York 1987.

Prognos Consult GmbH (Hrsg.): *Standort Deutschland. Eine Studie zum 50. Geburtstag des Handelsblatts*, Düsseldorf 1996.

Steinmann, H. / Olbrich, Th. (1995): Business Ethics in U.S.-Corporations, in: *Journal für Betriebswirtschaft*, 45, S. 317-334.

Steinmann, H. / Scherer, A. (1997): Intercultural Management Between Universalism and Relativism. Fundamental problems in international business ethics and the contribution of recent German philosophical approaches, in: Urban, S. (ed.): *Europe in the Global Competition*, Wiesbaden 1997, pp. 77-143.

United States Sentencing Commission (ed.) (1996): *Corporate Crime in America: Strengthening the "Good Citizen" Corporation*, Washington D.C. 1996.

Wieland, J.(1993): *Formen der Institutionalisierung von Moral in amerikanischen Unternehmungen*, Bern/Stuttgart 1993.

Doing Business in Different Cultures. Ethical Challenges of a Multinational Corporation

Peter Duncan

1. Introduction

Let me at the outset explicitly recognize the reason I am here in two words: "Brent Spar" and "Nigeria". Let me also recognize that in both cases Shell was faced with dilemmas and challenges for which it was, at least at the outset, culturally ill-equipped. I claim that in both cases our conduct was and is grounded in an attempt to strike a respectable balance between many conflicting imperatives. Certainly mistakes were made – particularly in our communications with, and responsiveness to the public. We have, I believe, learnt from our mistakes.

What is ethical "rightness" for a company? To what extent can and should this be influenced by public opinion? Well, I guess that is the subject of this talk. To begin with I'd like to quote from the introduction note of a little booklet titled 'History of the Royal Dutch/Shell Group of Companies': "From an alliance made in 1907 when Royal Dutch Petroleum Company and the Shell Transport and Trading Company, Ltd. agreed to merge their interests whilst keeping separate identities, the Royal Dutch/Shell Group has grown into one of the largest business enterprises in the world. It now operates in more than 100 countries; and in 1995 there were some 104,000 employees. The Group handles about one-tenth of the oil and natural gas in the world outside the former centrally-planned economies and has interests in nearly all aspects of the oil and chemical business, plus substantial investments in coal and forestry. It is characterised by its decentralised, diversified operations in which the operating companies have wide freedom of action, and where key operational decisions are

H. Lange et al., Working Across Cultures, 21–32.

always taken and implemented locally" This may give you an impression of the business setting I am working in.

2. Corporate Ethics Today

Ladies and Gentlemen, the potential dilemma between the profit motive of business and society's 'ethical' concerns has moved into a new phase in recent years. Over the last decade, environmental consciousness has increased dramatically. Modern communications have made the presentation – and sensationalisation – of information instantaneously global and visual.

At the same time unethical practices – real or perceived – such as insider dealing, bribery or environmental transgressions, have led to new discussions on corporate ethics and where they fit into business and, let's face it, a loss of credibility for business.

Today, economist Milton Friedman's comment in 1970 that a company's sole responsibility in society is to increase its profits, would be seen as a narrow view of the role of business.

Increasingly, business is having to deal with the redefinition of its ethical role in society. Corporations are being expected to provide more than employment, fair wages or working conditions.

A contribution to local services or infrastructure is being demanded of business by communities when governments are either unable or no longer prepared to provide such facilities. Some academics suggest this trend points to ethical business behaviour being increasingly seen to include consideration of society's broader needs – the agreed public good being given preference over private need.

Shareholders, too, are increasingly showing their displeasure over ethical abuses. Large corporate shareholders (pension funds, insurance companies) have begun to seek greater control over the day-to-day running of corporations seen as behaving unethically.

Some investors are no longer satisfied with a company assessment based purely on the balance sheet or the price-earnings ratio. Some investment fund managers are screening companies to concentrate investment in 'environmentally green' or 'best performing ethical funds'. Ethical funds are not investing in companies that, for example, make cigarettes, alcohol or weapons, or damage the environment.

Ladies and gentlemen, the ethics of business are the ethics of society. And, like the ethics of society, they are influenced by history and culture, are often difficult to define and can vary widely from country to country. This is not a comfortable world for companies which prefer clearly defined parameters. But it is the real world.

In the Western World, we take pride in the fact that the market economy is now displacing command economies which have demonstrably failed to meet the aspirations of the citizens in countries in which they have been the rule. Of course, the world of the market economy is not without its moral problems. In the most advanced countries we can see examples of blatantly unethical behaviour. But we should recognise that this behaviour is, in most cases, also outside the law – criminal in a word.

3. Shell Business Principles

I would now like to talk a little more specifically about business ethics in the light of the organisation I am working with.

A society, or nation, usually has a constitution, an established form of government that comprises a system of laws and customs. In many ways, that constitution is a reflection of the ethics of a society, developed over time from its religious and secular culture.

In Shell, we call our ethics, "business principles". They are, if you like, the truths that we hold to be self-evident. They have existed in an unpublished form at least as long as I can remember. But, since the mid 1970's, we have published them and made them available to Shell employees around the world. I was in fact involved in drafting the first version.

The so-called Royal Dutch/Shell Group Statement of General Business Principles applies equally to corporate decision-making and to the individual behaviour expected of employees in conducting Shell business. Shell operating companies may elaborate their own statements to meet national situations, but this Statement of General Business Principles serves as a basis on which, in their operations, they pursue the highest standards of behaviour.

The Policy Guideline on Health, Safety and the Environment, first issued in 1969 as an environmental policy statement, was broadened in 1977 into HSE Policy Guidelines which provide detailed guidance in the HSE field and were updated in 1991. Some other functions have a policy or mission statement.

Annually, general managers are asked to sign a Letter of Representation in which they confirm not only the probity of their accounts, but also that they have not been party to the offering, paying or receiving of bribery. Contrary to national laws and regulations these principles are applied worldwide within the Shell organization. This means, in a way, they are a powerful ethical tool in the process of globalisation.

The principles define four responsibilities, or areas of accountability, of Shell companies:

(1) Shell companies are responsible to *shareholders,* to protect their investment and give them an acceptable return.

(2) We have a responsibility to all *employees,* to provide good and safe working-conditions. We are required to develop and make best use of the talents of employees and to offer them equal opportunity, and to encourage their involvement in the planning and direction of their work.

(3) We have a responsibility to *customers* to provide products and services that give value in terms of price and quality, and which are backed up by the requisite technological and commercial expertise.

(4) And we have a responsibility to be good corporate members of *society,* to observe the applicable laws of the countries where we work and to give due regard to safety and environmental standards and societal aspirations.

I believe that the biggest contribution a company can make to the social fabric of a country is an economic one. By remaining profitable, it can provide jobs and revenue, and can help the nation gain prosperity. It is also right and proper that companies should make local contributions to the immediate communities in which they are located. And here I do not only mean financial contributions.

But in terms of broader social issues, the responsibility of corporate citizens becomes less clear-cut. Commercial enterprises certainly have no mandate in these issues. And I doubt whether they should play a direct role. Societal responsibility differs from one country to another, depending on the system or social fabric of the particular country, and these different societal values must be recognised.

4. Role of the Multinationals

The growth of the multinational enterprises is one of the distinguishing factors of the post-war world. Today they account for a significant percentage of the world's GDP and of the world's workforce.

There are some who still believe that the business corporation is amoral and exists for the sole purpose of maximising the return to its shareholders. I believe that this is not only nonsense, but also inconceivable. Business enterprises consist of people, and the latter bring their own sense of morality to the work place. Even if this were not so, sustainable acceptance – a pre-requisite for long-term success – requires acceptable behaviour.

In a multinational grouping like Shell, values are a subtle blend of those people working in their own countries and those of expatriates, who learn to develop a sensitivity to the values of their host countries. In this way, the multinational enterprises evolve and with that modify the values of society. Unless you believe that business people are inferior moral beings, this process can only be beneficial and create a better global understanding.

This may seem a bold claim to those accustomed to seeing the corporate sector, particularly the multinational part of it, vilified for its lack of morality. But business people, in my experience, are pretty much like any other group of people. Some are greedy, some altruistic, some aggressive, some not; some honest, some not. But to focus on the pathology of the situation is wrong. Do we judge the political world or the church only by corrupt politicians or errant vicars?

I do not believe that big businesses should try to assume a leading role in developing the social fabric of a country. They have no such mandate and I have said the best contribution a company can make to the community is to carry on its business efficiently and profitably – and ethically. After all, the very essence of business is competition. Continuity is only assured if competitive advantage is maintained, but this has to be within the law and according to standards of behaviour acceptable to society.

Neither do I claim that companies do not make mistakes including ones of moral judgement. That is human. Public scrutiny or criticism is a legitimate means of ensuring that these mistakes are minimised – but it should itself be honest and balanced.

5. Living in a Dilemma Situation

As global trade expands, corporations can find their ethical codes being seriously challenged by several forces. Today's world is one where society's expectations of business are constantly changing. Business is also having to deal with what it may view as the 'questionable' cultural norms of new international markets – particularly when involved in joint ventures. The dilemma is twofold: on the one hand, managers must strike a balance between what business wants and what society is prepared to accept; on the other, there is the balance between what a particular society wants and whether this can be reconciled with business ethics.

Life is not, of course, without its problems. Let's make no bones about the fact that trying to ensure the long-term future of any company in a competitive world can involve hard decisions about the careers of loyal employees with many years of service, a grave problem many companies have to face these days (number of employees in the Royal Dutch / Shell Group down to 104,000 in 1995 from 137,000 in 1990).

Another difficult area is the balance between the cultural values of different societies – or even parts of the same society. For the reasons I have already outlined, Shell companies work within a wide range of social, political and economic environments. We believe that our corporate structure is flexible enough to allow us to work well in different environments, provided those environments do not prevent us from adhering to our business principles.

The financial, political and cultural aspects are, of course, given full consideration in our business planning. But our work involves projects with long lead-times, huge initial investments, and in which profitability depends on conditions prevailing years into the future. So, in the lifetime of one project, governments may change or even be overthrown, economies may go through major downturns, there may be big changes in social attitudes, or complete reversals in attitudes to foreign investors.

In Shell, we try to plan for projects that will be secure and robust under a variety of circumstances but, of course, we can't predict what will happen in a particular country or under a particular regime. So we try to live with the prevailing conditions, carrying out our activities in what we regard as an acceptable way.

Companies sometimes find themselves in conflict with other parts of society. If I leave aside the differences with those who believe that our style of life is fundamentally immoral, I can still think of many examples. Fairly typical is the matter of having operations in countries with so-called oppressive regimes. Shell operates in more than 100 countries. Literally hundreds of thousands of people depend on us, directly and indirectly, for their living. The behaviour of some governments may appear objectionable to people living in other parts of the world.

How is a company going to react to this? Is it going to show loyalty to its employees – wherever they live? To its shareholders to ensure the continuity of the business? To its customers to ensure continuity of the business? To its customers to ensure continuity of supply? At times, these pull in different directions, not only because the time-frame of each is different.

But the idea of conflicting principles is nothing new – there can be nobody in this room who does not know the tension of an inner conflict – religious histories are full of them. All we can do is to use our judgement to reconcile our responsibilities as we see them at the time.

Shell's operations in Nigeria have been much publicised recently. It is a fact of life that the oil and gas industries, being private companies, are often partners of governments. The latter, after all, are the owners of the resources. Working closely with any organisation gives you the right to bring to its attention matters which affect the business, but there are limits beyond which partners cannot, and should not, go. Thus, while Shell companies can and do involve themselves in matters of energy policy and community services, they do not interfere in party politics. In this context, whereas there are those who criticise Shell for non-interference in Nigeria, there is also a long-standing and a considerable body of opinion that finds political interference by business unacceptable.

Some 92 countries have been identified by human rights groups as having violated human rights. If Shell was to become the arbiter of moral, social or political conduct, it would have difficulty in doing business as an international oil company.

Shell companies always endeavour to act commercially, operating within existing national laws in a socially responsible manner. As I mentioned before, a commercial organisation's main objectives must be commercial, not political or social.

We do, I believe, accept a broader view of our social responsibility than many companies. In particular we will act directly to protect the interests of those we employ. But we cannot substitute for government. Nevertheless, we acknowledge the concerns of those who say that Shell companies operate in countries where it is alleged there is a lack of respect for human rights and Shell is always ready to discuss these concerns.

And I have to admit, that this is a typical dilemma situation. Whatever one does, there are ethical "rights" and "wrongs" with it and one has to compromise somewhere. And as a company we should be open on this dilemma, attempt to share it with other interested parties and accept that our own view, while honestly held, may also be honestly disagreed with.

6. Environmental Aspects

Conservation of the environment is an integral part of the strategy of Shell companies and is central to the business principles that guide their activities. The first written policy statement on the environment was issued in 1969. Later initiatives have reflected the need to improve environmental performance continuously, through a management process of actively setting targets and executing detailed programmes.

Shell's Group Policy Guidelines on the Environment were first published externally in 1977, and have been revised from time to time to reflect increasing knowledge and changing public expectations. Since 1990, tough guidelines have established a strategy of continuous improvement in environmental performance, stressing this as a management responsibility. Environmental management systems have been developed to assist our companies.

We have taken it as an ultimate goal to eliminate – if possible – emissions, effluents and discharges that are known to have a negative impact on the environment. Similar guidelines were introduced in 1991 to ensure that products do not unduly affect the environment and are recycled if practicable, or disposed of safely.

We do not pretend that we operate in an identical manner around the world. It is rather a matter of aiming to improve each operation in the light of the individual circumstances.

Different environments will always have different ecological requirements. Different societies have different social and environmental values and priorities. Each local community or government will understandably place greater emphasis on one or the other environmental impact. The final decision requires judgement and close consideration. If no judgement were required, common global standards would have evolved long ago.

Of course, we should not pretend that we do not make mistakes. However high the standards, and however good the systems in place – unforeseen incidents can happen. The cause could be equipment failure, human error or management deficiencies. Here, the intention is to have a system that can rapidly take the appropriate remedial action, and also learn from the experience.

Ultimately, Shell's own commitment to continuous improvement underlines that we can never be satisfied with the status quo. By striving for continuous improvement, we are automatically rejecting consistency. To put it in other words: striving for consistency would be the kiss of death for continuous improvement.

Obviously the environment will continue to be a key issue and environmental protection should be an integral part of any responsible business strategy. It is, however, a shared responsibility, requiring cooperation between industry, governments, environmental groups and the public to find ways of balancing other needs of society and the requirements of environmental protection. Society itself, though, must determine the balance of risk and benefit in environmentally-sensitive activities, based on sound science and cost-effective use of resources.

Legislators have the role of monitoring industry's behaviour, setting the rules and protecting the public good. In business, we have the responsibility to participate in the debate on the resolution of environmental cost/benefit dilemmas and to show the way ahead through improved operational practices and better technologies. In this way, we hope to encourage regulators to move away from a technology-based prescriptive 'command and control' approach, and more towards setting objectives and targets that can be attained cost-effectively and which encourage the search for creative solutions and continuous improvement.

'Goal setting' is the way of the future, just as prescription was the way of the past. Under a 'goal setting' regime, the adversarial regulator-company relationship is replaced by a constructive relationship, but not a cosy one.

How to deal with the legacy of the past is one of the most difficult environmental problems. Facilities built up over decades were, of course, designed for and constructed to the environmental and technical standards of their time and to meet prevailing conditions. They can never match the latest technologies. The charge made by some critics of "double standards" is mistaken because it is based on the notion that there is a single "absolute environmental standard". But as long as we continue to improve, varying standards are inevitable.

Although Shell companies everywhere are committed to pursuing continual improvement in their environmental performance, how they approach it depends on their particular situation. The nature of their operations, their environmental hazards, the benefits of different improvement projects and, of course, the priorities of the country's regulatory authorities are all major considerations.

We should not forget that at the Rio Environmental Summit, developing countries insisted on maintaining their right to determine how their national resources are spent on environmental improvement and to decide for themselves how quickly their own regulations should catch up with those of the already developed world.

7. Need for Dialogue

Ladies and gentlemen, externally, Shell was challenged in the recent past by NGO's like Greenpeace, the media and also by the general public over the proposed deep-water disposal of Brent Spar as well as environmental and human rights concerns elsewhere. The events of the past year demonstrated the degree of complexity in the multinational operations of Shell companies and the need to gain broader understanding and acceptance of their activities. This is, in effect, Shell's licence to operate.

We learned that we need to have greater external focus if we are to create a better acceptance of Shell's business among varied audiences.

Shell companies must consult, inform and communicate better with the public. In such a dialogue they will need to point out the complexity of the issues and always balance human, environmental and economic considerations.

The events of last year remind us that improving operational standards is not enough. We have also to understand and respond to changing societal expectations. This means listening better, appreciating people's concerns and being more open to other views. We must communicate more effectively, so that we contribute to an informed debate on these complex issues. I acknowledge the contribution of many non-governmental organisations to this process of reasoned debate.

We live in a rapidly changing world. In many parts of the world there is considerable evidence of significant changes in people's attitudes and the way in which those attitudes are formed. People have more demanding expectations of big companies. It becomes an increasingly important question of how one relates to these changing societal expectations and how these can affect people's perception of a multinational company.

It is 20 years since our General Business Principles were first published. I believe that these principles, which have evolved over time, are fundamentally sound. Nevertheless, we are reviewing them now, to see whether they still meet changing societal values.

We are also discussing with human rights organisations the difficult and wider question of how companies should respond to concerns about human rights in countries in which they operate. However, while commercial organisations must have the right to express views on matters affecting their businesses, we remain convinced that it would be improper for them to interfere in the political process.

This year we shall also be reviewing our health, safety and environment management sytems in consultation with a wide range of interested parties.

In a world of change it is not easy to gauge social values and expectations on a global scale, with so many different cultural frameworks, points of view and clashes of interest. The issues of economic development, social justice and environmental progress are immensely complex, with no easy answers or straightforward solutions. Only too clearly, situations vary greatly from country to country.

The roles and responsibilities of commercial organisations, as opposed to governmental ones, are matters of profound consequence to society and must be discussed widely. I believe that it is vital that the business community as a whole takes part in this debate. Shell companies are always prepared to play their part and are already engaged in discussions in various business forums on such matters as sustainable development, combating extortion and bribery and liberalising world markets.

8. Closing

But we should never forget the prime purpose of commercial enterprise: to create wealth that enables society to progress. So, companies like Shell contribute to meet the energy needs of the world, they offer jobs and business opportunities, they contribute to national revenues and people's income by paying dividends. In developing countries, their role in transferring technologies and skills is a prime driver of development.

Discussion on the
Keynote Speech of Peter Duncan*

M = Moderation
Q = Question
A = Answer

M (Jürgen Weber):

Mr. Duncan, thank you very much, first for flying Lufthansa from Amsterdam to Frankfurt, but above all thank you for this excellent speech. It was very interesting for me as one of the responsible managers of a company which is under discussion almost every day because of the kind of problems you tackled here. Therefore I have learned a lot, and I am happy to coordinate questions and answers now as the moderator.

Q (Terry Bynum, Southern Connecticut State University, USA):

I was very pleased with the keynote speech that was just given, because I think it highlights what will probably be one of the themes of this conference. It is a really difficult problem that teachers of ethics had faced for a couple of thousand years, it's the problem of relativism versus absolutism, to use my professorial language here. On the one hand, you say that it is not appropriate for a multinational corporation to try to interfere in government, to try to take the place of the rulers of the country, and you point out that different types of governments may come and go, but the multinational corporation must continue to stay there and do business. You also point out that there are many different customs and mores, and different histories of different parts of the

---

* This chapter ist based on a transcript of the tape-recorded part of the opening session. To keep the discussion as authentic as possible, we made only some sligth adjustments in language and corrections on the spoken words. Thus, readers are kindly asked to be careful with their interpretation of the text.

H. Lange et al., Working Across Cultures, 33–51.
© *1998 Kluwer Academic Publishers. Printed in the Netherlands.*

world. Thus as a multinational corporation you have to do business in nundreds of countries with a wide variety of different customs and values.

Now, if you just stopped there, you would be stuck in a kind of relativism where you have to do business in hundreds of countries, and they all have different values, and it's not your place to go in and change their values, change their customs, and run their government. And so, whatever they do, if they bribe, if they pollute the water, if they allow the damage of the health of the workers, if that's built into their customs and mores and their laws, then what can you do? You just have to go and do business under circumstances like that.

On the other hand, you also said that no matter where you are around the world you are concerned about health, you are concerend about the environment, and there are certain things it seems to me that you have pointed to as universal values in every country where you do business. So this is exactly the difficult problem that teachers of ethics have, on the one hand to take account of the wide variety of histories and mores and practices, and at the same time to try to identify certain things that are universal, no matter what country you go to. I mean every country values life over death, every country values health over illness. So what I want to ask you is: can you say again what are the universal values that Shell is promoting in every country where you áre doing business?

A (Peter Duncan):

May I try to illustrate the point I am trying to make with an example. A universal value for us is "don't bribe", but we operate in countries where many peoplc bribe. We believe that the sustainable, if you like, morally acceptable way for us to operate in those countries is not to bribe. We will not operate in a country, neither will we engage in an investment project, where the only way we can achieve approval on that is by bribing. We have lost investments because of that attitude, but because that attitude is so clear, if the arguments brought forward by us to attract our investments are enough, we will be welcomed in that country without bribing. Should we there say that we are not going to operate in this country if other people bribe, or if a few government authorities accept bribes from other people, or not? You could debate this. You could say that it is a society which has lamentable moral standards, you shouldn't behave there. We would argue, and particularly because this course is not a question of going in or not going in, it's a question of pursuing our long term efforts in those countries, that the best contribution we can make to an improvement of standards in those countries is the demand that we will not come to those standards with our organization, we will sack people who engage in those practices.

Let me give another example, environmental behavior. The environmental behavior of Shell in Nigeria formed at least one of the dimensions in the debate which took place on that country. And it is true that there were failures in the environmental behavior of Shell there. I could talk at length about that. There were failures which have to do with, if you like, a judgement about cost-benefit, which I referred to, and I talked about that, which with the benefit of hindsight seem not to have been appropriate. They were always at the margin, and I believe there is independent evidence to confirm that. And there were never failures connected with destruction of the environment, but they were certainly standards which in retrospect we would wish to have seen better carried out. And we are of course taking active steps and had been doing so before the more recent controversy to ensure that that happens.

Generally, the best way we can operate in a country which may have environmental standards regarded as unacceptable is to try to draw a reasonable balance, behaving ourselves environmentally responsibly. It is more difficult than the bribery one, the bribery one is to my mind black and white. The environmental one is more difficult, because it is not necessarily true that the standards in Germany which would require the extraction of 99.99% of hydrocarbonates are appropriate standards for underdeveloped countries which want to retain some of their competitive advantages. And the point I am trying to make is that by the way in which we behave we can be a powerful influence of good over bad, and that there is a line to be drawn, and I accept that is not a clear black and white line between that, and the step which then goes further and engages actively in the process of saying the country's governmental system is wrong, the way you are organizing your industry is wrong, and so on, it's not a black and white line, because quite clearly, if you are in a country in which, for example human rights are at least to be questioned, and companies are made out of people, then people would be saying those things as well, they would not be saying it very publicly, but they would be doing this. But I think there is at least a conceptual distinction to be drawn which is supportable. The difficulty of course is then defining the specific subject.

Q (Peter Koslowski, Hannover Institute of Phil. Research, D):

I would like to ask a question to both speakers, Jürgen Weber and Peter Duncan, concerning your consensus that the process of globalization is unavoidable, uninvertible, that there is just no way to escape it. In some sense I agree with you, but one could also say that there are other possible developments, for example large continental trade blocks like the European Union, which in some sense can be interpreted as a means against globalization, and they are seen by some parts of the world as such. I would like to question the idea a little bit that this is simply a necessary process.

A second question relates to the kind of companies you are representing. It is clear that a company like Lufthansa that is working in worldwide traffic will be concerned and interested in globalization, and the same is true for an energy supply company like Shell. But, maybe this makes us blind to the fact that this process of globalization is not as necessary as we might think from the perspective of an airline, or an energy company. My question to both of you, with respect to your experience as representatives of these worldwide operating firms, would be: What are the causes of this process? Can you tell us from your experience why it happens now? Why does it happen with so much power and in this moment?

A (Jürgen Weber):

From our point of view I can see three main issues why globalization is coming up more and more, and why there is no way to say how we can stop it. The first reason in our business is liberalization. There are free markets, globalized business just will come, and it is a lesson of the whole history that you cannot stop it. The second driver for me is information technology. People in all parts of the world can inform themselves with cheap means about what is going on in other parts of the world, and they are getting interested more and more about these facts. Finally, I also think the traffic systems is important, the possi-

bility to fly within half a day to every point of the world out of Frankfurt. This has also been a driving force for globalization from our
point of view.

A (Peter Duncan):

I don't know that I can add a great deal to what you are saying. I think
information technology is key to this, and I would personally argue
more key than liberalization, because I would argue that liberalization
is partly a result of this as well. We in Shell work with scenarios in our
longer term planning, with attempts to derive internally consistent
worlds which examine issues which are important to us. The second
and last set of such scenarios examined precisely the issue of liberalization, thought through the consequences of a world that broke into
trading blocks, as against the consequences of a world which liberal-
ized in a global sense. Our latest set of scenarios had put that aside
because we regard that as now finished, that debate. It's now moving
in that direction, and I agree with you, I think transport is a large part
of it as well, I think it's all very connected.

You have to be careful when you talk about globalization of
course, because interestingly the transport and communication possibilities you have not only the opportunity for globalization, but also
for localization in many respects. You find, for example, that in Switzerland, Swiss-German is spoken more than it was twenty years ago,
and high German is spoken less well. There is a tendency in many
parts of the world because of the cheapness of processing information
to now go below what we previously regarded as for the mass. I can
now produce information for a small group of people, but I think in
the context that we are now talking about, and that is if you like to use
an expression reflective of the debate between socialism and capitalism, the commanding heights of the economy are globalized. And it is
in that sense that if the commanding heights of the economy are
globalized that we have no choice to react in a way on that subject,
which by the way Kenichi Ohmae, a distinguished consultant in Japan
has been writing about for years now. He has been talking for a long
time about the globalized economy.

So it is very much an area which you have got to differentiate and
look at in different ways. But for the purposes of our discussion about
ethics and about behavior it is quite clear of course now that a com-

pany cannot act in one country, in isolation at the impact in other countries. That was the lesson for my company last year.

Q (Horst Steinmann, University of Erlangen-Nuernberg, D):

I have a short question about the internal decision process and information process, which you have installed, to talk about something like ethical management. How do you ensure the integration of 100,000 people in different countries, so that you can get concrete actions according to what you intend with your business principles. What kind of information and early warning system is it, how does the communication process work, which you mentioned as so important for ethical behavior, to achieve the right decisions at the right time with respect to difficult ethical issues?

A (Peter Duncan):

I did mention one example of it in my speech, and that was the specific example of bribery. The significance more generally is in fact where we do ask the senior management of all our companies to sign every year an explicit statement that they have not engaged in that kind of behavior. Some of these activities are auditable, and some of them are not. Behavior in the environmental field is auditable in the sense that it is possible, and I made reference to that in my speech as well to devise management systems, that management process is a simple and conventional process, define your policy, implement your policy, and execute a feed back group to check what is going on is environmental policy. And that happens. We are subject to a process of scrutiny which is partly peer scrutiny, that is to say by other companies in a similar position, and partly Shell scrutiny to try and satisfy ourselves and themselves. That behavior in that respect does have processes behind it which are likely to achieve the desired end. In a broader sense we have processes described, as if you like, audit review, which take place on average every three years in every Shell company, by which a team of people often also including peers of other companies is sitting down and trying to go through all the management processes to try establish these things.

Now, that's one element. Another element is education, and that is to say bringing to the attention of people that these subjects are important to one. And I would say that our record in that respect is mixed and reflective of the priorities as they have been at a particular time. For example safety at work is a topic in which our company has made massive strides in recent years simply because we have made it very clear to people how important this is to us. Continuous improvement in environmental activities is another area of that type.

If we get into the areas which have become particular controversial: have you or have you not interfered in political processes – what does that mean? Then really the only way in which you can steer that is by a process of very general and continuous debate amongst companies of appropriate things to do, because it is not conducive to black and white answers. If I am standing up and making a speech about the environmental problems of "Standort Deutschland" you can argue I am interfering in the political process, and if I am criticizing the German government's support for the Leuna refinery, I am even more actively interfering in the political process, but there is clearly a line to be drawn between that and a process by which for example I am attempting actively to support particular members of Parliament or whatever. All we can try to do is to debate that more and it is quite true that as we move through the processes which have externally imposed on us in the last year, and the internal debates that are going on in Shell now we are trying to come back to terms with an acceptable form of behavior.

M (Jürgen Weber):

I am sure it is a very difficult task to communicate properly for such a big multinational company as Shell. We at Lufthansa are in a relatively good position, we have only a few percent of our people working in other countries. But, I can tell you that it is difficult enough to streamline the people in this country, and to get communication properly in the heads of everybody, as far as our company ethics is concerned.

Q (Gerhard Blickle, University of Koblenz-Landau, D):

I have a question to Mr. Duncan. You told us that you have a prohibition to bribe in your company. I have a question concerning the history of this prohibition. For how long have you had this prohibition, and how did you enact that prohibition?

A (Peter Duncan):

An interesting question for how long we have had it. You know the oil industry started off with a collection of robber barons and crooks, and if you go back to these very colourful figures, I recommend to you a book called "The prize", by a man called Daniel Jürgen, which describes all these sorts of people. I guess if you compare the Shell corporate ancestors with the rest of the corporate constellation we probably also had our share of rogues as well.

It's I guess in the post world-war years that the consciousness that a distinction has to be drawn becomes clear. I think that if you go back to the early years of the century the concept which you are talking about, if that's the practice in this country, I've got to live with it, was somewhat more prevalent. There are punctuation points as we move through the post war years in which oil companies, and that includes Shell, have been dragged into controversy concerning issues like political payment and so on, which strengthened our views, so that at some period as we moved through the 1950s to the late 1960s you get a switch in attitude from a company which – I don't think that the standards were in general bad – but I think you will find that the willingness to compromise on these issues switched to a pretty religious refusal to compromise on these issues. Not entirely I would admit out of a certain change from – as the Germans I think say – from Saulus to Paulus, but because of the recognition that the damage caused, not only externally but also internally, by a culture which commits that type of activity is far greater than the short term benefits that it can ever bring. That's an attempt to give you a reasonably honest laying out of the thing, and it's not to say that bribery does not take place within Shell now. We don't have an organization of 104,000 people without breaches, but it is to say true that our employees are made very clear about what our attitude is, and if we establish that it is taking place, then they will lose their jobs with us.

Q (Jack Mahoney, London Business School, UK):

I very much enjoyed Mr. Duncan's presentation. I think my question is about the ethics of responding to pressure, particularly since Mr. Duncan toward the end of his address mentioned the company's reputation as being its most precious asset. I have an MBA student in London who in fact was an employee of Shell UK. When I gave my class an essay assignment as their examination, he said he wanted to write me a paper on the ethics of Greenpeace. Now, toward the end of your address you said that the debate is in danger of becoming populist rather than moral. I wonder if you would care to enlarge on that.

A (Peter Duncan):

I was in a discussion group sometime ago with amongst others a certain Professor Rupert Lay, who will probably be known to many of the Germans here, but less to others, he is a Jesuit priest who has in that order some controversy as well, but also a thinker about these kinds of issues. I have mentioned it because in that discussion he drew a distinction between internal and exogenic morality, or ethics. In other words, ethics which are a measure of the expectations of society, and we have a little bit of a debate about what happens when you have a conflict between those two forms of morality, and in effect that particular case of Brent Spar.

We could argue that on the information available to Shell at that stage the only moral and ethical step there to take was exactly that step we proposed to take. On the other hand, the implications of taking that step, particularly in the population of Germany, but also in some other countries, as such I talk partly about violence, but not only as such, that the ethical arguments which were linked with risk to human life and the environment, for the one course became switched to the other course. It's quite clear that morality develops with different cultural views. On the other hand it must also be clear to me that there are certain common lines of thinking which I can hold to be absolute rather than relativist.

Theory is simple, the application is difficult. It is quite clear to me that a debate on ethics carried out against that kind of climate is inherently unhealthy. Therefore it was the right step for Shell, for some other reasons as well by the way, to terminate that exercise and allow that debate to calm down to a sensible one of pluses and minuses. The processes through which our sister company in the UK is going now to resolve that issue are different in kind from those it went through before in terms of transparency and terms of debate, in terms of discussion of different alternatives, and it is possible that out of that, and it is even probable, will come a disposal alternative which doesn't involve sinking it in the North Sea, and is not less safe for people or for the environment. Then I think Shell will have to ask for itself whether the processes to which it was subjected, which in my view had many scandalous aspects, but also had some positive aspects in that it forced the company to go through different kinds of processes in making decisions.

You are hearing from the kind of answer I give that the only way I can respond to this kind of thing has elements of waffle about it but I hope not too much. I am trying to describe what to my mind is a key problem, and I have no doubt a problem which you will debate in the next two or three days. And that's why I have put it in here. Where does an ethical debate move into populism? Both have an acceptable role, emotionalism has a role in my view which could be played, but ultimately there must also be space for a dispassionate debate about what is scientifically demonstrated to be the most acceptable view on the case.

Q (Georges Enderle, University of Notre Dame, USA):

Given the situation today, you said at the end of your very interesting keynote address that we learned how much we have to learn. Would you publicize such a report now, or how would you deal with those scientific research studies in the public debate? A second question which is connected with this is the Brent Spar case. I think it illustrated very clearly that there were different feelings in different countries. In early June I was in Ireland, and then I went to Amsterdam and to Germany. The feelings in Germany and in Ireland, and I assume in the UK, were very different. How to deal with those feelings in the public debate?

A (Peter Duncan):

Publicize such a report? The answer is more than a yes, but we are doing that. It takes too long to go into this process in detail, but they are pressing the process the way forward, which is an extensive process looking for suggestions, selecting companies, shortening the list down to a smaller group of companies, commissioning them to develop proposals with periodic and regular communications of those proposals to the public. Shell UK held its last press conference on this subject about six weeks ago. And I explained that documentation is extensively available. By the way if you have a look at the relevant about the history of Nigeria and how that country, when I say really country, then in inverted commas there, because it is a collection of countries bundled together at the convenience of British colonial administrators, and how that country has been put together, and all the background of things behind this. And there is Shell, and Shell discovers oil, others discover oil by the way as well, but Shell is the biggest. Shell becomes the operator in a consortium but is not the majority partner, the government is the majority partner, there are other companies, they are partners of Shell. Over the course of time regimes come and go in Nigeria, and there is one at the moment which many people would regard as the particularly difficult in many ways, and we have been through the processes with the Ogonies, and the tragedy of the Ogoni people, and the tragedy of the other groups there. All of these kind of things, and I'm not sure whether inherent in your questioning the word opportunism or cynicism is a perception that becomes some point in time where a company like Shell should say "I close up shop and go", because it is no longer acceptable to make the work in that kind of operation.

What would make you think that a company like Shell would operate and not put some pressure on the regime? I do really think you have to be a little bit careful, and I accept you can read a lot in the newspapers about Shell, and you can read a lot about Nigeria, and you can read a lot about the way they behave. I did say at one stage in my speech that long term acceptability is in the center of long term profits. I don't ask you to believe that Shell is a company which is a candidate for canonisation by the Catholic church. I do ask you to believe that Shell is not stupid. And I do ask you to believe that Shell would like to be in Nigeria in 30 years, and that it's highly likely that Nigeria will be governed by another five different regimes at different points of acceptability, and that Shell will therefore behave in Nigeria in a way which is most likely to show its sustained acceptability. That has to do with its behavior with respect to environmental pollution, it has to do with its attitude to the community where it works, it has to do with the kind of debate it has with the government, and the way in which they are behaving. It does not necessarily have to do with achieving head-lines in the newspapes which were satisfying the European publics, and I can accept even when I say that, you can say "well he would say that wouldn't he", he would say that they would do all that sort of

internet address you can get quite considerable information as well. There is a CD Rom which contains a great deal of information, from the original reports on that thing.

That is part of what I meant when I said that Shell was learning. Brent Spar of course is no longer a North Sea installation, Brent Spar is a symbol. And therefore it is subject to processes which aren't necessarily sensible processes in general. That it was sensible for Shell to do it in this particular case, because it was symbolic for itself for the outside world of a different way of behaving, which is not to say that my colleagues in Shell UK have not reached in a balanced and in my view honest and technically competent way a sensible decision earlier, which in their view is based on the fact that the environmental impli-cations of either route were marginal, and therefore other factors had to be taken into account and money played a role. And I do not believe that money should not play a role in these decisions. We are talking about the sensible allocation of resources. That's what we did learn out of this process, is that we have to be far more open earlier, listen far more, explain far more, and perhaps be prepared to consider again this debate about populism. When is it that the public view changes the decisions, which seem to be technically correct. Sometimes it must do so, everytime we market we are trying to convince customers to buy our goods, and if the customer likes what we happen to regard not as being technically optimum, then that's his choice, the customer is always right. So that is again part of the state of debate, transparency and openness have to be a large part of it, and large organizations, particularly of the Shell nature, are not brought up to lay open their decisions to the public, not brought up to share their dilemmas with the public. And, quite clearly, there are lots of things which we also don't want to share with the public, there are lots of things, far more things that we can, than we often realize, and I believe that multina-tional and large companies will achieve far more understanding if they are actually able to humanize themselves and demonstrate to people that they are also subject to the same uncertainty, to the same attempts, to the same compromise themselves, that's transparency and openness. And that's happening this way as well.

Different feelings in different countries? The answer is yes, and it's again part of that process of debate within individual companies, there were also different feelings, and these have been probably the most vivid examples in recent years, an action in one country raising almost hysteria in another country. But it is a precedent for processes of that type which will happen in the future. So we have somehow to draw a compromise between what is acceptable and discussed within an individual company and what is globally acceptable. That's part of operating within a global economy. And if we can do it better than our competitors then we will have a competitive advantage. So it's also partly a commercial decision.

M (Jürgen Weber):

Different feelings and different countries. Very interesting questions we can contribute with our airplanes, with environmental issues of our airplanes. Airplanes which are banned in Germany are welcomed in other countries because they bring in work and wealth. So that's a very difficult subject.

Q (Bettina Löhnert, Hannover Institute of Phil. Research, D):

I want to ask you, Mr. Weber, a question about your new program "Balance". As far as I understood it this program aims at identifying flight connections that Lufthansa wants to drop because of ethical or environmental reasons. I wanted to hear from you if there is any flight connection Lufthansa actually ever dropped because of environmental and ethical reasons, and sacrificing a good revenue it could make on this connection.

A (Jürgen Weber):

With "Balance" we wanted to communicate, in a first step to our own people, but then in a second step also to the general public, the Lufthansa opinion on many general questions, environmental questions, but also other questions which are of interest to the public. And your direct question, if we have stopped any flight connections due to environmental reasons, I am very sorry to say: a lot. It's a pity, we are not allowed to fly into some of the German airports after ten o'clock at night, and we divert with a full airplane from Hamburg to Berlin with children in this airplane, because it is two minutes beyond the threshold in the evening, and then those people fly to Berlin. Then they are packed in a bus and transported, 50 people with a bus, straight through

Northern Germany: very "environmentally friendly". This is one of the pending problems we have to solve, in our society a typical example. I would like to discusss this subject with you for some hours, I can give you good examples.

Q (Peter Ulrich, University of St. Gallen, CH):

Mr. Duncan, you said Shell has learned that listening is important. I tried to listen too, and so please excuse me if I ask you to be a little bit more precise. In some of the statements you made, which are completely consistent with what we could read and hear from Shell all about, things remain unclear for me. One statement was that activities of Shell are commercial, and not political. I think you stressed this sentence to say Shell wants to be ethically and politically neutral. But, if you stress this sentence, isn't that the problem rather than the solution? Because I think from an ethical point of view every activity of a big institutional corporation is factually political, and I am thinking here on the context of Nigeria.

A second statement, you said we try to live with changing regimes in host countries. Again, in Nigeria, how do you make a difference between your policy to live with these regimes against opportunism, or even cynicism?

A (Peter Duncan):

I don't think I used the question ethically and politically neutral, but I think I know what you mean. I don't think ethically neutral is a kind of philosophy to which I would subscribe at all, if you mean by that some kind of wishy-washy adapting to whatever acceptable or unacceptable circumstances that may be in different countries. I thought I answered that in connection with another question.

I also accept and accepted that the subject of political neutrality is a very difficult point. And you have mentioned Nigeria, and Nigeria happens to be one of the most controversial such cases at this point of time, but there are all sorts of other cases as I said in my speech. There are 92 countries, let's call it round about 100 countries, which are held to have regimes which are oppressive. Now, Shell has been operating in Nigeria since the 1930s, and has been producing oil in Nigeria since 1958. And you will know how many regimes and systems Nigeria has gone through since then. And I don't know how many of you know thing, but I don't see any evidence of it. And that is a plausible view from your point of view. I only ask you to accept that you don't have to believe that Shell is good morally. You only have to believe that Shell is sensible, and in it for a long term. Who is going to suffer from the human rights violations of the Nigerian government if it is not Shell. Do you think Shell is going to sit back and do that?

That's the best I can respond to you on that, and please I don't wish to sound pompous or arrogant on that subject, because I recognize that seen from the outside the impression can be given of a large, mono-lythic, amoral, and anonymous organization pursuing its economic and profit maximization where the public can't do anything particularly if, I regard to the in my view scandalous publicity about Nigeria that takes place. I just tried to put this in front of you.

M (Jürgen Weber):

This was, I'm sure, a very good but a difficult question, and this was a good and honest answer. I am very sorry that I have to announce that we have to stop with our interesting discussion now. I would like to thank once more Mr. Peter Duncan for the excellent presentation and discussion.

Intercultural Business Ethics. Lessons from Nigeria

Workshop-Statement by Nicola Pless and Thomas Maak,
Institut für Wirtschaftsethik, University of St. Gallen, CH

Mr. Duncan admits that Shell has made some mistakes throughout their activities in Nigeria and he believes that they have learnt from their mistakes. Nevertheless we assume that Shell is still neither aware of the political dimension, nor fully aware of the moral dimension of managing across cultures.

1. Need for Dialogue: Public Relations as a Suitable Approach to Face Ethical Dilemma Situations?

As a result of Ken Saro-Wiwa's devotion to the matters of the Ogoni and the information policy of NGO's like Greenpeace the Ogoni case has attracted worldwide attention and became a matter of growing public concern. Shell and other multinational oil companies are now aware of the fact that by means of public pressure and consumer boycotts such events could lead to heavy losses of image and profit. In order to prevent that and to gain public acceptance or rather to calm down the critical public Shell has intensified their public relations activities in both cases, Nigeria and Brent Spar. We are convinced that this is no suitable way to solve the problematic situations and that it won't be a suitable basis to communicate better with the public or even to communicate more effectively as Mr. Duncan has announced in his keynote address. Let us explain why.

Firstly, the Public Relations (PR)approach is mainly a one-way-form of communication which aims at increasing confidence in and acceptance of a company's policy in some crucial parts of the public. The company shapes this one-way-dialogue according to their interests and goals. PR therefore does not enable a constructive dialogue between equal participants and causes a communication asymmetry. Secondly, and closely connected with the first argument, PR follows the traditional stakeholder approach. The stakeholder approach is based on a result- or profit-oriented attitude of the parties involved. Only such groups are seen as relevant stakeholders that are economically influential and potentially powerful, insofar as they can take sanctions against the company, or, as Freeman puts it, insofar as they can affect the achievement of the firm's obejctives. Thus the stakeholder dialogue remains a bargaining approach, and therefore it is of a merely strategic character. If the company gets a short-term strategic acceptance at all, it is but far away from long-term ethical legitimacy. The latter of course is the decisive prerequisite for any business activity in the future. As a result the company's dialogue with *all* stakeholders has to be based on the regulative idea of a reasonable dialogue of understanding. This implicates that *every* group with possible legitimate claims becomes a relevant group in the dialogue.

The case of Shell Nigeria illustrates impressively the moral shortcomings of the PR-approach. The Ogoni as a politically suppressed and marginalized group did not have any bargaining power. That's why the PR-approach disregards the Ogonis and turns down a constructive dialogue of understanding with the key group in this conflict. Now, if Shell has learned to communicate better with the public, this can only mean to take into consideration every legitimate claim made by a person or a group which is somehow affected by the company's activities. And this cannot mean to communicate more effectively the usual and tested way. On the contrary, this requires a growing awareness of the moral and political dimension of economic activities, and the insight that corporate communication can only take place on clarified normative grounds. On such a sound basis Shell should radically change its business principles to give expression to an ethically enlightened understanding of public relations, e.g. like "we have the responsibility to take into consideration every legitimate claim made by a person or a group irrespective of race, class, gender, religion, and political or economic power and to discuss whenever possible together their position in a reasonable dialogue of understanding". This insight of course can only grow on appropriate intercultural normative grounds, which means that Shell has to overcome its cultural relativism.

2. Towards an Intercultural Minimal Ethos of Human Coexistence

When Mr. Duncan explains that he believes that the biggest contribution a company can make to the social structure of a country is remaining profitable, that social responsibility differs from one country to another, governments come and go, and situations vary greatly from country to country, that Shell has been involved in matters of energy policy and community services, but (that) political interference is unacceptable, he refers to two closely interwoven ethical shortcomings. Firstly, the assumption that there are no intercultural moral principles and that considering the applicable laws of the countries in which Shell companies operate is sufficient. Secondly, the myth of the unpolitical economic activities of one of the world's largest companies. We cannot go deeper in the latter but it should be clear that the political dimension of the company's activities in Nigeria didn't emerge out of the blue, but is inseperately connected with its economic activities. Beside that, even the statement not to be political is a political one.

But do we have the possibility to establish intercultural moral principles which are so fundamental in their nature that they take precedence over every culture-specific tradition and can claim universal validity? Yes, we have. The very fact of being human provides a platform for an intercultural, universally applicable standard of ethics which is not open to rational question. Whatever the cultural slant of moral issues and values, whatever culture-specific moral tradition the Ogoni people have, nobody can for instance reasonably dispute that all individuals are human beings. It is therefore reasonable to propose the categorical preservation of human dignity and enjoyment of basic human rights as a minimum ethical standard which requires no further justification. It is imperative that each person, Ogoni or Shell employee, be acknowledged and respected as a physically and emotionally vulnerable human being. The point here is for people to acknowledge each other as subjects, as beings of equal dignity.

Shell's behaviour in Nigeria simply disregards the necessity of a minimal ethos of human coexistence. It reduces human relations to an object-oriented bargaining approach and therefore violates the principle of ethical reciprocity, expressed in the categorical imperative formulated by Kant: "Act in such a way that you always treat humanity, whether in your person or in the person of any other, never simply as a means, but always at the same time as an end."

The categorical precedence of the other's human dignity and autonomy over egocentric concerns should be acknowledged for its own sake. Since within discourse ethics this reciprocity principle is interpreted as part of the social context of human beings who acknowledge each other as people capable of and open to argumentation, discourse ethics is especially well suited as a form of intercultural minimal ethics and therefore as a basis for intercultural business ethics, through which each multinational company's behaviour, like Shell's, should be constantly and critically (self-) reflected. Modern business ethics thus comes to life as an intercultural ethical discourse about the moral foundations and political implications of a multinational company's activities. This leads us to the insight that, since everybody is recognized as a human being, no suppression of minority rights or violation of basic human rights can be accepted. Every

legitimate claim made by a person or group has to be taken into consideration. Last but not least an enlightened understanding of corporate relations leads us to a reasonable dialogue of understanding, and
thus to the insight that the corporate dialogue between all those
affected directly or indirectly by the internal and external costs and
benefits of a company's activities is essential.

On such clarified normative grounds the consequences for Shell in
Nigeria would be the following: Shell has to acknowledge the Ogoni
people as human beings with human rights and a culture-specific
identity, whatever the political conditions might be. Since the activities of a large multinational company are of public interest, Shell
should admit that their economic activities always have a political
dimension. Shell should furthermore try to establish a potential for a
dialogue of understanding between representatives of the company,
the Ogoni and all those groups who might lay legitimate moral claims
to the company. This of course would require a radical change of their
general business principles. In the end Shell should be aware of their
ethical responsibility and of their political co-responsibility.

In an era of accelerating globalization the case shows very clearly
that there is a need for redefining cross-cultural relating and understanding between companies and all those groups which are affected
or could be affected by a company's activities. No disregard of legitimate claims can be justified by the fact that customs and way of life or
political conditions are simply different elsewhere.

PART II

International Corruption

Introduction: The Challenge of International Corruption

Peter Eigen

Had this book been published say seven or eight years ago, it would have looked very different − if it had been published at all. At that time, with countries just waking up in the aftermath of the cold war, corruption was just emerging as an issue on the international agenda. It will not come as a surprise to readers to learn that corruption is one of the greatest challenges the world is facing today. It is true that corruption has been a prominent feature of social and political life probably ever since humankind began to differentiate between public and private life. Without corruption many wars would never have been fought, many fortunes we would never have been amassed, many revolutions would never haven taken place, many empires would have enjoyed a more robust health. But it is today that people from North and South, from all walks of life and all sectors of society come to see corruption as the threat and the challenge it is. Why is that so?

A commonly used definition describes corruption as the abuse of public power for private gain. It is obvious that this leads to the distortion of the decision-making process and that it is the general public, the welfare of nations that suffers from that distortion: Private pockets are stuffed as schools are being built at sub-standard quality, roads are washed away with the first rain as ministers caress their bank accounts in Northern tax havens and corrupt manufacturers can sell technologically outdated equipment at above-market prices as their innovative but clean competitors are swept from the market in a competition of bribery. This list could be prolonged, extended with tales of children in a hospital being left untreated by corrupt physicians, of haemophiles being treated with HIV-infected plasma sold by corrupt businessmen. Yet, until seven or eight years ago, all this took place behind a veil of ignorance, was explained away as excessive in a system that was

55

H. Lange et al., Working Across Cultures, 55–58.
© 1998 *Kluwer Academic Publishers. Printed in the Netherlands.*

otherwise working, or even portrayed as a necessary transition stage in the process of modernisation.

All this has changed. Today, we see more clearly that international corruption is fuelled by both supply and demand, we sense that there is a system behind the excessive acts of a few and we realise that if we don't find the means to fight and to prevent corruption, we will endanger our own future. This change has occurred because it is no longer allegedly necessary to prop up corrupt leaders simply because they happened to fight on the right side in the cold war. The rise of democracy and human rights is further supporting this – as people in many different countries have come to realise that they do have inalienable rights to share in their nation's wealth and to participate in the decision-making process of their societies corrupt leaders have come under increasing pressure. And as the world's problems become more pressing with every day – especially as the global economy still is far from a state sustainability – we begin to understand that we simply cannot afford to waste scarce resources through corruption.

The title of this book – Working Across Cultures – may seem at odds with a widely held perception of corruption. Many may see corruption mainly as a domestic problem: a policeman trading in parking tickets, a revenue officer trading in reduced tax assessments, local government officials trading in licences for market stalls. Less apparent, however, is the much deeper international corruption, which usually does not take place as openly and as unashamedly as does petty corruption.

Corruption can be enormously profitable, and often its proceeds represent public monies which have been diverted in huge amounts to overseas "accounts" to the detriment of the social and economic development of the country concerned. A recent United Nations report estimates that as much as 30 billion US-$ has been stashed away internationally by political leaders from some African countries alone.

In such cases, more than a sense of simple justice dictates that a policy of tracing, seizing and confiscating the proceeds of crime be implemented. To do so effectively, the fight against corruption must involve more than the successful detection and prosecution of offenders in one's own country. Why? Because, frequently, the corrupt official has partners in crime abroad who, as a general rule, are beyond the reach of local authorities. The proceeds of corruption are stashed in bank accounts in industrialized countries, and the techniques of money-laundering (perfected mainly by drug traffickers) are brought into play. Therefore, deterrence, no less than justice, dictates that a country should try to put itself in a position where it can successfully bring criminal or other proceedings against such persons through international assistance arrangements.

Therefore effective anti-corruption work involves work across cultures – sometimes legal cultures seem to have much higher walls between them than any other cultures. But working across cultures should also be understood in a more general sense. By doing so, we will be starting to see that we all stand to gain from a commitment against corruption. And in that fight we can draw on experience common to people from all cultures. One of that basic experiences is that there is no culture in the world that allows or condones corruption. This is encouraging as many apologists of international corruption still want us to believe that bribery is necessary for business abroad as it allegedly forms part of local culture. Yet, this isn't to reject cultural relativism out of hand. At least one should try to understand the motivation for some people to come into conflict with the interests of the group they belong to as opposed to the public at large. Where there can be no doubt however, is about the detrimental effects of corruption – the maleducated child will be as disadvantaged in Egypt as it will be in Indonesia. And we can also relate across cultures to sense where the fight against corruption finds its limits – shall we kill, shall we corrupt our souls to fight corruption, as is common practice in China, or in Vietnam?

It is therefore most appropriate and timely that EBEN has made international corruption one of the central themes of its 9th Annual Conference. For international corruption is an important ethical challenge, in particular for leaders in Europe, where so much grand corruption has its principal source.

How important is the ethical dimension of corruption? Last year, in this same venue, we heard some voices of defence for the need to bribe abroad. Some prominent authors on business ethics wanted us to believe that the moral condemnation of corruption is culturally relative, that it is considered unethical only in our European culture and that our exporters should therefore feel free to bribe abroad. These voices have since become thinner – and this forum, the EBEN forum, has made a contribution to this change.

The discussion with EBEN also helps us to learn further about the ethical dimension of international corruption. This will sharpen our conceptual and practical tools to control it – perhaps in the sense of "building the enabling enviroment for ending corruption", as postulated by Karl Homann, including incentives for ethical behaviour. We at *Transparency International* call this enabling environment a *National Integrity System* against corruption. Coming from a more practical experience orientation, we also believe that a holistic systemic approach is needed to induce integrity and accountability.

To strengthen the integrity system of society, a *coalition of government, business and civil society* is required. It is therefore most fortunate that we have brought together excellent representatives from all these players to discuss the problem.

Many of the people that have been contributing to this book have met in the past seven or eight years that have proven so decisive in the fight against corruption. And it is heartening that both the European Business Ethics Network as well as Transparency International have been able to provide a forum for these people. Already, they have walked their first steps together, and a global consensus about what steps need to be taken is gradually evolving. Thus I am certain that the islands of integrity we find in all cultures will have grown, should this book be reprinted in seven or eight years.

We are fortunate and privileged to be introduced to the complex theme of international corruption by the *Hon. Dr. Frene Ginwala*. She comes from special country, South Africa, which has for our subject a special importance. South Africa is in a process of dramatic change. In many ways it is particularly vulnerable to the onslought of corruption. But far from accepting it, as some cultural relativists might suggest, South African society is deeply concerned and determined to build up an integrity system against it. This determination unites government, business and civil society – from top to bottom.

Dr. Ginwala is one of the most prominent leaders of this movement. As Speaker of the National Assembly she has sponsored a number of initiatives that are exemplary in the world – and we will be privileged to hear from her first hand where this complex and dramatic effort of building an integrity system in the new South Africa stands.

The Role of Governments in International Corruption

Frene Ginwala

Comparative experience indicates that radical political transitions are usually accompanied by an increase in corruption, crime and instability, and on occasion by a total breakdown in law and order. The former Soviet Union and Eastern Europe provide many examples. South Africa is another, but in our case the legacy of apartheid has given our problems a particular shape and design.

Since the negotiations to end apartheid began, we found an increase in crime, corruption, racketeering and drug trafficking, as well as political violence, though some of this apparent increase is due to a greater degree of revelation and reporting.

The levels and type of criminal activity can be attributed to the legacy of the apartheid state. In saying that I do not wish to simply blame the past, but rather to explain how that past has shaped and contributed to the situation in which South Africa now finds itself.

Apartheid was a criminal system and was maintained by criminal means, with scant regard for public or private morality, or respect for human life. The activities of agents of the state were unconstrained, institutions lost their legitimacy, and growing numbers of citizens abandoned previously accepted norms of behaviour as they were required to condone, rationalise and legitimise injustice and oppression. The "Total Strategy" put in place to defend Apartheid knew no bounds and both legal and illegal methods were acceptable. As Steven Ellis explains: "That grand corruption, sometimes masquerading as *raison d'Etat*, shapes the environment in which individual politicians, diplomats and business people are obliged to operate."

Front companies were established in South Africa and abroad. They provided the paper cover for the purchase of embargoed oil, strategic minerals, and technology (including the nuclear weapons programme) and for the overt export of South African products. Air-

59

H. Lange et al., Working Across Cultures, 59–72.

lines were set up, ships registered under flags of convenience, "private" mercenary armies and security companies were established and used as surrogate forces, or as assassins. Covert attempts were made to purchase a major US newspaper, and journalists and opinion makers were "bought".

The legal and social system in South Africa was designed to facilitate illegal operations. Ours has been a closed society, with no extradition, poor controls on the movement of funds, no disclosure of nominee companies or transactions, and even the easy establishment of covert banks. This situation also provided the perfect opportunity for private deals and personal enrichment.

South African Defence Force generals were prominent in the illegal trade in ivory, rhino horn and weapons in Angola and Namibia. Another more notorious example is that of Eugene De Kock, a former security police commander whose name has become synonymous with apartheid's death squads (and who in his current trial described himself as apartheid's most effective assassin).

De Kock was an agent in the counter-insurgency forces in Rhodesia, and Namibia. Later he commanded the infamous Vlakplaas, the base from where the euphemistically named Civil Cooperation Bureau, the CCB, operated. According to De Kock's own evidence its operatives fomented infighting within sectors of the black Population. They operated in South Africa and abroad and were responsible for assassination of leading anti-apartheid activists and leaders, car-bombings, supplying arms to Inkatha, poisoning, bank-robberies, disposal of bodies, and handing out booby-trapped hand grenades to black civilians. De Kock faced 121 charges, many of them activities for private profit. They include eight counts of murder, insurance fraud, car theft, theft from the state of proceeds of selling Rhino horn, dealing in false dollar notes and various Eastern Bloc weapons.

Apartheid South Africa opened its doors to smugglers and gave refuge to wanted criminals. In their turn, they put their skills to use, providing for the defence of apartheid. In oil, arms and covert financial transactions, there were well known Mafia connections, as well as with the P-2 Italian operations. Sanctuary was provided to known criminals and often citizenship as well. If there was an occasional public outcry, then citizenship was easily provided by one of the so-called independent Bantustans.

For South African business, apartheid was profitable. To legitimate profits were added the opportunities provided by high tariff protection, by sanctions-busting, by availability of secret funds and accounts, and no public accountability for national resources. A study on South African Business Ethics reported in the South African Journal of Economic and Management Scientists found: "The country started to lose its way in the late 1970's. Dishonesty in business had always been there at the margin, but the fallout from the "Muldergate Scandal" and the lack of direction in the country's political affairs plus overseas pressure all combined to send out a signal that corrupt practices could move into a higher gear". And they did.

Bantustan leaders also had their snouts in the trough and provided their own havens and opportunities for international fugitives and criminals. Our heritage has thus been the complete subversion of public morality, and now democratic South Africa suffers the consequences. We battle a civil service that engages in activities which weaken the democratic order. We have uncovered widespread criminal behaviour in the system of welfare payments, the collection of public revenue, the functioning of the criminal justice system, the theft of drugs and medicine from public hospitals and from salaries and wages.

Most seriously, the police force is riddled with corruption making investigation difficult. Now special task forces have been appointed, and growing numbers of police officers are being charged.

For international drug syndicates and other criminals, South Africa, coming out of decades of isolation, has been virgin territory, fertile ground for exploitation and the establishment of new criminal empires. The climate of criminality, the absence of controls and legal frameworks, and known corrupt elements within the enforcement agencies have attracted them to South Africa.

Most South Africans are justly proud of our efforts to create a new society based on a culture of respect for human rights. Now we find the prevalence of crime and corruption being used to undermine our democratic transition.

There are those who echo our authoritarian and fascist past, and loudly proclaim that the reason we have so much crime is because we are now too soft on criminals. Instead of just locking people up, suspects now have too many rights, bail conditions are too lax, sentences are too lenient, parole is easy and the death penalty has been declared unconstitutional.

The racists in our society have also climbed on the bandwagon: declaring a black government does not know how to govern, it is inept, and there are too many incompetent people in power. Blacks are also more corrupt. It's "their culture" we are told.

Political opportunists combine racism, and authoritarianism in their propaganda projecting the ANC as the party of the black majority, which encouraged lawlessness, made the country ungovern able, allowed the youth to run wild and now cannot cope. Therefore put the old (white), experienced politicians back in power.

Corruption and crime now pose a threat to the government's strategic objectives of development, reconciliation, investment. The loss of public support for the civil liberties essential for democracy could undermine the progress we have made in building a human rights culture in South Africa. Now a legitimate, democratic and honest government is trying to address the problems, but finds that our efforts could be foiled unless the countries of the north also take measures.

Developed countries and their companies tend to see corruption as a problem mainly in the South, and in particular of poorer countries. Sometimes this is attributed to weak institutions and state structures, or more often, to a racist perception that corruption is part of the cultures of particular peoples.

The fact is that despite national and international concern and condemnation, corruption is widespread. Earlier this year Commonwealth Law Ministers considered corruption as a "serious multidimensional national and international problem which inhibits development, creates poverty, and undermines good government".

Globalisation, and relatively stagnant economies in what has been referred to as the developed world, has led to fierce competition among national and multinational companies for a greater share in international trade and in the large construction and other projects in Asia, Africa, Latin America, and now Eastern Europe.

Regrettably, both governments and companies have engaged in corrupt practices to retain or expand their share. Company officials have bribed politicians, public servants, and businessmen in order to secure lucrative contracts. Some politicians from the developed

countries have gone beyond a justifiable attempt to influence and per-
suade, and themselves engaged in corrupt practices.

Mickey Kantor, the US Secretary of Commerce indicated in March
this year that the US government was aware of almost 100 cases in
which foreign bribes undercut the ability of US firms to win contacts
valued at $45 billion in the 12 months before May 1995. A recent UN
study estimates that between 1988 and 1992 the top ten arms exporters
sold US $20 billion of arms to ten developing countries. The study
assumes that at least 15% of this was paid to politicians and military
chiefs as bribes. These are some examples. The scale and extent of
corruption forces us to consider whether there is now a crisis in ethical
practice, both, within the business community and the public sector.

There is an undoubted link between corruption and other forms of
crime. Where you have corruption of government officials, money
laundering, counterfeiting, drug trafficking, the illegal selling of pro-
prietary economic information, illicit arms sales and other organised
and international crime will tend to be more commonplace. The start is
corruption.

Corruption also encourages the penetration of legitimate business
by organised criminals, eager to cover up the paper trail leading to
their ill-gotten gains, thereby corrupting legitimate business as well.
This has already happened in many countries (for example, Colombia,
Mexico, USA, Italy and the former Soviet Union), where organised
crime has become an investor under dubious conditions in privatised
state assets.

Popular definitions and perceptions of corruption are themselves
culturally value-laden, focusing on those who receive the cash or pay-
offs, and away from those who make the payments in order to secure
benefits for themselves or their companies. Thus we hear that corruption is the "use of an official position for purposes of private enrichment or illegitimate advantage." The other side of the transaction,
namely bribery, is ignored and thus is less blameworthy. The dictionary makes no such distinction, and I am glad to say, neither does
Transparency International. Let me offer a personal and Southern
definition: *"Any transaction or attempt to secure illegitimate advantage for national interests or private enrichment through subverting
or suborning public officials from carrying out their proper functions
and acting in the interest of the public."*

In these terms, the picture looks different, and is a more accurate portrayal of the problem and attributes responsibility more even-handedly. Let us be honest and admit that there are two parties to the transaction, the giver and the recipient, the corrupt businessman or company, and the equally corrupt politician or official.

The truth is that international corruption is in many instances tacitly supported and actively encouraged by many Western countries. While most countries have laws against domestic corruption which outlaw the tendering of bribes and the receipt thereof, as far as I am aware only one, the USA, has made it illegal to bribe foreign officials.

What is worse is that many countries consider bribes to be legitimate business expenses that are deductible for tax purposes. This is the case in, Austria, Australia, Belgium, Canada, Denmark, France, Germany, Greece, Ireland, Luxembourg, the Netherlands, New Zealand, Norway, Spain and Switzerland. Thus governments actively encourage their companies to indulge in bribery instead of taking steps to stop them.

Outrageously, Lord Young, a former cabinet minister in Britain and now chairman of Cable & Wireless is reported to have claimed that bribery abroad is job creation at home, while a German priest could say to German businessmen, that it is positively immoral not to bribe abroad if this means a loss of jobs in Germany.

The OECD has made a number of recommendations, but has stopped short of recommending the criminalisation of transnational bribery and corruption. The OECD recommended in 1994 that members take effective measures to deter, prevent and combat bribery of foreign public officials in connection with international business transactions. This decision was not binding on members and remains to be implemented. In May 1996, OECD member countries, supported by the International Chamber of Commerce, agreed to stop allowing companies to deduct the payment of foreign bribes from tax assessments. However, this agreement still does not criminalise transnational bribery and corruption and we do not know when this will be implemented, as tax rules will have to change.

Uncertainty prevails over another recommendation of the OECD's Development Assistance Committee that governments take action to introduce anti-corruption provisions into contracts funded by their aid budgets. We should note the case of war-torn Mozambique, a country where 98% of the country's GNP comes from foreign aid, and where, according to the World Bank, a total of $160 million – a sum amounting to 90% of the government budget – was paid to corrupt civil servants.

In the West, drug-trafficking and international terrorism are seen and promoted as global issues while corruption is not placed on the same pedestal. Consequently, corrupt leaders who are more often than not, perpetrators of human rights abuses can find safe haven with their ill-gotten fortunes. The knowledge of such sanctuary serves as an inducement for leaders to continue with their corruption.

Why don't the developed countries act? Could it be that their politicians and political parties have in their turn been corrupted and benefit directly from corruption in the poorer developing countries?

The connection of corruption in the South with the political parties and decision makers of the North is most clearly demonstrated in the case of Italy, with the disclosure of a sophisticated system developed over many decades. The main political parties received "kickbacks" for the awarding of public contracts from businesses and parastatal corporations.

The scheme included dividing the political oversight of the development budget among the parties – with the Socialist Party benefiting from projects in Somalia, and another party from Mozambique and so on. As part of the political spoils system, Italy's leading political parties also divided along geographical lines the political oversight of the large Italian development budget, with the Italian Socialists Party taking Somalia, for example, and another party, Mozambique. Each party thus took its cut of kickbacks from contacts given to Italian companies, as did the relevant officials and politicians in Africa itself.

There are many cases of governments as well as multinational corporations involved in corruption. I have referred to activities of security and other state agencies in South Africa. You are no doubt familiar with the activities of the C.I.A. and other western intelligence agencies. The support for corrupt leaders, autocratic dictators, drug traffickers and other criminals is well known – Guatemala, Colombia, Nicaragua, Panama, Zaire. Prominent leaders and politicians have been exposed in the US, UK, France, Italy, Spain, Japan, and elsewhere.

The arms industry survives by kickbacks and payment of exorbi-
tant commissions. Arms shipments to developing countries are worth
$35 billion a year from which companies in the North make huge
profits. According to Mark Pieth, weapons sales in Europe require 5 to
8% "augmentation", in the Middle East it is about 10%, while in
Africa it amounts to between 15 % and 25%.

While arms sales have declined in some regions, military expenditures are still going up in two of the poorest regions of the world –
sub-Saharan Africa and South Asia. Developing countries that are
relatively high spenders in the field of military and armaments, receive
twice as much ODA per capita as more moderate military spenders.
Are we expected to believe this is just co-incidence?

Corruption in general hinders the development of international
trade and investment by raising transaction costs and distorting the
operation of free markets. Corruption of government officials has
often been cited as the reason for socio-economic deterioration in
much of Africa and the persuasiveness of corrupt practices within
development programmes in developing countries is believed to be
one of the major reasons for the escalating debt crisis.

Participants at the African Leadership Forum Seminar on Corruption considered that the funds illegally acquired and deposited in off-
shore accounts alone could pay for Africa's debts and serve its development programmes, if they could be brought back to the continent.

While in developed countries the state may be able to withstand
the loss of revenue resulting from bribery induced tax-deductions and
the financing of aid to corrupt countries, or even offset these through
other gains, the consequences in developing countries at the end of the
day is very different. It is the citizen in developing countries who bears
the costs of bribery, directly through the increased costs of government
procurement contracts, consumer products or economic infrastructure
in the host country, and indirectly through loss of state revenue which
the developing state can ill-afford.

Corruption, which is by its very nature covert, thrives under conditions of secrecy and unaccountability. However, it also actively sub-
verts open and transparent societies and threatens the democratic process and democracy itself. All of the 80 coup attempts in Africa
between 1960 and 1982 were justified by their perpetrators as reac-

tions to corrupt regimes, though the governments or juntas which took over were not less corrupt.

There is a link between drug trafficking, national debt, organised crime and corruption in Colombia. We have seen the corruption of the democratic process through provision of massive campaign funds by the drug cartels, where the government was effectively annexed by an interest group. In present-day Russia, organised crime has been known to put up candidates, while the criminalised banking sector has also backed certain political campaigns. The experience of Nigeria also demonstrates how corruption can lead to expanding realms of illegality and criminality.

Thus, while corruption is a moral issue, its consequences extend far beyond questions of personal or business morality and the borders of the South. Corruption is against the long term interests of companies. It loads the dice against efficiency and free competition. As it threatens and undermines democratic governance it also restricts economic development and hence limits the market. You may win one contract, clinch another deal – but what will that market be like in 5 or 10 years – and where will your company be? Rather than allow them selves to be undermined, more governments may follow the Singapore route and simply ban companies and businessmen guilty of corruption.

Over the last decade there has been an increase in international efforts to combat all forms of international crime, including corruption. National and international efforts have tried to contend with difficult questions of national sovereignty and boundaries, differences in legal systems and economic policies in trying to come up with mechanisms and provisions to combat international crime and corruption. It is only recently that some of these efforts are beginning to bear fruit.

In July 1995, the UN urged states to develop comprehensive measures to combat corruption in the corporate, state and private sectors. It noted the draft international code of Conduct for public office holders, which was submitted for further comment and submission to the UN Commission on Crime Prevention and Criminal Justice for implementation after its sixth session.

Under the initiative of President Rafael Caldera of Venezuela the Organisation of American States adopted the Inter-American Convention Against Corruption in March 1996. Parties to the convention agree to criminalise acts of corruption and to cooperate in anti-corruption efforts through extradition, mutual legal assistance, seizure of assets, and technical assistance. The accord also encourages adoption of agreed standards of conduct for public employees. All OAS members are expected to sign the convention.

The convention is particularly significant in that "it will no longer be possible to justify the crime of corruption as political persecution". By committing governments to share evidence and other judicial assistance, the convention will help to overcome the problem that allows the corrupt to go free because the evidence exists in another country and cannot be obtained because there has been no charge or indictment in that country. It will also deny those charged with corruption the benefit of the practice of bank secrecy which has been used to hide illicit transactions.

In Southern Africa, the SADC Countries have set up a Ministerial Forum Against Corruption. This recognised the need to safeguard public integrity and the need for appropriate disclosures of interests of political leaders and decision-makers. It identified "international public procurement as an area which is particularly vulnerable to corrupt practices, and so requiring continual monitoring to ensure through techniques of transparercy and accountability that abuse is kept to a minimum".

Member States agreed to review and develop administrative and regulatory mechanisms for the prevention of corrupt practices; to review the adequacy of criminal laws and procedural Legislation to combat corruption, to adopt procedures for the detection, investigation, and prosecution of corrupt officials and those involved with them; provide for the forfeiture of funds and property derived from corrupt practices; and establish anticorruption agencies in member countries.

Importantly, SADC called upon the "industrialised countries" to criminalise "the bribery of our citizens and ending the tax deductibility of bribes and further by assisting us to recover corruptly-obtained funds placed in havens in their countries". President Mandela has just assumed the Presidency of SADC and will I am sure take this process further.

Within the public sector, governments have a major role to play: the responsibility for the prevention and detection of illegal acts and irregularities ultimately lies with them. They also have a duty to foster practices consistent with high ethical standards within the body of public functionaries. Africa, especially its leadership cannot escape the collective blame for the current state of affairs, nor can the institutions and members of civil society be absolved from blame.

Bureaucracy and a plethora of rules open up avenues for corruption, by creating a core of officials with discretionary authority to apply regulations that are usually framed in a way that few ordinary citizens or businessmen can understand. According to the World Bank, seventy separate steps may be necessary in some countries to take goods across a border legally which, in the case of Nigeria, led to the loss for the government of US $480 million in 1976 from goods smuggled to neighbouring countries. Recently President Mkapa of Tanzania has tried to simplify the system of clearing goods through the port of Dar-es-Salaam.

Ultimately, developing countries will have to ensure sufficient economic growth to address the living needs of citizens and provide decent wages for workers. The collapse of the economy and institutions in many countries has driven those on the margins to engage in petty corruption simply to survive. Unless poverty and deprivation are addressed, the phenomenon of corruption will simply persist.

While governments can put morality on the agenda, and even set the moral tone, morality like values cannot be legislated. There needs to be a voluntary submission to a higher code of probity, which goes beyond strictly legal prescriptions. Let me once more say, that attributing corruption to our cultures is both arrogant and racist – as well as convenient and self-serving. It says more about the culture of the North than our own.

Governments can, however, impose behaviour by providing the legal framework to regulate commerce, enforce anti-corruption and bribery laws etc. Ethical behaviour is about following the spirit of the law as much as the letter.

Ethical behaviour needs to be entrenched throughout society and here organs of civil society have an important role. NGO's, professional organisations, business organisations, have a crucial role in developing public awareness of corruption and its national consequences. Transparency International is mobilising civil society on a global scale. In South Africa business is mobilising against crime.

Mechanisms we can use must include business codes of conduct. These require monitoring procedures. Too many companies have codes which are either ineffective or inadequately followed. For many it is more of a PR exercise.

The role of a free press is fundamental to the fight against corruption. It has a special role to expose corruption. But the press corporations are themselves open to corrupt practices, and need to monitor each other, and we need to monitor them.

To return now, to where I began: South Africa. The promotion of ethical behaviour is part of the renewal of South African society, and is fundamental to our vision of a transformed society. Integrity, Openness, Transparency and Accountability underpin our Constitu tion. The ANC made clean government part of its election manifesto.

We believe, where there is weak social control over government (and business) corruption will flourish. A strong civil society will ensure that government and the corporate world conduct their business in a way which does not harm the well-being and integrity of society. A society, aware of its rights, and organised to give expression freely and fearlessly, will be able to stem the rot of systemic corruption. The South African government is fully committed to combat corruption in public administration and to promote integrity in public life. This resolve is underscored by various provisions of the new constitution, by policy initiatives and legislation of the government.

Our Constitution provides for "Watchdog" structures, such as a Human Rights Commission, an Auditor General and Public Protector. The latter is responsible for the investigation of any alleged maladministration in connection with affairs of government, improper conduct by public officials, improper acts with respect to public money, improper or unlawful enrichment of public officials and an act or omission by a public official resulting in improper prejudice to another person.

An Office for Serious Economic Offences was established to provide for the swift and proper investigation of serious economic offences, and has recently been strengthened.

All government departments, as part of their main functions, are obliged to adopt measures to combat corruption. The Public Service Commission intends establishing a code of conduct which will be included in the Public Service Regulations during 1996.

Parliament has recently adopted its own Voluntary Code of Conduct which provides for disclosure by Parliamentarians of all assets, income, and gifts. This will be extended and will cover all those who hold public office, as well as public employees, and later will be enforced by legislation.

The Justice Committee of Parliament will be spending the entire Spring recess (next month) processing a series of Bills dealing with money laundering, extradition, the proceeds of crime, and much more, providing the legal framework that we lack.

A joint effort, utilising the anti-corruption units set up within the police service, is confronting corruption within the criminal justice system with the establishment of 10 internal anti-corruption units These units have already resulted in more than 800 cases being investigated this year alone.

Within the National Crime Prevention Strategy, we have a National Programme on corruption and commercial crime. The aims of this programme are, inter alia, to reduce the incidence of corruption within the private and public sector. The programme will set up a fully inclusive Programme Team involving representatives of all key stakeholders. This task force will address:
- the development of a code of conduct for business, which requires reporting of cases to the commercial branch, encouraging sectors to address internal criminality openly;
- the co-ordination of training of police, security personnel and internal auditors to maximise the use of investigative and regulatory capacity;
- the provision of an information service on latest trends and developments in commercial crime;
- upgrading legislation to address new technology-based crimes;
- sharing resources between agencies to co-ordinate detection and investigation of commercial crime;
- the development of a comprehensive strategy to deal with government corruption based on international practices and structures.

Fighting crime and corruption falls within the mission of our RDP, and is one of the 6 pillars of the government's Growth and Development Strategy.

Political systems which allow for political patronage and clientelism lend themselves to corrupt practices. These systems have the tendency to perpetuate themselves. They allow the political and bureaucratic class to manipulate the process of resource distribution to favour themselves and their clients. They will forestall any challenges to the system to bring about change and broader economic development.

Only democracy can ensure open and transparent government. In a democratic environment, people will not vote for corrupt politicians or government officials. But democracy is itself threatened by corruption. It is ironic that in the new South Africa, the disclosure of more corruption resulting from open government policies and practices, has resulted in the perception of more corruption.

Corruption in the developing world is linked to corruption in the West. The problem of corruption can thus only be addressed on both the international and national levels.

As a government we have made significant gains against forces, but we have not yet achieved satisfactory levels of honesty and accountability in our public service. In this task we need the support of the international business world which has in the past contributed to the undermining of many government policy initiatives for the sake of short term profits. Let the business world not be responsible for the demise of democracy which is currently in resurgence in the developing world.

The developing world holds as yet untapped economic potential of great importance to the economies of developed countries which are in constant search for new markets. Africa has 600 million people, all of whom are potential customers. By the year 2000, four out of five consumers will be in what is now the developing world, many of them in Africa. Through democracy and development, people become more productive and have greater spending potential. In cultivating markets, business needs to take a long term view, rather than taking quick profits with disastrous consequences for millions of people and ultimately for yourselves.

The European Union and the Fight Against Corruption in International Trade *

Ugo Draetta

1. Premise: Corruption as an International Crime Phenomenon

On a strictly economic level, totally aside from any ethical evaluation, it is almost unanimously accepted that corruption causes considerable damage to the economies of the countries in which it occurs, by impeding international trade and hindering fair competition[1]. In addition to the wasting of scarce resources, in developing countries corruption also damages the growth of democracy, so that it is generally

---

* This article was published first in *Revue De Droit Des Affaires Internationales / International Business Law Journal No. 6/1995*, and is reprinted here with the kind permission of the Chief-Editor of this Journal.

[1] For some interesting socioeconomic thoughts on corruption see J.T. NOONAN, *Bribes - The Intellectual History of a Moral Idea*, University of California Press 1984; S.R. ACKERMAN, *Corruption: A Study in Political Economy*, N.Y. Academic Press, 1978; D. DELLA PORTA & Y. MENY, *Démocratie et Corruption in Europe*, Editions La Découverte, Paris 1995, R. KLITGAARD, *Controlling Corruption*, University of California Press 1988; G. *SAPELLI, Costanti storico sociali della corruzione e peculiaritá nazionali*, unpublished speech at the Conference "Corruption in International Trade", organized by ISDACI in Milan, on November 8, 1994; F. CAZZOLA, *Della Corruzione*, Einaudi 1987; A. ROGOW & H. LASSWELL, *Power, Corruption and Rectitude*, Englewood Cliffs 1966; J.C. PETERS & S. WELCH, *Political Corruption in America: A Search for Definition and a Theory*, in: The American Political Science Review 1978, p.13ff.; D.H. LOWENSTEIN, *Political Bribery and the Intermediate Theory of Politics*, in UCLA Law Review 32 (1985), p.805ff.; S. McMULLAN, A *Theory of Corruption*, in: The Sociological Review 1961, p.96ff.; A. VANNUCCI, *Fenomenologia della tangente: la razionalitá degli scambi occulti*, in Etica degli affari e delle professioni, n.1/1993, p.40ff.

H. Lange et al., Working Across Cultures, 73–91.
© 1998 *Kluwer Academic Publishers. Printed in the Netherlands.*

accepted that to fight underdevelopment one must first fight corruption[2].

It is extremely difficult to calculate the economic damage produced by corruption, due to the secrecy surrounding the illicit payments

---

[2]   See the inspiring (but unpublished) study by G. MOODY-STUART, *Grand Corruption in Third World Development,* prepared for the UNPD Human Development Report 1994. See also S. LABINI, *Il sottosviluppo e l'economia contemporanea,* Bari 1983, p.192, where the argument is made that the reform of developing countries' public administrations is unavoidable to save these countries from the abyss of poverty, and that the purpose of such a reform is not only to improve efficiency, but also "to reduce the possibility of corruption, which is an economic and social issue, before than a moral one". In the same vein J. BHAGWATI, *L'economia dei paesi sottosviluppati,* Edizioni il Saggiatore, 1966, p.85. Enlightening, and dataintensive, is a study written under the auspices of the World Bank by D. GOULD, *The Effects of Corruption on Administrative Performances: Illustrations from Developing Countries,* World Bank Staff Working Papers, Management and Development Series, n. 7, 1983.

Starting from the 1960s, researchers on corruption and its impact on the progress of developing countries appear to be divided into two schools of thought. On the one side, the so-called "moralists" condemn corruption without appeal, for it produces political chaos and economic standstill. To this school belong, among others, G. MYRDAL, *Il dramma dell'Asia,* il Saggiatore, 1971; G. BENSON, S. ANDRESKY and J. DOBEL, *The Corruption of a State,* in: The American Political Science Review 1978, p.973ff.).

On the other side, the second school of thought, the so called "revisionist" or "structuralist", considers that corruption presents specific structural hindrances in developing countries and that, therefore, structural corrective interventions are needed to confront it, beyond repression of isolated episodes. Sharing this orientation is J.S. NYE, *Corruption and Political Development: a Cost-Benefit Analysis,* in: The American Political Science Review 1967, p.419ff.; S. ACKERMAN (op. *cit.); D.H. BAILEY, The Effects of Corruption in a Developing Nation,* in: The Western Political Quarterly 1966, p.726ff.); T. NAS, A *Policy-Oriented Theory of Corruption,* in: The American Political Science Review 1986, p.109ff.; N.H. LEFF, *Economic Development Through Bureaucratic Corruption,* in: The American Behaviorist Scientist 1964, p.8ff.; C. LEJS, *What is the Problem About Corruption?,* in: A. HEIDENHEIMER, *Political Corruption Readings in Comparative Analyses,* New York 1978, p.59ff.; A. HEIDENHEIMER, J. SCOTT, *Corruption, Machine Politics and Political Change,* in: The American Political Science Review 1969, p.1142ff..

On corruption, with regard to specific developing countries, see T. SMITH, *Corruption, Tradition and Change in Indonesia,* in A. HEIDENHEIMER, *Political Corruption Readings in Comparative Analyses,* New York 1978, p.427ff.

system. Nonetheless, interesting investigations are being carried out by a Berlin-based, non-governmental international organization called *Transparency International ("TI")*, which was established in May 1993 to promote the fight against corruption at an international level. These investigations are aimed at calculating the cost to developing countries arising out of the diversion as a result of corruption from welfare-producing uses of community resources to the enrichment of the few. These studies indicate – as was expected – that corruption-related costs to the world economy have reached significant levels, estimated at several billions of US dollars per year[3].

---

[3] Although these are approximate figures, they are nonetheless adequate to provide a rough idea of the dimension of the phenomenon. Reliance is placed on the data furnished by S.R. ACKERMAN, *Proposal for Research on the Leyel and Impact of Corruption in International Business,* unpublished report presented at the annual meeting of *Transparency International,* held in Milan, on March 27-28, 1995. The author, in her report, describes the criteria of an analysis undertaken by some American economists, aimed at determining the economic cost of corruption in international trade, and gives a rough estimate of it, using data supplied by the International Monetary Fund. According to these data, the direct foreign investment in developing countries has exceeded $40 billion per year between 1990-1992. Assuming that 5% of this amount is attributable to illegal payments, the total volume of corruption would reach $2 billion per year. Considering, moreover, that illegal payments are associated not only with investments, but also with importation of goods, the cost of corruption would amount to $45 billion per annum (5% illegal payment rate applied to the $908 billion worth of goods imported every year by developing countries in 1990-1992).
The author also cites other interesting data. In Italy, for instance, according to studies carried out by the Istituto Einaudi, in 1993 $4.4 billion were spent in illegal payments to obtain contracts. In Mozambique, in 1993 corrupt public officials have obtained illegal payments of some $160 million, an amount equal to 90% of the governmental budget, in a country where 98% of the Gross Domestic Product comes from foreign aid. See also G. MOODY-STUART, *op. cit.,* who maintains that illegal payments to obtain transnational contracts have increased considerably over the last years, reaching on average 10-15% of the contract price from the previous 2.5%, and offering more specific data concerning Brazil, Pakistan and Japan. Nor is it possible to argue, as some commentators do, quoting the Somoza family case in Nicaragua (J.S. NYE, *op. cit.,* p.419), that the money illegally received is reinvested so as to benefit developing countries' economy. The truth is that, to consider Swiss banks only, some $20 billion are deposited there in the name of leaders of African countries, as a Swiss report, quoted in the document *Corruption and Development* (1993 draft) by *Transparency International,* has recently shown. Another dramatic aspect is the growth of

It is also known that, in many industrialized countries, illegal payments abroad by national enterprises in order to obtain contracts are tolerated, or even encouraged. The rationale behind this approach is that winning orders abroad increases the work-load of national manufacturers, fosters employment opportunities and improves the country's balance of trade. In this regard, it is interesting to point out that these arguments have been widely recognized as mistaken even from a strict economics perspective. Namely, this approach is the result of pressure groups who take into account their own interests rather than those of all citizens. The interests of the entire community, in fact, would be better served by developing a genuinely-competitive commercial and industrial structure, instead of an artificial one, which is kept alive by practices which are illegal, at least in the countries to which they are directed[4].

This point leads us to the issue of the global dimensions of corruption, which is the focus of this study. Although corruption obviously exists and produces effects at a domestic level, a national legal system has the means to fight and repress this kind of corruption. The only problem in this respect is the effectiveness of the enforcement of these means, which in turn depends on the political conditions and the degree of social development of the State in issue. Corruption at the national level is an issue dealt with differently by each country and, if contained at that level, should have no international significance.

The phenomenon dealt with here is instead corruption in international trade, a phenomenon which, along with the globalization of commercial and, more generally, economic activities, has itself reached a global dimension. We are witnessing therefore international business transactions making provisions for highly complicated contractual schemes. The only purpose of these arrangements is to assure that a money payment or the conferring of other benefits by the party obtaining a contract (usually an enterprise from an industrialized coun-

---

developing countries' indebtedness as a consequence of their having paid bribery-inflated contract prices. According to an estimate given by the Vice President of Ecuador, almost one third of these countries' indebtedness has to be considered the result of illegal payments (see D. FRISCH, *Les effets de la corruption sur le dévelopement,* presented to the Regional Seminar on "Corruption, Democracy and Human Rights", held in Cotonou, Benin, on September 19-21, 1994).

[4]   See the vast majority of commentators quoted supra, fn. 1 and 2.

try) to individuals (usually public officials) having the power to affect the decision of the client (usually the government or a public entity of a developing country) is not easily retraceable. The parties' creativity in this respect has no limits, and nowadays cases of up-front cash payments from the corrupter to the corrupted are very rare indeed. To conceal these payments, agreements of distribution, agency, other kinds of brokerage, pre and post-sale assistance, subcontracts, various sorts of partnership or advice are usually simulated. The only or main purpose of similar arrangements is to make formally legitimate payments whose actual consignee is a person different from the recipient[5].

Frequently such payments are effected via international banking transactions in countries where bank secrecy is jealously guarded for reasons not always easy to acknowledge, or where lax regulatory controls exist, if at all, on financial transactions. Consequently, there is less risk of the illegal payment being discovered.

Thus, corruption in international trade qualifies as a phenomenon of international crime, whose detrimental effects are usually much more serious than those arising out of purely "domestic" corruption, not least because of the larger dimension that international trade, in a context of a globalized economy, has reached in comparison to domestic trade.

2. Inadequacy of National Instruments to Confront International Corruption

It is surprising that, in light of the above, the instruments to confront corruption exist essentially at the national level only, and that the struggle to combat corruption at an international level is still at an embryonic stage.

Analysis shows that the vast majority of national laws limit their consideration of corruption to the bribery of national public officials, whereas it does not constitute a crime to bribe public officials of another country. Moreover, in almost every State, possibly illegal

---

5   See S.J. RUBIN, *International Aspects of the Control of Illicit Payments* (Symposium: *The Foreign Corrupt Practices Act: Domestic and International Implications,* March 19-20, 1982), in Syracuse Journal of International Law and Commerce 9 (1982), p.315ff.

payments (in the country of destination) made to obtain contracts are deductible for tax purposes by the payer, without any duty imposed on the tax authority to exercise any oversight over the legitimacy of the payment. As a result, if illegal payments can be treated as "transaction costs", less tax is recoverable. Thus, the cost of the illegal payments, in reducing revenues to the State, is borne by the entire community. It is as though the country as a whole, abets corruption by subsidizing illicit payments.

Some years ago, when currency restrictions were in force, in many European countries including Italy even the authorizations required to transfer abroad foreign currency, necessary to promote the award of contracts by foreign public officials, customarily were issued without any control over the lawfulness of these payments.

The rationale for this kind of approach by the national legislator is apparently unexceptionable, for it is linked to the principle of territoriality of criminal law, which would preclude criminalizing conduct occurring outside a State's national territory. Corruption of a foreign government official, therefore, could be prosecuted only in the public official's national State.

At this point, two observations are noteworthy. First, at a purely conceptual level of analysis, nothing prevents a State from considering as a crime the conduct of its own citizens in another country, especially when it would not be difficult to identify that conduct's links with the State's national territory, for instance, as the place where the payments qualified as illegal originate. This is for example the direction followed by both the United States and Swedish legislators, as discussed below.

Secondly, at a substantive level of analysis, such an approach by the industrialized countries reflects a certain degree of hypocrisy. In fact, the issue of corruption has reached the current dimension in international trade precisely because of the reluctance by the governments of client states (often – though not necessarily – developing countries), to enforce rigorously their own domestic anti-corruption regulations.

In other words, if developed countries were fully aware of the economic damage caused by corruption as a phenomenon of international criminality, it would be reasonable to expect a more responsible approach from the developed countries.

As recent case law has shown, in some European countries the actual recipients of illegal payments made abroad were politicians of the same European country of the bribing enterprise. In this way, all or part of these payments would end up "coming back home" after a long series of transactions aimed at concealing the identity of the ultimate recipients. This element induces the belief that, underneath the developed countries' formal invocation of the principle of the territoriality of criminal law, might be concealed little more than simple hypocrisy – of essentially protecting their own narrow interests.

The problem we are dealing with, moreover, is aggravated by a number of additional circumstances. Attention must be paid to the fact that many international transactions enjoy public financing or foreign trade credit guarantees and insurance from entities managing taxpayers' funds, and that the concession of such financing or foreign trade credit guarantee and insurance is never subject to any control as to the inexistence of illegal payments. Thus, under this aspect too, the citizens of the State allowing such benefits bear the relative burdens, as long as the underlying contract or the possibly uncollectible credits are being financed with public money.

The conclusion is that, as corruption takes the form of an international crime, its suppression is still regulated to national legal instruments inherently territorial in nature and, therefore, largely inadequate to confront it.

3. Need for Internationalization of the Battle Against Corruption in International Trade

As can be seen from the previous discussion, an effective campaign against corruption in international trade may be undertaken only by means of the internationalization of legal instruments. This could be done following the methods adopted for repressing other violations in the international arena. One could consider as examples: antitrust regulation, the fight against environmental crimes, drug smuggling, money laundering, insider trading, and human rights' violations.

All these violations feature a common element. With the globalization of economies and the steady increase of international transactions, even the facts constituting these violations have assumed a global dimension. The result is a tension between the global dimension of these violations and the territoriality of the domestic rules against them. Simply summing these territorially limited norms (which are in addition not co-ordinated among each other, but simply juxtaposed) is not enough to provide an adequate normative answer to unlawful situations of a transnational nature.

Returning to the examples referred to above, it becomes self-evident that (i) competition-infringing agreements and monopolistic positions do not produce their most detrimental effects upon national markets only, but also on international trade, (ii) environmental harms do not stop at States' national borders, and those crossing them are very often the most severe, (iii) drug smuggling and money laundering (the latter being often directly linked to the former), thrive exactly because of territorially-limited bite of national laws fails to contain their global dimension, (iv) it would be impossible to suppress insider trading on an exclusively national basis, in a world where telecommunication systems easily permit every possible form of securities' transaction around the globe, and finally, (v) human rights' protection is today recognized as a value to be promoted universally, one which is no longer considered as belonging to that "domestic jurisdiction" left to the rules of each State.

As a consequence, the internationalization of the fight against these kinds of violations has long since been achieved, especially within those geographic areas, such as Europe, where it has been possible to reach an advanced degree of integration. National rules have not disappeared, of course, but have ended up playing what we would call a residual role.

It is perhaps worth now offering some examples of this internationalization of the fight with regard to each of the situations referred to supra.

In the matter of *antitrust,* regulation now exists throughout the European Economic Area. In addition, some statutes, such as the *Sherman Act* in the United States, contain remarkable elements of "extra-territoriality", at least in so far as they strike down agreements, whether concluded abroad or between foreigners, producing any effect in a given State. The normative framework is completed by international instruments, such as the agreement between the EC and the US, striving to assure cooperation between their respective agencies in charge of enforcing domestic antitrust rules[6].

Environmental protection is now an objektive falling expressly within the jurisdiction of the EU and, at a broader level, is the subject of a growing number of international conventions, both bilateral and multinational[7]. Likewise, the fight against *drug smuggling* and *money laundering*, besides being the subject of international agreements, is within the framework of the judicial cooperation in the EU and, at least so far as money laundering is concemed, is specificaffy addressed by EU legislation[8]. In addition, measures against *insider trading* are being taken at the EU level. Moreover, the relevant EC Directive concerned has given rise to the promulgation of new legislation within Italy[9].

Finally, there is little need to mention that *human rights'* protection is guaranteed by a number of international instruments, both within the United Nations and at the regional level, and more specifically within the European context[10]. Active in this field is also an international non-governmental organization, Amnesty International, whose organ-

---

6   Competition Laws Co-operation Agreement, signed in Washington on September 23, 1991, between the United States and the Commission of the European Communities. See A.A. GRIKSCHEIT, *Are We Compatible? Current European Community Law on the Compatibility of Joint Ventures with the Common Market and Possibilities for Future Development,* in: Michigan Law Review 92 (1994), p.968f.

7   With the passage of the Single European Act, Title VII on environment has been added to the EC Treaty. As far as EC legislation on the issue is concerned, it is worth mentioning Directive 85/337/EEC, introducing mandatory assessment of the effects of certain public and private projects on the environment, and Directive 82/501/EEC on the major-accident hazards of certain industrial activities. As for conventional international law, we quote the Declaration on Environment and Development, issued following the 1992 UN Rio Conference, the 1976 Barcelona Convention for the protection of the Mediterranean Sea against pollution, and the 1979 Geneva Convention on long-range transboundary air pollution

8   Directive 91/308/EEC on the prevention of the use of the financial system for the purpose of money laundering.

9   Directive 89/592/EEC, coordinating regulations on insider dealing, implemented in Italy by the Law no. 157/1991.

10   See principally the 1948 UN Universal Declaration of Human Rights and the European Convention for the Protection of Human Rights and Fundamental Freedoms of November 4, 1950, with further additional Protocols.

izational structure has provided the model for Transparency International.

The foregoing examples are not meant to be exhaustive, but further examples would appear unnecessary. The point is that, as the structure of the illegal conduct becomes increasingly international, so do the legal instruments. It seems odd, therefore, that this process has not yet taken place, or at least has done so very narrowly, in relation to corruption in international trade.

With respect to international trade, in fact, we have on record only some UN soft-law projects, along with some more recent documents, such as an OECD Recommendation and a Council of Europe Resolution, both without binding effect.

More specifically, the United Nations General Assembly adopted in 1975 Resolution no. 3514, which "condemns all corrupt practices, including bribery, by transnational and other corporations, their intermediaries and others involved in violation of the laws of the host countries", and requests that all Governments cooperate against corruption[11]. An ambitious 1979 draft treaty on corrupt practices was drawn up but not adopted[12]. Should it be approved, this project would

---

[11] One year later, the Economic and Social Council adopted Resolution 2041 (August 11, 1976), entitled "Corrupt practices, particularly illicit payments, in international commercial transactions", and decided to establish an ad hoc Intergovernmental Working Group to conduct an examination of the problem of corrupt practices. However, within the UN bodies a code of conduct for multinational enterprises dealing expressly with corrupt practices has yet not been adopted. In 1988, the Secretary General transmitted to the ECOSOC a report by the chairman presiding at the special session of the Commission on Transnational Corporations, recommending that further consultations be undertaken to resolve the outstanding issues in the draft code of conduct (Doc. E/1988/39). Still in draft forrn is a UN international code of conduct on the transfer of technology (Doc. TD/CODE/TOT/25 of June 2, 1980) inviting the parties to "observe fair and honest business practices" (p.15). Another general invitation to abstain from abusive practices (and, therefore, corruption) is in the UN code against Restrictive Business Practices, based on a UNCTAD report and adopted by a General Assembly resolution of December 5, 1980. Thus, Resolution no. 3514 of December 15, 1975, is the only UN document squarely addressing corruption. Although lacking any binding effect, the document provides for the Secretary General to present the General Assembly, via the Economic and Social Council, with reports on the implementation of the Resolution.

[12] See the text in Doc. E/1979/104. The draft treaty was prepared in May, 1979, by a Working Group established by the Economic and Social Council. Its enactment

oblige the signatories to the treaty to forbid bribes to foreign public officials by their citizens.

As far as the OECD is concerned, this organization had already dealt with corruption, albeit in a broader context, in the 1976 "Guidelines for Multinational Enterprises"[13]. The OECD Recommen-

---

has so far been prevented by conflicts which have arisen in the past among the member States. Articles 1, 2 and 4 of this draft require the signing States to modify their domestic anti-corruption criminal laws so as to make them applicable to corruption prosecutions against foreign public officials, if the crime occurs on their territory, and the contracting State is allowed to prosecute the crime of corruption of a foreign public official committed abroad by one of its own citizens (art. 4.1. (c)). This provision establishes a nationality-based criminal jurisdiction, as is provided for in some American statutes, among them the 1977 Foreign Corrupt Practices Act (Pub. L. No. 95-213, 91 Stat. 1494, codified at 15 U.S.C. 78dd-1 & 78dd-2, as amended), which is discussed below. The draft treaty binds the signatories to cooperate actively in the field of criminal investigations, to exchange information about corruption cases, and to communicate the measures adopted on the matter. Hence, it is clear that the approval of such a treaty would require a serious and explicit commitment on behalf of all contracting States to confront corruption in international trade, and it is no surprise that some States may show some reluctance to go forward with it. For comments on the draft treaty, see D. SLADE, *Foreign Corrupt Payments: Enforcing a Multilateral Agreement*, in: Harvard International Law Journal 22 (1981), p.148ff.; A. HERITIER, *Les pots-de-vin*, Mémoires de la Facultd de Geneve, 1982.

13 *Principes directeurs à l'intention des enterprises multinationales, OECD*, Paris, 1976. The text has been revised in 1979, 1982 and 1984. These Guidelines are non-binding recommendations jointly addressed by the OECD governments to multinational enterprises operating in their territories. In setting standards of behavior and practice, their objective is to provide guidance to multinational enterprises and to help to ensure that the operations of these enterprises are consistent with the policies of the countries where they operate. In doing so, the Guidelines seek to strengthen the basis of mutual confidence between enterprises and host States, so as to create favorable conditions for foreign investments. In this regard, enterprises are required to abide by certain conduct standards, among which are those described in sections 7 and 8. Of these sections, the former specifies that multinational enterprises should "[n]ot render – and they should not be solicited or expected to render – any bribe or other improper benefit, direct or indirect, to any public servant or holder of public office". The latter provides that "[u]nless legally permissible, [multinational enterprises should] not make contributions to candidates for public office or to political parties and other political organizations". See *The OECD Guidelines for Multinational Enterprises,OECD, Paris,* 1976, p.13. Of interest is the institutional mechanism devised for the enforcement of the OECD Guidelines. A Committee on International Invest-

dation of May 27, 1994, instead, has as a specific object corruption in international trade transactions, and contains a General invitation to OECD States to adopt effective provisions penalizing the corruption of a foreign public official. Even if this recommendation is of political and moral value only, it addresses, with the invitation and its other provisions, what appears to be the crucial issue of the anti-corruption battle on the international scale[14].

The Council of Europe also adopted a resolution at its 19th Conference of European Ministers of Justice, held at Malta on the 14-15th of June, 1994, where a proposal was put forward to establish an interdisciplinary study group with the task of formulating an international action scheme against corruption[15].

---

ments and Multinational Enterprises (CIME) has been established as a forum, open to all enterprises, where all issues concerning the enforcement of the Guidelines are discussed. (Ibid., n. 11, pp. 12, 29). Although the CIME is not authorized to issue evaluations on the conduct of individual enterprises, the publication of its discussions might work as an effective deterrent against enterprises persisting in the violation of the OECD Guidelines. For an overall discussion of these Guidelines, see NGUYEN HUU TRU, *Les codes de conduite: un bilan,* in: Revue générale de droit international public 1992, p.51ff.; R. BLANPAIN, *The OECD Guidelines and Labour Reiations: Badger and Beyond,* Kluwer, Deventer, 1980. On the limited effectiveness of anti-corruption *soft* law norms such as those of conduct codes or guidelines, see W. SURREY, *The Foreign Corrupt Practices Act: Let the Punishment Fit the Crime,* in: Harvard International Law Journal 1979, p.245ff.

[14] The definition of corruption contained in the OECD Recommendation is partially borrowed from the U.S. Foreign Corrupt Practices Act. The Recommendation invites the member States to modify their domestic legislation not only so as to make illegal the corruption of a foreign public official, but to prevent the tax deductibility of illegal payments, to improve transparency of enterprises accounting as to major payments, and to deny public aid (financing, foreign trade credit insurance, etc.) to enterprises involved in corruption cases. The CIME fulfills a monitoring duty, by verifying every year the extent to which member States comply with the OECD Recommendation.

[15] "Resolution concerning private, administrative and criminal law aspects of anti-corruption", 19th European Ministers of Justice Conference, Valletta, Malta, 14-15 June, 1994, adopted on the basis of a report by the Italian Ministry of Justice, comparing different anti-corruption criminal rules and pointing out the ties between corruption, money laundering and organized crime. The Resolution also sets forth guidelines for the interdisciplinary study group. This is in charge of preparing, after having undertaken a thorough study of criminal, private, administrative and tax law issues, model-laws, codes of conduct, administrative regula-

Finally, non-governmental organizations, for instance the Paris based International Chamber of Commerce (ICC), have occasionally dealt with corruption in international trade[16].

Such efforts at the international level ought to be viewed as unsatisfactory. Indeed, the time has come for much more effective measures against corruption in international trade. While waiting for such developments at the international level, or as an alternative to them, we propose that States should, at a minimum, follow the example offered by the United States and Sweden, where a national legislative answer has been given by sanctioning as illegal the bribing of foreign government officials to obtain commercial benefits by those States' citizens[17]. In these countries, the legislature has clearly considered as concrete measures unavoidable to combat corruption in international trade, despite the private interests of their national enterprises, which suffer at the hands of third-country competitors who lack any such legal constraint.

With regard to these laws, "extra-territoriality" is alleged to be incompatible with the notion of the territoriality of criminal law rooted in our legal tradition. Nonetheless, we note that in these laws, apart from the principle of nationality as the legal basis for extending jurisdiction, there always exists a nexus between the factual structure of the illicit conduct and the territorial domain of the rule governing it.

---

tions and a draft international convention to promote cooperation among member States' administrative and jurisdictional bodies in dealing with corruption cases.

16 The ICC adopted on November 29, 1979, the *Rules of Conduct to Combat Extortion and Bribery,* as a part of the report *Extortion and Bribery in International Transactions,* creating for the occasion an expert panel in charge of the their enforcement. These Rules had a small following, and only as late as the end of 1994 the *ad hoc* committee for their revision was nominated. In so far as ICC-administered international commercial arbitrations are concerned, arbitrators have frequently faced invalidity claims against agreements to effect illegal payments. Arbitrators have not delivered univocal awards on the issue; see A. CRIVELLARO, *Intermediazione illecita ed arbitrato internationale,* report to the Conference on "Corruption in international trade", organized in Milan by ISDACI, on November 8, 1994.

17 With specific regard to the United States, see the 1977 Foreign Corrupt Practice Act, commented by SURREY, *op. cit.,* and F.F. HEIMANN, *Should Foreign Bribery Be a Crime?,* report to the Conference on "Corruption in international trade", organized in Milan by ISDACI, on November 8, 1994.

For example, in the United States Foreign Corrupt Practices Act this criterion consists of the use of an instrumentality of interstate commerce (including the U.S. mail and Telephone and means of Transport) by the corrupter, in order for one's conduct to fall within the scope of the statute. On a closer inspection, the argument concerning the territoriality of criminal law looks more and more like a shield for those States which, pressurized by the needs of lobbying groups, do not intend to provide a satisfactory answer to the issue of corruption in international trade.

4. Legal Foundations of and Possible Developments in EC Anti-corruption Regulation

The EU represents, in light of the high level of integration achieved among its member States, a perfect testing ground for an effective action to repress corruption in international trade – at least within the common market established by it. Strangely, however, the issue of corruption has so far been barely considered by the EU bodies, so that, essentially, the EU has not as yet taken any official stand on such a serious issue.

EU authorities have instead paid attention to the adjoining issue of fraud to the Community[18]. The new article 209 A of the EC Treaty, added by the Treaty of Maastricht, binds the member States to "take the same measures to counter fraud affecting the financial interest of the Community as they take to counter fraud affecting their own financial interest". Fraud to the EC is an example of a course of conduct being criminalized at the national level, as a consequence of an international treaty, even when the constituent elements are no longer exclusively those dictated by national law. This example demonstrates that there exist conditions for an analogous process of internationalization at the EC level for the crime of corruption.

However, since every individual European Union statutory initiative requires its own legal foundation, we will begin by indicating briefly the norms of the European Union Treaty where such a legal

---

[18] The annual report on frauds presented by Commissioner Anita Gardin on March 29, 1995, indicates 1,032 millions ECU discovered in 1994, equal to 1.2% of the entire European Union annual budget.

foundation can be found, that is to say, to underline the relevance of corruption at the EC level. Then, we will try to sketch a series of concrete measures which, without distorting the existing laws, could be adopted by the EU to combat corruption.

4.1.   Legal basis for EU anti-corruption initiatives.

Article 235 of the EC Treaty provides for the possibility of an action by the EC when it "should prove necessary to attain, in the course of the operation of the common market, one of the objectives of the Community and this Treaty has not provided the necessary powers...". As a preliminary step, therefore, it seems to be necessary to assess briefly how corruption in international trade (or among member States) might jeopardize the functioning of the common market and the achievement of the purposes of the European Community. Without trying to cover all the issues involved, in the following sections we will draw attention to several EC rules which would be violated, or whose enforcement would be endangered, by corruption-tainted business transactions.

(a) Rules on competition (arts. 85 ss.)

We consider it settled that corruption obstructs trade among Member States and restricts competition within the common market, so long as the Arrangement between corrupter and corrupted is aimed at excluding from the competitive arena those who do not agree to effect payments qualified as illegal in the country where they are demanded.

(b) State Aids (arts. 92 ss.)

Tax-deductible illegal payments, public financing of international contracts obtained through illicit compensations, credit insurance by public agencies on such contracts are all cases of State aid to bribing enterprises, punishable under art. 92 of the EC Treaty as designed to favor those enterprises, thus distorting competition within the common market.

(c) Principle of non-discrimination

Allowing corruption in international trade results in the violation of the principle of non-discrimination – one of the pillars of the EC legal system. Discrimination affects those exporters who do not agree, in order to obtain contracts, to make payments deemed to be illicit in the countries where they are demanded.

(d) Development co-operation (EC Treaty, Title XVII)

Corruption, as noted at the outset, is universally recognized as one of the main causes of underdevelopment. It does not only cause the waste of scarce economic resources, with devastating effects on the economies of developing countries, but it also hinders the growth of a democratic consciousness in the citizens of these countries. Failure to prosecute corruption in international trade, using all available means, represents a retreat from the principles which should guide the EC action in the matter of co-operation for development, as described in Title XVII of the EC Treaty.

(e) Public Procurement Directives

One of the objectives effectively pursued by the EC with a series of important directives is assuring transparency in public procurement within the Community, and equal access to all EC enterprises. There is little need to underline that anti-corruption initiatives are the logical corollary of such a policy, as corruption is one of the major obstacles towards transparency and freedom of access. It is not surprising, therefore, that within the GATT negotiations there have always been efforts to link "procurement code" rule to an effective anti-corruption agenda.

(f) Transparency of corporate accounting

The EC has enacted several directives, with the purpose of harmonizing corporate legal regimes law among member States, dealing with transparency of corporate accounting. It is evident, as case law in Italy and in other countries has demonstrated, that illegal payments, due to the impossibility of being recorded as such, are often connected with the falsification of accounting documents, which violates the principles underlying these directives.

(g) Cooperation in the fields of justice and internal affairs

Anti-corruption action undoubtedly falls within those objectives of judicial cooperation in criminal matters and of police cooperation directed at the prevention and the fight against international crimes set forth in art. K 1, nn. 7 and 9, of the Maastricht Treaty.

(h) Approximation of laws

EC anti-corruption initiatives could also be justified on the basis of the arts. 100 and 100 A of the EC Treaty, so long as corruption directly affects the creation and the functioning of the common market (art. 100), or of the internal market (art. 100 A).

4.2.   Proposal for EU intervention

Having identified the legal basis for an EU anti-corruption initiative, we would like to indicate some measures which could be taken immediately by EC bodies, at the very least to take eventually an unequivocal stand on the matter, instead of the rather agnostic approach currently being maintained.

(a) At the level of the *European Parliament*, it seems that the time has come for this body to adopt a resolution whereby corruption is denounced as an international crime and domestic anti-corruption measures are declared insufficient to deter corruption.

The European Parliament should take a firm stand against the opportunistic approach grounded in the territoriality of criminal law, which would prevent domestic courts from punishing the corruption of foreign officials. Such a resolution should also acknowledge the strict ties between a country's anti-corruption actions and its democratic development, as well as the devastating impact of corruption on the development of the world economy. The European Parliament should, consequently, in the name of the people of all the States of the European Union, provide explicit support to all the international organizations, governmental and non-governmental, engaged in the struggle against corruption, and to stimulate EU intervention in the field, making use of the new powers to initiate a legislative process conferred upon it by the Treaty of Maastricht.

(b) As far as the Commission is concerned, it should issue proposals – both for directives and regulations – with the aim of correcting the most troublesome aspects of the current situation.

A directive, for example, could harmonize member States' criminal laws in relation to the crime of corruption, by embracing into the concept of "territory", necessary to determine the *locus commissi delicti,* the territory of all member States. Such a harmonization would make it illegal in every State to corrupt a government official of any other member State. Modifications to some national penal codes which, in the matter of fraud to the EC, treat it equal to a domestic fraud, go in the same direction. The issue is to keep going on this path to arrive, eventually, at a uniform European law making it illegal to corrupt a govermnent official of every country. There is no need to stress the fact that, in other fields, the notion of national territory has already been broadened, by replacing it with that of Member States' territory, for purposes of determining the field of application of some uniform rules. For examples, the industrial property field (European patent, European trademark) and the corporations field (European Economic Interest Groups, European Corporation Articles project).

A second directive could prevent Member States from allowing tax-related deductions for illegal payments. This could take place via a system of checks or, more easily, by subjecting the deduction to a declaration as to the lawfulness of the payments, possibly undersigned by the receiving foreign agent or middle-man. Should such a declaration be later ascertained as being false, all criminal-law-related consequences provided for false declarations of this kind would apply. An identical solution could be devised where state financing or credit insurance in international business transactions is funded with public money.

Other rules should strengthen the uneven control system currently in force as to the lawfulness of payments related to contracts financed or somehow subsidized by the EC via the European Investment Bank, various structural funds, or other types of EC financial support.

c) At the level of the *Council*, but especially of the *European Council*, the issue of corruption should be included on the agenda in order to obtain a declaration of common intent to fight it.

The foregoing are only guidelines for EU intervention against corruption which could take place without undue delay, and which would have the advantage of providing a clear indication of the EU approach on the issue. It is also evident that these actions should work as emergency measures only, and should be the prelude to more organic legislation by the European Union to address corruption as an international crime. Among these more far-reaching actions, we would certainly consider the promotion among the member States of an international agreement, whose content should be equivalent to the 1979 UN draft treaty on corrupt practices, or should give binding effects to the norms of the OECD Recommendation of May 27, 1994. EC action for the uniformity of member States' anti-corruption legislation, following the Swedish or the U.S. model of the Foreign Corrupt Practices Act, would point towards the same target. This would be an important step in the direction of an Europe which does not want to be only the Union of governments and multinational enterprises, but mainly the Union of European citizens.

Co-ordinated Steps to Prevent Transnational Corruption. Consequences for the Business Community

Mark Pieth

I. This summer the media reported extensively on the gastronomic highlights of the Lyon Summit of G7. As we were told, the heads of State dined for eight hours and worked in session for six hours, but sometimes the shorter debates are the more productive: They achieved a rather astonishing breakthrough on a delicate issue: The topic of bribery in international business relations. In their final communiqué of June 28 we can read that they are "resolved to combat corruption in international business transactions, which is detrimental to transparency and fairness and imposes heavy economic and political costs. In keeping with the commitments of OECD Ministers to *criminalise* such bribery in an *effective and co-ordinated manner"*, presidents and prime-ministers urge, as the text runs on, "that the OECD further examine the modalities and appropriate international instruments to facilitate criminalisation and consider proposals for action in 1997". To those who have been involved in the discussion on international commercial corruption over the last two decades this commitment – for all its diplomatic jargon – clearly marks a milestone in the development of meaningful concepts against corruption.

You might remember that the UN drafted a world-wide convention against international corruption after 1975. It was an ambitious project – too ambitious at the time – as one soon realised. In 1979 the UN had to admit failure and abandon the initiative. A project developed at the same time by the international business community – the International Chamber of Commerce (ICC) – was finalised in 1977. Without the seconding of intergovernmental action it remained, however, more or less dead letter. We will come back to the updated version of 1995 in just a moment. A further initiative, this time in the context of indus-

H. Lange et al., Working Across Cultures, 93–112.
© 1998 *Kluwer Academic Publishers. Printed in the Netherlands.*

trialised states, focusing primarily on establishing a level playing field
of commerce, the *OECD action against corruption* faced similar difficulties in its first stages in 1986 and 1989. Many countries feared,
their industry might suffer from a competitive disadvantage if they
were to take the lead against transnational corruption. Yet in 1994,
after five years of preparatory work, a dramatic breakthrough was
achieved: For the first time a considerable number of countries
committed themselves to take "concrete and meaningful steps" against
the bribery of foreign public officials. The 1994 *OECD-Recommendation* was – as you can see from the documentation – still vague in
terms and only politically, not legally binding. However, it initiated a
process, helped along by peer-pressure, especially by a tight follow-up
mechanism.

A series of in-depth analyses of sub-topics like *criminalisation* of
the bribery of foreign officials, *banning tax deductability* of such
bribes, developing *bookkeeping- and auditing standards* to promote
transparency as well as minimal rules on *public procurement* are only
a selection of such items. What made the instrument internationally
relevant was its potential to break taboos, to provoke political debate
and suggest compromise. This is the mechanism that lead to generate
the political resolve for the *1996 OECD-Recommendation* to ban tax
deductability of bribes, finalised by Ministers in May of this year, as
well as the program for 1997 to evaluate the 1994 Recommendation
and to develop concrete ways to criminalise international corruption.
However, in a competitive context an outreach-program is just as
essential to link efforts to other international organisations as well as
to include *non-member countries*, especially the so-called economies
in transition (Mexico has joined, Korea is in the process of joining the
OECD; several other, especially Eastern European countries are taking
part in the efforts of OECD as observers). OECD is also seeking the
cooperation of the business communities and NGO's such as ICC and
Transparency International (TI).

The breakthrough in 1994 of course is no mere coincidence. It has
not only been promoted by a general shift towards *globalisation* of
markets but also by the general *fatigue* with local corruption in the
North just as in the South. No longer the business communities and
their representatives in national trade departments are opposing the
combat against international corruption in principle. The tendency is

to seek effective and co-ordinated means to take such a delicate step without leaving short term trade advantages to those who linger behind.

Since 1994 a key element to further development of stringent rules against corruption is the concurrent action by regional international organisations, namely the *Council of Europe* (including the countries of Eastern Europe), the EU and the OAS. We are approaching the issue of a convention once again, however, with far more chances to success than in 1979. In some respects the process runs along the same lines as the action against money laundering, during the last ten years: Recommendations and model-legislation have paved the way, helped to generate the political will that lead to a system of co-ordinated binding rules, a world-wide minimum standard.

When placing the OECD-instruments in the context of other international initiatives I should also highlight the *differences*: First of all, the OECD approach is motivated by a fair trade rationale – establishing a level playing field of commerce. At the same time it should contribute to limit the risks to *good-governance* especially in vulnerable political and economic environments by "drying up" the corruption market from the supply-side: Of course the OECD counts on other, especially regional organisations like the OAS or the major lending institutions to develop complementary schemes; unlike the regional initiatives, however, it does not depend on reciprocity of action by the "victim-country". Active corruption abroad may be prosecuted even if the victim-country does not request such action.

II. What will be required from member-countries? What do the new standards mean for companies?

1) The aim of the OECD-Recommendation is certainly not to bring as many businessmen as possible to court. The aim is to raise the costs of transnational corruption in a co-ordinated way, in order to make such practice risky and uneconomic. However, the discussions over the last decade have shown, that member-states hesitate to establish economic sanctions, like banning tax deductability or blocking companies from public procurement procedures, without a clear distinction between licit and illicit behaviour, best established by *criminalising*
– the active bribery of a foreign public official and
– international corruption-money laundering.

I will not go into the details of how to define the offences – this is a technical discussion taking place currently in the different organisations; I would rather sketch two further issues with direct implications for business entities:

2) The OECD has been concentrating on *bookkeeping and auditing standards* lately. The aim is to establish a level that makes it more difficult to create "slush funds", to effect "off-the-book"-transactions. Beyond the work done by relevant international professional associations to coordinate rules on bookkeeping and auditing the OECD is fostering integral approaches developed under the wider chapeau of *corporate governance* – especially complex systems of *internal control* to allow management, board and shareholders a realistic view of what is going on in a company. *Compliance* to a no-corruption policy will be essential even where bribes could be called immaterial to the balance of a company in a traditional sense: Corruption, if clearly forbidden, might lead to contingent liabilities.

3) There is a direct link to the next topic currently examined in greater detail: *public procurement-rules,* both, to establish the principles of international competitive bidding and to allow the exclusion of unreliable companies. Introducing sound internal controls will help remove companies found to be unreliable from a "black list" deluring them from access to procurement contracts.

The extent to which companies could be blocked from bidding internationally is under discussion. This example indicates, however, that co-ordinated action against corruption could be very effective. Of course, it will be under all circumstances vital to secure fair proceedings.

III. Clearly, an effective structure to prevent international corruption in a business context cannot be built on a legislative and regulatory basis alone; it depends on the business community to take responsibility.

Intergovernmental and national action can establish a framework for fair trade; developing compliance-structures, however, is for business organisations and specialised professional associations (like the international, regional and national federations of accountants) as well as individual companies.

The ICC in its new guidelines of 1995 has laid the groundwork. The topics should be taken up regionally and possibly by business sectors specifically. It is essential that business entities should not stop at writing company codes, but should introduce anti-corruption policies down to the operational level of day to day work.

Note: A revised and expanded Recommendation of the Council of the OECD on combatting brivery in international business transactions has been adopted on 23 May 1997, including the issues mentioned above, sub. II (cf. Annex 4.).

Annexes

1. OECD PRESS RELEASE (1994):
OECD GOVERNMENTS AGREE BRIBERY

OECD governments today agreed to take collective action to tackle the problem of bribery in international business transactions. The OECD Recommendation on Bribery in International Business Transactions is the first multilateral agreement among governments to combat the bribery of foreign officials and represents a breakthrough in a difficult area. While nearly all countries have laws against the bribery of their own officials, most do not provide legal sanctions for the bribery of foreign officials by their nationals or their domestic enterprises.

Bribery presents moral and political challenges and, 'in addition', exacts a heavy economic cost, hindering the development of international trade and investment by raising transaction costs and distorting the operation of free markets. It is especially damaging, to developing countries since it diverts needed assistance and increases the cost of that assistance.

The Recommendation calls on Member countries to take effective measures to deter, prevent and combat bribery of foreign public officials. Such measures include reviewing their criminal, civil and administrative laws and regulations and taking "concrete and meaningful steps" to meet this goal, as well as strengthening international co-operation. The Recommendation appeals to non-Member countries to join with OECD Members in their efforts to eliminate bribery in international business transactions. It also provides for a follow-up mechanism to monitor implementation.

The OECD believes that this initiative could act as a catalyst for global action and could help companies refuse to engage in such practices in host countries by setting standards of behaviour to which they could refer. Combatting bribery through firm and joint actions by Member countries can also strengthen the multilateral system for trade and investment by ensuring equitable competitive conditions. The Recommendation will also help to promote good governance.

2. RECOMMENDATION OF THE COUNCIL OF THE OECD
On Bribery In International Business Transactions (1994)

THE COUNCIL

Having regard to Article 5 b) of the Convention on the Organisation for Economic Co-operation and Development of 14th December 1960;

Having regard to the OECD Guidelines for multinational Enterprises which exhort enterprises to refrain from bribery of public servants and holders of public office in their operations;

Considering that bribery is a widespread phenomenon in international business transactions, including trade and investment, raising serious moral and political concerns and distorting international competitive conditions;

Considering further that all countries share a responsibility to combat bribery in international business transactions, however their national might be involved;

Recognising that all OECD Member countries have Legislation that makes the bribing of their public officials and the taking of bribes by these officials a criminal offence while only a few Member countries have specific laws making the bribing of foreign officials a punishable offence;

Convinced that further action is needed on both the national and international level to dissuade both enterprises and public officials from resorting to bribery when negotiating international business transactions and that an OECD initiative in this area could act as a catalyst for global action;

Considering that such action should take fully into account the differences that exist in the jurisdictional and other legal principles and practices in this area;

Considering that a review mechanism would assist member countries in implementing this Recommendation and in evaluating the steps taken and the results achieved;

On the proposal of the Committee on International Investment and Multinational Enterprises.

General

I. RECOMMENDS that Member countries take effective measures to deter, prevent and combat the bribery of foreign public officials in connection with international business transactions.

II. CONSIDERS that, for the purposes of this Recommendation, bribery can involve the direct or indirect offer or Provision of any undue pecuniary or other advantage to or for a foreign public official, in violation of the officialls legal duties, in order to obtain or retain business[1].

Domestic Action

III. RECOMMENDS that each member country examine the following areas and, in conformity with its jurisdictional and other basic legal principles, take concrete and meaningful steps to meet this goal. These steps may include:

i)   criminal laws, or their application, in respect of the bribery of foreign public officials;

ii) civil commercial administrative laws and regulations so that bribery would be illegal;

iii) tax legislation, regulations and practices, insofar as they may indirectly favour bribery;

iv) company and business accounting requirements, and practices in order to secure adequate recording of relevant payments;

v)   banking, financial and other relevant provisions so that adequate records would be kept and made available for inspection or investigation; and

vi) laws and regulations relating to public subsidies; licences, government procurement contracts, or other public advantages so that advantages could be denied as a sanction for bribery in appropriate cases.

International Co-operation

IV. RECOMMENDS that Member countries in order to combat bribery in international business transactions, in conformity with their jurisdictional and other basic legal principles, take the following actions:

i)   consult and otherwise co-operate with appropriate authorities in other countries in investigations and other legal proceedings, concerning specific cases of such bribery through such means as sharing of information (spontaneous or "upon request"), provision of evidence, and extradition;

ii) make full use of existing agreements and arrangements for mutual international legal assistance and where necessary, enter into new agreements or arrangements for this purpose;

iii) ensure that their national laws afford an adequate basis for this co-operation.

---

[1] The notion of bribery in some countries also includes advantages to or for members of a law-making body, candidates for a law-making body or public office and officials of political parties.

Relations with Non-Members and International Organisations

V. APPEALS to non-Member countries to join with OECD Members in combating bribery, in international business transactions and to take full account of the terms of this Recommendation,

VI. REQUESTS the Secretariat to consult with international organisations and international financial institutions on effective means to combat bribery as an aid to promote the policy of good governance.

VII. INVITES Member countries to promote anti-corruption policies within and beyond the OECD area and, in their dealings with non-Member countries, to encourage them to join in the effort to combat such bribery in accordance with this Recommendation.

Follow-up Procedures

VIII. INSTRUCTS the Committee on International Investment and Multinational Enterprises to monitor implementation and follow-up of this Recommendation. For this purpose, the Committee is invited to establish a Working Group on Bribery in International Business Transactions and in particular:
i)   to carry out regular reviews of steps taken by member countries to implement this Recommendation, and to make proposals as appropriate, to assist Member countries in its implementation;
ii) to examine specific issues relating to bribery in international business transactions;
iii) to provide a form for consultations;
iv) to explore the possibility of associating non-Members with this work; and
v)   in close co-operation with the Committee on Fiscal Affairs, to examine the fiscal treatment of bribery, including the issue of tax deductibility of bribes.

IX. INSTRUCTS the Committee to report to the Council after the first regular review and as appropriate thereafter, and to review this Recommendation within three years after its adoption.

3. REPORT OF THE COMMITTEE ON INTERNATIONAL INVESTMENT AND MULTINATIONAL ENTERPRISES TO THE COUNCIL AT MINISTERIAL LEVEL (1996)

Implementation of the Recommendation on Bribery in International Business Transactions

I. Introduction and Summary of Progress

1. At its meeting in 1995, the OECD Council at Ministerial level invited the OECD to strengthen work on bribery and corruption in international transactions and to provide the 1996 Ministerial meeting with a full progress report on the implementation of the 1994 OECD Recommendation.

2. The 1994 Recommendation on Bribery in International Business Transactions instructs the OECD Committee on International Investment and Multinational Enterprises to monitor implementation and follow-up, and, in particular:

i)   to carry out regular reviews of steps taken by Member countries to implement this Recommendation, and to make proposals as appropriate to assist Member countries in its implementation,

ii) to examine specific issues relating to bribery in international business transactions;

iii) to provide a forum for consultations;

iv) to explore the possibility of associating non-Members with this work;

v)   in close co-operation with the Committee on Fiscal Affairs, to examine the fiscal treatment of bribery including the issue of tax deductibility of bribes.

3. Since 1994, progress has been made to implement the Recommendation: the OECD examined a wide range of national measures which can apply to international bribery; the Council approved a new recommendation to re-examine tax rules with the intention of disallowing the deductibility of bribes to foreign public officials; analysis of the criminalisation of bribery of foreign public officials resulted in a consensus that it is necessary to criminalise the bribery of foreign public officials in an effective and co-ordinated manner. These results are reported more fully below.

4. A Symposium on Corruption and Good Governance held in March 1995 stimulated the interest of non-Members in OECD work. Since then, Argentina and Bulgaria have requested to adhere to the OECD Recommendation. To follow-up the Symposium, the OECD also established an informal network to share information on anti-corruption activities among organisations such as the World Bank, the IMF, EBRD, regional development banks, the United Nations, the Council of Europe, the Organisation of American States and others.

5. In other related work, the Development Assistance Committee is presently considering a proposal for adoption by the DAC's High Level Meeting to combat corruption in the securing and implementation of aid-funded contracts (see separate report).
The Public Management Service is conducting a comparative analysis of how ethics
and conduct are managed in the public service in selected OECD countries. Interest
in this issue was underscored by ministers at the March PUMA Ministerial Symposium on the Future of Public Services. Programmes of the Centre for Co-operation
with Economies in Transition are assisting countries from Central and Eastern
Europe and the New Independent States to put in place systems which will help them
combat corruption.

6. Further progress needs to be made. Over the coming months the OECD will continue to analyse specific issues related to international bribery, including accounting
and auditing, the modalities for criminalisation of bribery of foreign public officials,
public procurement, commercial and competition law. It will also monitor the progress of Member countries in implementing the 1994 Recommendation and the new
recommendation on tax deductibility, and continue its outreach to non-Members and
the private sector. These activities will form the basis for the review of the 1994
Recommendation which is to be presented to Ministers in 1997.

II. Progress in Implementing the 1994 Recommendation on Bribery in
International Business Transactions

A. *Survey of measures to combat bribery in international business transactions*

7. The Committee on International Investment and Multinational Enterprises
(CIME), through its Working Group on Bribery in International Business Transactions, completed a first examination of measures which could be used to combat
bribery in international business transactions.

The examination covered participating countries' criminal, civil, and commercial
laws, administrative laws, accounting requirements, banking and financial provisions
and laws and regulations relating to public subsidies and contracts. Although the
information is still partial, it is the most complete survey done to date. It reveals a
more positive situation regarding the potential reach of]aws to the bribery of foreign
public officials than was previously known. In a number of countries existing laws,
including criminal laws, may apply, even though they do not specifically address the
bribery of foreign public officials.

8. Countries have made some progress in implernenting the Recommendation, but
further efforts are needed. Most participating countries have established intermini-
sterial bodies to review national laws and regulations and many are considering
changes in order to extend their laws to reach international bribery. Particular atten-

tion is being given to the feasibility of amending criminal law provisions. The ongoing analysis by the Working Group of the various areas of domestic law and regulations and of issues in international co-operation, will permit the Committee to make proposals to assist Member countries in implementing the Recommendation. This analysis will also help set the stage for the review of the Recommendation which will be presented to the meeting of the Council at Ministerial level in 1997.

B. Tax deductibility of bribes

9. In response to the 1994 Recommendation, the Committee on Fiscal Affairs reviewed tax measures which may influence the willingness to make or accept bribes. The Committee summarised the current practices of Member countries, examined the related tax principles and analysed two possibilities to use tax provisions to combat bribery of foreign officials: to disallow the tax deductibility of such bribes or to subject them to disclosure conditions; to use cross-border exchange of tax information to discover and prosecute illegal bribery.

10. In January 1996 the Committee on Fiscal Affairs agreed on a draft recommendation on the tax deductibility of bribes of foreign officials; it was welcomed by the CIME at its meeting on 5 February. The Council approved the recommendation as set forth below at its meeting on 11 April 1996.

I.   RECOMMENDS that those Member countries which do not disallow the deductibility of bribes to foreign public officials re-examine such treatment with the intention of denying this deductibility. Such action may be facilitated by the trend to treat bribes to foreign officials as illegal.

II. INSTRUCTS the Committee on Fiscal Affairs, in co-operation with the Committee on International Investment and Multinational Enterprises, to monitor the implementation of this Recommendation, to promote the Recommendation in the context of contacts with non-member countries and to report to the Council as appropriate.

C. Criminalisation of the bribery of foreign public officials

11. The CIME Working Group on Bribery analysed issues related to the criminalisation of the bribery of foreign public officials at meetings in October 1995 and February 1996. The latter meeting included the participation of prosecutors responsible for anti-corruption cases. The discussions with the prosecutors reinforced the conviction that criminalisation of the bribery of foreign public officials would be a significant means to deter, prevent and combat bribery in international business transactions by providing a basis for criminal prosecution of such acts and by improving the basis in national law for mutual international legal assistance. It would also facilitate the implementation of the recent OECD recommendation on the tax deductibility of bribes.

12. The analysis by the Group of various means to criminalise bribery of foreign public officials showed that a certain latitude can be allowed, consistent with different legal systems. At the same time the Group emphasised that criminalisation should be carried out effectively and co-ordinated in substance. It worked on several methods for criminalisation which could achieve a sound basis for prosecution of such bribery and which are set forth in a report. Co-ordination should also help to ensure conditions of a „level playing field", with respect to business interests. Action by Member countries to criminalise and to enforce their laws should be subjected to appropriate follow-up and multilateral monitoring.

13. The Working Group and the CIME reached the following conclusions:
1) Member countries agree it is necessary to criminalise the bribery of foreign public officials in an effective and co-ordinated manner in order to combat corruption in international business transactions;
   For that purpose, the CIME through its Working Group on Bribery in International Business Transactions should further examine the modalities and the appropriate international instruments to facilitate criminalisation, taking into account work done in other fora;
   Proposals should be submitted as part of the 1997 Review of the 1994 Recommendation;
2) Mernber countries should review existing procedures to ensure the provision of timely and effective mutual legal assistance in matters relating to allegations of bribery;
3) Member countries should consider including bribery as a predicate offence under their money laundering Legislation.

4. REVISED RECOMMENDATION OF THE COUNCIL (1997)
On Combating Bribery in International Business Transactions

THE COUNCIL,

Having regard to Articles 3, 5a) and 5 b) of the Convention on the Organisation for Economic Co-operation and Development of 14 December 1960;

Considering that bribery is a widespread phenomenon in international business transactions, including trade and investment, raising serious moral and political concerns and distorting international competitive conditions;

Considering that all countries share a responsibillty to combat bribery in international business transactions;

Considering that enterprises should refrain from bribery of public servants and holders of public office, as stated in the OECD Guidelines for Multinational Enterprises;

Considering the progress which has been made in the implementation of the initial Recommendation of the Council on Bribery in International Business Transactions adopted on 27 May 1994, and the related Recommendation on the tax deductibility of bribes of foreign public officials adopted on 11 April 1996, as well as the Recommendation concerning Antlcorruption Proposals for Bilateral Ald Procurement, endorsed by the High Level Meeting of the Development Assistance Committee on 7 May 1996;

Welcoming other recent developments which further advance international understanding and co-operation regarding bribery in business transactions, including actions of the United Nations, the Council of Europe, the European Union and the Organisation of American States;

Having regard to the commitment made at the meeting of the Council at Ministerial level in May 1996, to criminalise the bribery of foreign public officials in an effective and co-ordinated manner;

Noting that an international convention in conformity with the agreed common elements set forth in the Annex, is an appropriate instrument to attain such criminalisation rapidly.

Considering the consensus which has developed on the measures which should be taken to implement the 1994 Recommendation, in particular, with respect to the modalities and international instruments to facilltate criminalisation of bribery of foreign public officials; tax deductibility of bribes to foreign public officials; accounting requirements, external audit and internal company controls; and rules and regulations on public procurement;

Recognising that achieving progress in this field requires not only efforts by individual countries but multilateral co-operation, monitoring and follow-up;

General

I. RECOMMENDS that Member countries take effective measures to deter, prevent and combat the bribery of foreign public officials in connection with international business transactions.

II. RECOMMENDS that each Member country examine the following areas and, in conformity with its jurisdictional and other basic legal principles, take concrete and meaningful steps to meet this goal:

i)   criminal laws and their application, in accordance with section III and the Annex to this Recommendation;
ii) tax Legislation, regulations and practice, to eliminate any indirect support of bribery, in accordance with section IV;
iii) company and business accounting, external audit and internal control requirements and practices, in accordance with section V;
iv) banking, financial and other relevant provisions, to ensure that adequate records would be kept and made available for inspection and investigation;
v)   public subsidies, licences, government procurement contracts or other public advantages, so that advantages could be denied as a sanction for bribery in appropriate cases, and in accordance with section VI for procurement contracts and aid procurement;
vi) civil, commercial, and administrative laws and regulations, so that such bribery would be illegal;
vii) international co-operation in investigations and other legal proceedings, in accordance with section VII.

Criminalisation of Bribery of Foreign Public Officials

III. RECOMMENDS that Member countries should criminalise the bribery of foreign public officials in an effective and co-ordinated manner by submitting proposals to their legislative bodies by 1 April 1998, in conformity with the agreed common elements set forth in the Annex, and seeking their enactment by the end of 1998.
DECIDES, to this end, to open negotiations promptly on an international convention to criminalise bribery in conformity with the agreed common elements, the treaty to be open for signature by the end of 1997, with a view to its entry into force twelve months thereafter.

Tax Deductibility

IV. URGES the prompt implementation by Member countries of the 1996 Recommendation which reads as follows: "that those Member countries which do not disallow the deductibility of bribes to foreign public officials re-examine such treatment with the intention of denying this deductibility. Such action may be facilitated by the trend to treat bribes to foreign officials as illegal."

Accounting Requirements, External Audit and Internal Company Controls

V. RECOMMENDS that Member countries take the steps necessary so that laws, rules and practices with respect to accounting requirements, external audit and internal company controls are in line with the following principles and are fully used in order to prevent and detect bribery of foreign public officials in international business.

A. *Adequate accounting requirements:*
i)   Member countries should require companies to maintain adequate records of the sums of money received and expended by the company, identifying the matters in respect of which the receipt and expenditure takes place. Companies should be prohibited from making off-the-books transactions or keeping off-the-books accounts.
ii) Member countries should require companies to disclose in their financial statements the full range of material contingent liabilities.
iii) Member countries should adequately sanction accounting omissions, falsifications and fraud.

B. *Independent External Audit*
i)   Member countries should consider whether requirements to submit to external audit are adequate.
ii) Member countries and professional associations should maintain adequate standards to ensure the independence of external auditors which permits them to provide an objective assessment of company accounts, financial statements and internal controls.
iii) Member countries should require the auditor who discovers indications of a possible illegal act of bribery to report this discovery to management and, as appropriate, to corporate monitoring bodies.
iv) Member countries should consider requiring the auditor to report indications of a possible illegal act of bribery to competent authorities.

C. *Internal company controls*
i)   Member countries should encourage the development and adoption of adequate internal company controls, including standards of conduct.
ii) Member countries should encourage company management to make statements in their annual reports about their internal control mechanisms, including those which contribute to preventing bribery.
iii) Member countries should encourage the creation of monitoring bodies, independent of management, such as audit committees of boards of directors or of supervisory boards.

iv) Member countries should encourage companies to provide channels for communication by, and protection for, persons not willing to violate professional standards or ethics under instructions or pressure from hierarchical superiors.

Public procurement

VI. RECOMMENDS:

i) Member countries should support ihe efforts in the World Trade Organisation to pursue an agreement on transparency in government procurement;

ii) Member countries' laws and regulations should pennit authorities to suspend from competition for public contracts enterprises determined to have bribed foreign public officials in contravention of that Member's national laws and, to the extent a Member applies procurement sanctions to enterprises that are determined to have bribed domestic public officials, such sanctions should be applied equally in case of bribery of foreign public officials. [2]

iii) In accordance with the Recommendation of the Development Assistance Committee, Member countries should require anti-corruption provisions in bilateral aid-funded procurement, promote the proper implementation of anti-corruption provisions in international development institutions, and work closely with development partners to combat corruption in all development co-operation efforts. [3]

International Co-operation

VII. RECOMMENDS that Member countries, in order to combat bribery in international business transactions, in conformity with their jurisdictional and other basic legal principles, take the following actions:

i) consult and otherwise co-operate with appropriate authorities in other countries in investigations and other legal proceedings concerning specific cases of such bribery through such means as sharing of information (spontaneously or upon request), provision of evidence and extradition;

ii) make full use of existing agreements and arrangements for mutual international legal assistance and where necessary, enter into new agreements or arrangements for this purpose;

iii) ensure that their national laws afford an adequate basis for this co-operation and, in particular, in accordance with paragraph 8 of the Annex.

---

[2] Member countries' systems for applying sanctions for bribery of domestic officials differ as to whether the determination of bribery is based on a criminal conviction, indictment or administrative procedure, but in all cases it is based on substantial evidence.

[3] This paragraph summarises the DAC recommendation, which is addressed to DAC members only, and addresses it to all OECD Members and eventually non-member countries which adhere to the Recommendation.

Follow-up and institutional arrangements

VIII. INSTRUCTS the Committee on International Investment and Multinational Enterprises, through its Working Group on Bribery in International Business Transactions, to carry out a programme of systematic follow-up to monitor and promote the full implementation of this Recommendation, in cooperation with the Committee for Fiscal Affairs, the Development Assistance Committee and other OECD bodies, as appropriate. This follow-up will include, in particular:

i)   receipt of notifications and other information submitted to it by the Member countries;

ii) regular reviews of steps taken by Member countries to implement the Recommendation and to make proposals, as appropriate, to assist Member countries in its implementation; these reviews will be based on the following complementary systems:

*   a system of self-evaluation, where Member countries' responses on the basis of a questionnaire will provide a basis for assessing the implementation of the Recommendation;

*   a system of mutual evaluation, where each Member country will be examined in turn by the Working Group on Bribery, on the basis of a report which will provide an objective assessment of the progress of the Member country in implementing the Recommendation.

iii) examination of specific issues relating to bribery in international business transactions;

iv) examination of the feasibility of broadening the scope of the work of the OECD to combat international bribery to include private sector bribery and bribery of foreign officials for reasons other than to obtain or retain business;

v)   provision of regular information to the public on its work and activities and on implementation of the Recommendation.

IX. NOTES the obligation of Member countries to co-operate closely in this follow-up programme, pursuant to Article 3 of the OECD Convention.

X. INSTRUCTS the Committee on International Investment and Multinational Enterprises to review the implementation of Sections III and, in co-operation with the Committee on Fiscal Affairs, Section IV of this Recommendation and report to Ministers in Spring 1998, to report to the Council after the first regular review and as appropriate there after, and to review this Revised Recommendation within three years after its adoption.

Co-operation with non members

XI. APPEALS to non-member countries to adhere to the Recommendation and participate in any institutional follow-up or implementation mechanism.

XII. INSTRUCTS the Committee on International Investment and Multinational Enterprises through its Working Group on Bribery, to provide a forum for consultations with countries which have not yet adhered, in order to promote wider participation in the Recommendation and its follow-up.

Relations with international governmental and non-governmental organisations

XIII. INVITES the Committee on International Investment and Multinational Enterprises through ist Working Group on Bribery, to consult and co-operate with the international organisations and international financial institutions active in the combat against bribery in international business transactions and consult regularly with the non-governmental organisations and representatives of the business community active in this field.

ANNEX:
Agreed Common Elements of Criminal Legislation and Related Action

1) *Elements of the offence of active bribery*
   i)   **Bribery** is understood as the promise or giving of any undue payment or other advantages, whether directly or through intermediaries to a public official, for himself or for a third party, to influence the official to act or refrain from acting in the performance of his or her official duties in order to obtain or retain business.
   ii) **Foreign public official** means any person holding a legislative, administrative or judicial office of a foreign country or in an international organisation, whether appointed or elected or, any person exercising a public function or task in a foreign country.
   iii) **The offeror** is any person, on his own behalf or on the behalf of any other natural person or legal entity.

2) *Ancillary elements or offences*
The general criminal law concepts of attempt, complicity and/or conspiracy of the law of the prosecuting state are recognised as applicable to the offence of bribery of a foreign public official.

3) *Excuses and defences*
Bribery of foreign public officials in order to obtain or retain business is an offence irrespective of the value or the outcome of the bribe, of perceptions of local custom or of the tolerance of bribery by local authorities.

4)   Jurisdiction

Jurisdiction over the offence of bribery of foreign public officials should in any case be established when the offence is committed in whole or in part in the prosecuting State's territory. The territorial basis for jurisdiction should be interpreted broadly so that an extensive physical connection to the bribery act is not required.

States which prosecute their nationale for offences committed abroad should do so in respect of the bribery of foreign public officials according to the same principles.

States which do not prosecute on the basis of the nationality principle should be prepared to extradite their nationale in respect of the bribery of foreign public officials.

All countries should review whether their current basis for jurisdiction is effective in the fight against bribery of foreign public officials and, if not, should take appropriate remedial steps.

5)   Sanctions

The offence of bribery of foreign public officials should be sanctioned/punishable by effective, proportionale and dissuasive criminal penalties, sufficient to secure effective mutual legal assistance and extradition, comparable to those applicable to the bribers in cases of corruption of domestic public officials.

Monetary or other civil, administrative or criminal penalties on any legal person involved, should be provided, taking into account the amounts of the bribe and of the profits derived from the transaction obtained through the bribe.

Forfeiture or confiscation of instrumentalities and of the bribe benefits and the profits derived from the transactions obtained through the bribe should be provided, or comparable fines or damages imposed.

6)   Enforcement

In view of the seriousness of the offence of bribery of foreign public officials, public prosecutors should exercise their discretion independently, based on professional motives. They should not be influenced by considerations of national economic interest, fostering good political relations or the identity of the victim.

Complaints of victims should be seriously investigated by the competent authorities. The statute of limitations should allow adequate time to address this complex offence. National governments should provide adequate resources to prosecuting authorities so as to permit effective prosecution of bribery of foreign public officials.

7)   Connected provisions (criminal and non-criminal)

* *Accounting, recordkeeping and disclosure requirements:* In order to combat bribery of foreign public officials effectively, states should also adequately sanction accounting omissions, falsifications and fraud.
* *Money laundering:* The bribery of foreign public officials should be made a predicate offence for purposes of money laundering legislation where bribery of

a domestic public official is a money laundering predicate offence, without regard to the place where the bribery occurs.

8) *International co-operation*

Effective mutual legal assistance is critical to be able to investigate and obtain evidence in order to prosecute cases of bribery of foreign public officials.

Adoption of laws criminalising the bribery of foreign public officials would remove obstacles to mutual legal assistance created by dual criminality requirements.

Countries should tailor their laws on mutual legal assistance to permit co-operation with countries investigating cases of bribery of foreign public officials even including third countries (country of the offeror; country where the act occurred) and countries applying different types of criminalisation legislation to reach such cases.

Means should be explored and undertaken to improve the efficiency of mutual legal assistance.

Multinational Corporations, Governance Deficits, and Corruption: Discussing a Complex Issue from the Perspective of Business Ethics *

Klaus M. Leisinger

Corruption is a worldwide problem. To restrict this lack of social control to the developing countries alone would be to take an unfittingly optimistic view of the pestilence. Hans-Ludwig Zachert, head of the German Federal Bureau of Criminal Investigation, has likened corruption in his country to corrosion: initially it only crops up here and there and frequently makes inroads beneath the surface. "No matter how much government apologists may maintain otherwise", he has stated, "corruption in the public service is not just a matter of 'a few black sheep' but an alarmingly everyday occurrence in Germany."[1] According to Zachert, the cases uncovered to date already number in the thousands. The main profiteer is organized crime which, aided by civil servants on the take, seeks to gain massive influence over the authorities. "Practically no sector is spared corruption or quasi-corrupt practices. Hardly a day passes without new cases coming to light."[2] If timely countermeasures are not set in motion, he fears, the canker will become so widespread as to subvert the very pillars of the system.

---

* This article is a revised and translated version of chapter II.5 of the author's recently published book *"Unternehmensethik: Globale Verantwortung und modernes Management"*, Munich 1997. Publication with kind permission of Verlag C.H. Beck, Munich.

[1] SCHERER, P.: *Korruption fast alltäglich*. In: DIE WELT, 16 February 1995, No. 40-7, p. 1.

[2] Ibid.

H. Lange et al., Working Across Cultures, 113–139.

In July 1995 a German newsweekly reported that highly paid executives in the country's automotive industry were under suspicion of having enriched themselves by demanding and pocketing "commissions", i.e. kickbacks. The magazine thought to discern signs of a "culture of corruption"[3] – this, be it noted, in the Federal and not some remote Banana Republic. Other instances of corruption in the Federal Republic of Germany have even been elaborated in the form of case studies.[4]

In emergent countries such as South Korea and Mexico former top officeholders have been arrested or are suspects in connection with corruption; likewise in France, Italy, Belgium and Japan.[5] American analyses see corruption as a problem for the United States too.[6] Further publications[7] in the same vein from the United Kingdom, Japan and The Netherlands, as well as a voluminous documentation on Italian tangentopoli (more than 1,300 top managers were arrested), point to the supposition that virtually every society on earth knows corruption in one guise or another.[8]

Transparency International, an organization established to combat corruption, publishes national listings that grade the intensity of corruption ascertained in a country on a scale going up to 5 points for the worst. No fewer than eight countries qualify for the maximum. In other words, no baksheesh, no business.

The global dimension of corruption thus stands proved. But what is an apposite definition of the phenomenon?

3   "Der Spiegel" No. 28 / 1995, 10 July 1995, pp. 22-29.
4   Cf. RÜGEMER, W.: *Corruption in Waste Water Treatment. A Case Study from Germany.* In: Transparency International (Ed.); TI Newsletter, Dec. 1995, p. 3.
5   Cf. Business Week, International Edition, 18, December 1995, pp. 25-34; see also *Kursbuch,* Issue 120, Rowohlt Verlag, Berlin 1995.
6   BANFIELD, E.C.: Corruption as a Feature of Governmental Organizations. In: *The Journal of Law and Economics,* Vol. 18 (1975), pp. 587-605.
7   Cf. MAHONEY, J.: Ethical Attitudes to Bribery and Extortion. In: Stewart, S./Donleavy, G. (Eds): *Whose Business Values?,* Hong Kong University Press, Hong Kong 1995, pp. 223-246.
8   Cf. reports in TI-Newsletter, available from Transparency International e.V., Heylstrasse 33, Berlin.

1. Defining the Beast: Basic Considerations

First off, without beating about the bush or prettifying the subject one can define corruption as misuse of power for private benefit or advantage.[9] This power may, but need not, reside in the public domain. Besides money, the benefit can take the form of protection, special treatment, commendation, promotion, or the favors of women or men.

A more differentiated approach discloses a remarkably multiplex cluster of mores that is value-judged quite differently from culture to culture and, where its ramifications are concerned, accordingly heterogeneous. In some cultures presents and reciprocal personal favors are a part of the code of expected conduct and social behavior. In others the person who wishes to show gratitude for professional assistance rendered with personal gifts can quickly bring discredit on himself and the beneficiary.

Whereas some countries permit bribes to be deducted from taxes as "operating expenses" or "special outlays", other countries such as the United States have anti-corruption legislation that even makes the bribing of foreigners in a foreign country a punishable offense. For companies based in diverse parts of the world this legislative motley leaves them with varying degrees of elbow room in coming to terms with corruption. In the Federal Republic of Germany bribing an official is a criminal offense for which both briber and bribed can be punished. If the bribe changes hands abroad, however, it is (still) tax-deductible, a fact that would seem to indicate a certain understanding on the part of the lawgivers that double standards are a fact of life.

Under the German law against unfair competition so-called "commissions", i.e. fees paid for favors done in business dealings – for example, to a company employee who in his or her job capacity gives preferential treatment to a certain firm – also open both parties involved to punishment. Because the arrangement includes granting possible price reductions to the firm placing the order, however, this sort of wrongdoing might better be defined as fraud or breach of trust and punished accordingly. Since such deals are shadowy and the parties to them are locked in conspiracy (briber and bribee both in the same boat), it is extremely difficult to prove their existence, so that

---

9 Thus GALTUNG, F.: *Zum Beispiel Korruption*, Lamuv Verlag, Göttingen 1994, p. 11.

relying solely on legal redress is inapposite. For this reason it is useful to consider the problem in the context of corporate ethics.

In sum, generally speaking corruption encompasses four main distinguishing features:[10]
- Misuse of a position of power;
- Gaining of advantage for those who, actively and passively, are parties to the misuse;
- Undesirable effects on third parties (ramifications);
- Secrecy of the transaction.

Because both the dimensions of a position of power and the undesirable consequences can vary greatly and because of its significance for moral reasoning, we need to differentiate further.

Before we consider the moral differences among the various forms that the phenomenon of corruption takes, two further provisos. Not every business is susceptible to it to the same degree. Experience shows that construction firms that specialize in infrastructure and other large-scale projects and manufacturers of big-ticket capital equipment such as turbines or aircraft are especially vulnerable, most notably when the decision on a contract hinges on just a few people or even on one person alone.[11] Ailing companies with uncompetitive products and services are more likely to stoop to corrupt behavior than healthy companies who enjoy a salient marketing edge thanks to excellent products and services.

Sweeping statements about "the" developing countries, for example, and "everyone" there who carries responsibility are out of place as well. Payments tainted with corruption may indeed occur more frequently and involve various officeholders more often and to that extent be a condition of business. This does not mean, however, that corruption is practiced everywhere and in every case and that upright officials are nowhere to be found.

---

[10] See also SCHMIDT, K. / GARSCHAGEN, Ch.: Korruption. In: *Handwörterbuch der Wirtschaftswissenschaften*, Vol. 4, Gustav Fischer Verlag, Stuttgart 1978; JOHNSON, H.L.: Bribery in International Markets: Diagnosis, Clarification and Remedy. In: *Journal of Business Ethics*, Vol. 4 (1985), pp. 447-455; D'ANDRADE, K.: Bribery. In: *Journal of Business Ethics*, Vol. 4 (1985), pp. 239-248.

[11] LANE, H.W. / SIMPSON, D.G.: Bribery in International Business: Whose Problem is it? In: *Journal of Business Ethics*, Vol.3 (1984), p. 36.

2. Differences in the Various Forms of Corruption

First of all it is pertinent to draw a purely quantitative distinction between "small" and "big" corruption. And qualitatively we can distinguish between corruption for legal and for illicit ends.

2.1. "Petty" corruption

This form is defined as "small" payments intended to get someone empowered to take and enforce decisions to see to it that something he or she is duty-bound to do is actually done within a reasonable period of time. The payments are made because without this additional "stimulus" nothing would happen, or else its happening would be inconscionably delayed. Hence the expression "speed-up gratuities."

The word "petty" in "petty corruption" refers to both the size of the financial transaction and the size of the obligation that the transaction buys. In many poor countries petty corruption pervades every segment of society. In an impoverished society many people's success in the daily struggle to survive can depend on doing things that they would not be constrained to do if they were better off. In this light petty corruption appears as a defensive strategy that people must resort to because their income does not suffice to feed and clothe their families.[12]

Professionals working for Switzerland's official development aid agency have described the concrete implications in strikingly candid fashion. They pointed out that "... the responsible Ministry officials (can) cause us very serious difficulties by dragging out procedures if friendly relations are not cultivated – with an invitation to attend the Swiss national holiday celebration on August 1st, say, or a small Christmas present. Such token gestures have an immediate effect on the dispatch with which our requests are dealt with at the administrative level."[13] If someone takes a firm line in resisting demands his work is impeded. Sometimes this can be offset by extra personal effort, sometimes not. "Each person has to find out for himself how

---

[12] Cf. Directorate for Development, Cooperation and Humanitarian Aid (DEH): *Entwicklung - Developpement*, No. 38, November 1992, p. 26 ff.

[13] As recounted by a DEH delegate who works in Honduras: Ibid., p. 27.

clean he wants to stay – and how firm he can remain."[14] A case history from Mexico illustrates the consequences that can ensue from a demonstration of "firmness":

"All over the country it is difficult to obtain a telephone extension. The price set by Teléfonos de Mexico, which has the monopoly, is 500 dollars, inclusive of installation. Only 5 out of 100 applicants try this route. The rest prefer to shell out 1000 to 1500 dollars on a huge black market controlled by employees of the monopoly itself. For 1500 dollars you get your phone within days. But if you pay Teléfonos de Mexico 500, you can wait 12 months – if you are lucky. The workers, who install the illegal extensions at incredible speed, earn 400 dollars a month.[15] A Mexican political analyst's commentary: "Everything can be fixed like that – whether you want to enroll a child in secondary school, evade a traffic fine, or leave the country without having to show your military identity card. Every victory over hopelessness has its price."[16]

One may justifiably wax indignant about corruption in connection with humanitarian aid, yet, taking every aspect into consideration, it becomes clear that *simple* solutions are not possible here either. A former deputy director of the Swiss Federal Directorate for Development Cooperation and Humanitarian Aid (DEH) has admitted to carrying on the mission even under conditions tarnished by corruption. "Development cooperation is necessary all the same", he said. "If one went so far as to declare that we shall cease helping countries where corruption exists, then there would be practically nothing more we could do. But the whole point is to bring about improvements."[17]

Terminating a development assistance program because of "small" exactions seldom has an impact on those who are the intended target anyway. Instead the brunt falls on those whose chances for a better life depend, sometimes critically, on humanitarian aid. Here again the social consequences of an alternative course of action in a given case have to be weighed in a situation ethics framework. Private enterprise,

---

[14] Statement by a DEH delegate who works in Madagascar: Ibid., p. 27.

[15] Cf. LEYVA, C.G.: Die Korruption blüht nach wie vor. In: DEH: *Entwicklung-Developpement*, No. 38, November 1992, p. 8 ff.

[16] Ibid., p. 9.

[17] Cf. DEH: *Entwicklung-Developpement*, No. 38, November 1992, p. 31.

too, should follow this guideline. The *following case* can serve as an example from the real-life world of doing business:

An official of the central bank of a developing country has the authority to grant import licenses. In public bidding a company has obtained a contract to supply life-saving drugs to the national hospitals and now wishes to import them. To secure the needed foreign exchange, however, an import license is required; but the central bank official is prepared to issue one only if he profits personally. Because patients' lives depend on the timely delivery of the medicines the company comes under pressure, while the official drags his feet. In this situation the manager of the drug company decides to bribe the official with an "expediting" payment. For the sum of 500 US dollars the import license is authorized on the very same day. As I reason it, handing over the 500 dollars creates an ethical problem. However, weighing the "sin" of paying against the benefits of risk-averting for innocent patients, I consider it to be a lesser evil than risking even one patient's life.

Corruption can have a direct influence on business success. With its help the whole climate of doing business can be changed in the bribers favor. Without resort to corruption well-nigh insurmountable problems can arise: deliberate foot-dragging instead of friendly treatment (in passing on information or granting approvals, for example); holding back information rather than imparting it in time (for example, in connection with a crucial deadline such as the latest date for submitting a tender in a public bidding competition); or shelving vs. approving applications (e.g. for import or export licenses or sales authorizations). All this can add up to the decisive difference between business success and failure.

In the sphere of "petty" corruption gifts present a delicate special problem, in that there is always the possibility that they may be given without ulterior motives as tokens of personal sympathy.

2.2. Gifts

In many cultures gifts given directly, as in the form of an invitation to dinner or other favors of this order, are frankly expected as marks of respect or as proof of amicable relations. Refusing them can be taken as a sign of rejection or even as an affront. In other cultures the fact

that a company presents potential customers with gifts may be criti-
cized as bordering on corruption, or at least as ethically suspect.[18] The
problem lies not in the giving as such but in the value of what is given.
Unproblematic under a certain limit, as soon as this is exceeded the
practice may be looked upon askance.

Various organizations have drawn up guidelines on how their
employees should act with respect to the gifts they give to customers
or business friends as well as those they themselves receive. The practice may be expressly forbidden, pointers to what is appropriate given,
or an upper limit specified-value must not exceed 100 dollars, for
example. A critic of the pharmaceutical industry once put it thus:
"Whatever you can eat or drink in a day does not constitute corruption." As both recreations can be enjoyed at differing levels of quality,
however (a 1947 vintage Bordeaux is in a loftier league than, say, a
bottle of last year's Valpolicella), purists may well regard this way of
demarcating the borderline with scepticism.

Guidelines are never the whole answer to the question, though, on
account of factors such as a different standard of living between giver
and receiver, cultural dissimilarities and divergent social norms, or
quite simply the grey areas inherent in giving and receiving. What
always remains is a latitude of interpretation and discretion that
demands an independent exercise of judgment on the part of the
person concerned.

The intention of the giver is always a pertinent consideration in
evaluating the merits of a case. If a gift is meant simply as a friendly
gesture, free of any expectation that a reciprocal situation might arise –
one need not always have ulterior motives in mind – then there is not
much of a problem. Still, such gifts are not altogether unproblematic
either, since they do serve to generate good will that can pay off later
in some other connection. The sociologist Neckel refers in this nexus
to the "Don Corleone Principle", describing how subtly habit-forming
gifts can get to be.[19]

---

[18] Cf. HAZLET, Th.K. / Sullivan, S.D.: Professional Organizations and Healthcare
      Industry Support: Ethical Conflict? In: *Cambridge Quarterly of Healthcare
      Ethics*, Vol. 3 (1994), pp. 236-256.

[19] "I am doing you a favor now and expect nothing in return – other than that you
      help me should I once need your help." Cf. NECKEL, S.: *Der unmoralische*

If on the other hand gifts are bluntly intended to spur the receiver into performing or omitting to perform a certain action within a relatively well-defined period of time in the interest of the giver, clearly what we have is a corrupt maneuver. As a general rule one is best advised to desist from giving or accepting gifts that go beyond small kindnesses and friendly gestures.

The second test that acceptability has to pass is, as already noted, a gift's value. Obviously a ballpoint or fountain pen – assuming it is not a chic designer model – is not in the same class as computer equipment given for private use or airfare to coveted destinations.

In my experience a good way to stay clear of any suspicion of corruptibility is to have the gifts that employees have been given personally turned over to the company and made available to everyone – through a raffle, for example. During an assignment in a developing country in Africa I was, to my utter surprise, showered with gifts. At the end of my first year I had them put on display in the company conference room, numbered, and raffled off among the full workforce. In this way everyone from the night watchman to the secretaries to management staff got the chance to acquire desirable items that would otherwise have been beyond their means.

Most of the gifts came from customers who knew that a certain discretionary elbow room existed where the provision of goods in short supply (on account of lacking import licenses) or the granting of discounts were concerned. Without wishing to insinuate that our customers hoped to point me in a certain direction with their gifts, I can report that there were no more gifts once the word had got around about how they had been disposed of.

As a preventive measure companies and other organizations are well-advised to oblige employees whose decision-making authority leaves them particularly exposed to temptation to inform their superiors of any gifts received. With the matter out in the open one can decide on how to handle it fairly.

Tausch. Eine Soziologie der Käuflichkeit. In: Kursbuch. Rowohlt Verlag, Berlin 1995, Issue 120, p. 15.

2.3. *"Big" Corruption*

Although the transition from "petty" to "big" corruption is fluid in the individual case, the latter presents a distinct problem area.[20] In the worst case a parasitic political and economic upper stratum ruthlessly exploits its privileges and the clout that goes with them to funnel huge sums into its own pockets. In order to bag loot on that scale corrupted and corrupters shop for ways to buy goods and services with the highest possible price tag.

Everyone involved has an interest. The supplier sells pricey, perhaps overpriced, goods and services, while the "customer" takes his cut in the form of illicit "commissions".[21] Development ruins in many a poor country testify to the deplorable results of such wheeling and dealing. Most of them are relatively useless, ill-adapted and lavishly expensive installations, colossal prestige projects and outsized construction schemes, or armaments that far exceed a country's legitimate defense interests. In most cases the purchase transaction as such is perfectly legal.

The illicit nature of such dealings consists in this: by dint of loyalty to their charge, and in view of the scarcity of resources, the officeholders or those empowered to make decisions would be duty-bound to serve the public interest, fending off whatever is harmful to it. For selfish reasons they fail to do so, however. Instead of seeking the most cost-effective solution to a problem – for example, by publicly inviting tenders and straightforwardly appraising the offers that come in – they give preference to the most expensive variant. The overblown dimensions, technical complexity, lack of a flanking infrastructure before and after, or simply a non-existent need – all these factors often make it highly unlikely that such investments will ever be efficiently used.

Since the "commissions" are normally high and, being underhanded, do not show up on any tax declaration, the direct effect on the beneficiary's income is substantial – and the harm done to the public welfare usually great. The devious practice is considered to have added massively to the foreign indebtedness of many developing

---

[20] LLOYD, B.: Corruption: Where to Draw the Line?, In: *Business Ethics: A European Review,* Vol. 2 (1993), No. 2, pp. 97-100.

[21] Cf. MOODY-STUART, G.: *Schwere Korruption in der Dritten Welt.* In: Kursbuch. Rowohlt Verlag, Berlin 1995, Issue 120, p. 118 ff.

countries while seldom contributing to bettering the lot of their people. The upshot is the notorious "privatization of profits and socialization of losses", with the public costs of corruption outweighing whatever private benefit it may bring many times over.[22]

The privatization/socialization caper takes on especially opprobrious dimensions when large-scale corruption is carried on – that is, when payments are made in order to transgress the law. Again, an example will show what is meant:

A company in an industrial country wants to spare itself the high investment costs of building a special wastes incineration plant on its own turf and mounts a search for an alternative, cheaper way to dispose of the waste. In this situation a highly placed ministry official of a developing country approaches the company with a proposal: for a consideration of three million dollars he would arrange for the trouble-free importation of all of the waste into his country for a five-year period. He would also see to it that the special waste was buried in a remote and, in his perception, secure site. In his native village he owns enough land that would be well-suited to the purpose. True, the import (and since the "Basle Convention" of 1989, the export as well) of such toxic substances is officially prohibited. However, he, the Deputy Minister for Economic Promotion, sees no cause for worry since, first, the waste can be mixed with other materials such as gravel or sawdust and, second, the waste dump would bring jobs and so benefit the people of his village.

After briefly considering the economic advantages of the proposal the company assents to it. The sequel: a few years later the people living in the vicinity of the disposal site fall victim to a mysterious ailment - later diagnosed as severe poisoning. The deputy minister swears that he knew nothing of the special wastes' toxicity and that he was misled by the multinational corporation. The company is indited in the "host" country and becomes a focus of public protests at home as well as in numerous industrial countries.

At the beginning of this discussion we pointed out that, far from being confined to developing countries, corruption is a world-wide phenomenon. Nevertheless, it does constitute a special problem in the developing world.

---

[22] Cf. NYE, J.S. Jr.: Corruption and Political Development: A Cost-Benefit Analysis. In: *The American Political Science Review,* Vol. 61 (1967), pp. 417 ff.

3. Corruption In Developing Countries

Corruption is to all appearances widespread in developing countries and has very serious repercussions on their peoples' quality of life – above all that of the poor and disadvantaged.[23]

3.1. The background

Gunnar Myrdal, the late, great, committed social scientist, saw how corruption in the developing world triggers a chain of deplorable effects. He emphasized two in particular:[24]
– Habitual corruption paves the way for authoritarian regimes. It works thus: by exposing the corrupt character of the old crowd and undertaking to punish the guilty the new crowd manage to wrap themselves (temporarily) in a mantle of legitimacy. Parenthetically, this charade underscores the important fact that the broad mass of people in developing countries reject corruption, precisely because they suffer under it.
– Exaggerated notions of how pervasive corruption is and of how corruptible civil servants (for example) are – what Myrdal calls the "folklore of corruption" – produce resignation and fatalism among the "little people" and reinforce their conviction that this form of asocial behavior is normal.
    Myrdal saw the roots of corruption in developing regions such as South Asia in the remnants of the traditions of pre-modern societies, where presents, tribute and other social obligations were a customary and normal part of social networks. Where fundamental loyalties are due the family, the village, co-religionists or one's own ethnic group or caste, rather than the state or society as a whole, then for someone holding office favors done for and preferential treatment given to kinsmen are more important than fidelity to the state and its organs. Where culturally sanctioned gifts denote respect toward higher-ups and taking care of protégés by way of reciprocating are the done thing

---

[23] More on the subject in: THEOBALD, R.: *Corruption, Development and Under-development.* Macmillan, London 1990.
[24] MYRDAL, G.: *Asian Drama. An Inquiry into the Poverty of Nations.* Pelican Book (Penguin), Harmondsworth 1968, 3 vols. Here Vol. 2, Chap. 20, p. 937 ff.

it becomes especially difficult to pinpoint just where these customs slide over into corruption. Added to this, in many developing countries government employees are so poorly paid that they are unable to maintain even a modest standard of living. In consequence they have almost no other recourse than to seek to augment their income. And when the payroll is not met, for many of them loyalty to their employer ceases. They then start looking out for opportunities to feather their nest. Myrdal recalled that 200 years ago corruption was widespread in England, Holland and Scandinavia. It took improved governance and a firming up of moral standards, especially among the higher echelons of their civil services, as well as pay reforms to curb the rot.[25]

The confluence of poverty, relics of old and outmoded traditions, and bad governance, together with the fact that in this conflation, too, Myrdal's principles of cumulative causation and circular interdependence intensify the effects of the problem components, have disastrous consequences.

3.2. Effects of corruption in developing countries

Reality in many developing countries today is still shaped like this: relatively underdeveloped public institutions, small upper class elites, and huge differences in wealth and income – with the concomitant possibilities of wielding power and exercising authority. Under these conditions corruption has especially deplorable effects.[26] Where it spreads, no bedrock remains in the long run; habituation to dishonesty destroys all sense of honesty. The disposition to corrupt and be corrupted rather than qualifications comes to determine relations between people. Corrupt conduct in office ends up as flagrant disregarding of community interests.

The ones short-changed by all this are the socially powerless and decent people, for they either cannot or will not join in playing the

---

25 MYRDAL, G.: *Asian Drama. An Inquiry into the Poverty of Nations.* Pelican Book (Penguin), Harmondsworth 1968, 3 vols. Here Vol. 2, Chap. 20, p. 957.

26 For early examples from Sub-Saharan Africa see LEYS, C.: What is the Problem about corruption? In: *The Journal of Modern African Studies,* Vol. 3 (1965), pp. 215-230.

crooked game. Because of their poverty or uprightness they constantly get short shrift in comparison with those who have the wherewithal to influence decisions and the way things are handled to their advantage and are not shy about doing so.

When it comes down to cases this often means that quite normal services to which all citizens are nominally entitled by the constitution and the law are denied persons from the underclass, already under severe social duress, unless they cough up. It starts with giving someone who needs a certificate of birth or death a hard time, continues where children are enrolled in school, testimonials are required for job applications or positions with government are filled, and does not stop even when, following a catastrophe, the state distributes free or subsidized relief goods such as food.

Those, on the other hand, who thanks to their connections and social status and the pull these confer, are better off and in a position to dispense pecuniary or other favors need not fear mistreatment. Oftentimes they do not even have to pay their full taxes or other levies. Thus privileged, they regularly enjoy the benefits of government-provided services that, in view of their social position, they ought not and certainly have no need to profit from.

The same mechanisms are in play at the institutional level, for example in connection with official approvals, authorizations, prohibitions and the like that are of importance to business companies' operations, among other things. Wherever muzziness prevails in the awarding of contracts for goods and services by officeholders possessing discretionary authority, power centers take shape that positively invite corruption. And again, this has consequences.

Only select circles of clients get to benefit from services that government, by virtue of the job it was set up to do, should provide without discrimination. For certain companies approvals are not forthcoming, no matter that all legal requirements have been fulfilled. Conversely, other companies get the stamp of approval without having met the requirements. Some firms, wondrously, are spared tax audits and technical inspections for years and years, although it is obvious for all to see that they are precisely the ones who should be controlled. Others have to undergo controls three or four times a year, no explanation given – and never mind that there is no detectable evidence of anything amiss.

What a business enterprise, be it large or small, has to contend with in a state-dominated economy with its profusion of laws, decrees, regulations and implementation directives, and how corruption can trammel the life of the economy, was described graphically a few years ago by Hernando de Soto, taking Peru as an example:[27]

De Soto induced a "typical Peruvian small businessman" to petition for permission to operate a tailoring establishment, specifying that all legal requirements should be fulfilled. In order to obtain a permit the entrepreneur had to "pay his respects" to no less than 11 ministerial or municipal departments, one after the other. Ten of 11 officials were only prepared to perform their duty in return for an additional financial consideration. Two of them even threatened to "bury" the application if the businessman did not pay up. In the end it took 289 days, and the expenditure and lost working time came to US $1,231, i.e. 32 times the Peruvian minimum wage at the time.

Contrary to stereotype, a want of governance and corruption hit the small people hard, not the bigwigs. Large companies can hire experts to cope with the bureaucratic hurdles and obscure rules of play. They also have the means, should they wish to employ them, to "oil" the administrative machinery and speed up long drawn-out decision-making processes.

In earlier discussions of the problem of corruption in developing countries this fact led some authors to perceive positive aspects of it as well. Their argument ran that corruption overcomes bureaucratic indifference and accelerates decisions, reduces uncertainty about deciding whether or not to invest, and thus serves to mitigate the consequences of poor government policies.[28]

---

[27] Hernando de SOTO et alia.: *El otro sendero*. Lima 1985 (Caracas 1987).

[28] LEFF, N.H.: Economic Development through Bureaucratic Corruption. In: *The American Behavioral Scientist,* Vol. 8, November 1964, pp. 8-14.

4. Elements of Ethical Assessment

4.1. Basic premise: corruption is immoral

As we have said, corruption occurs in societies the world over. Most people, and not only those in the realm of Occidental culture[29] are in agreement[30] that it is iniquitous and abhorrent. (Unless, that is, they happen to be among those who profit from it.[31]) Corruption is socially destructive. It saps the foundations of probity and leads to disregard of the public interest. In the markets it warps competition to the point of stultifying it, to the detriment of the economy. By thwarting rational ways of deciding things and getting them done it puts a further strain on the network of interaction, cumbersome enough to begin with in many developing countries. From the perspective of development policy it is particularly to be deplored that repercussions emanating from corruption hurt the underdogs of society worst because of its inherent tendency to twist decisions in favor of those who, thanks to their pocketbook or social position, can bring influence to bear.

Small businesses and poor people lack the resources to prod the decision-making mill to work in their interest; they are helplessly at the mercy of capriciousness and corruption. So they must try to make a go of it in the outlaw zone of the shadow economy, living in constant fear of criminal prosecution or forced to "protect" themselves by greasing the palms of the servants of the state. As de Soto has shown, the poor of Lima, like those in other big cities in developing countries, have built up an informal shadow economy because "official channels" leave them no chance of survival, what with too much government and too many conditions, approvals and decrees serving mainly to satisfy

---

[29] Cf. EIGEN, P.: *Das Nord-Süd-Gefälle der Korruption.* In: Kursbuch. Rowohlt Verlag, Berlin 1995, Issue 120, p. 155 ff. See also letter by Olusegun Obasanjo, Ex-President of Nigeria, to the Financial Times, 14 October 1994.

[30] One reflection: recent reference works such as the Concise Oxford Dictionary give both a specific and a more sweeping definition: "*corrupt* a. rotten, depraved, wicked; influenced by bribery ... *corruption* n. decomposition, moral deterioration, use of corrupt practices..." (Seventh edition, reprinted with corrections, 1983).

[31] Concerning this ambivalence see NECKEL, S.: *Der unmoralische Tausch. Eine Soziologie der Käuflichkeit.* In: Kursbuch. Rowohlt Verlag, Berlin 1995, Issue 120, footnote 24. p. 9 ff.

the bureaucrats' own interest and opening up opportunities for corruption to them. The deleterious impact of corruption on development is beyond doubt.[32]

The business world as well can only view corruption as an evil. For one thing it undermines every effort to do business with the customer in mind, aiming to achieve the optimal customer satisfaction that translates into market success. A business that can flourish merely by "greasing" has no incentive to strive for quality. In a climate of corruption the quality and competitive price of products and services do not determine market success, but rather how much bribe-money changes hands; not the reliability and integrity of a company, or other gauges of genuine competence, but rather the unscrupulousness of corrupt individuals. This game does not deserve the name of competition: its true name is fraudulent competition. Corruption can tie up sizable financial and organizational assets[33] indefensible in any normal climate of operations. Without the impediment of corruption those resources could be employed elsewhere or used to improve profitability.[34]

Last, it is too much to expect of employees that they should perform corrupt acts and submit to making payments. Especially employees of multinational corporations who do so can run a high personal risk, for it is probable that even though two people may be doing "the same thing" it will not be considered quite the same. A bribe passed to a government employee by a countryman is generally looked at in a different light than the identical act with an expatriate doing the bribe.

In the long term no society can subsist as an orderly whole if corrupt mores dictate the tenor of economic, social and political life. It always comes down to shady practices used to procure an unfair advantage for one side at the expense of someone else. Both the Eco-

---

[32] More on this in NYE, J.S.: Corruption and Political Development: A Cost-Benefit Analysis. In: *The American Political Science Review,* Vol. 61 (1967), p. 417 ff.; also BAYLEY, D.H.: The Effects of Corruption in a Developing Nation. In: *The Western Political Quarterly,* Vol. 19 (1966), pp. 719-732.

[33] Gunnar Myrdal pointed this out with reference to South Asia almost 30 years ago. See MYRDAL G.: *Asian Drama. An Inquiry into the Poverty of Nations.* Pelican Book (Penguin), Harmondsworth 1968, 3 vols., here vol. 2, Chap. 20, p. 942 ff.

[34] Unless, that is, tacking the additional costs on to prices is part of the deal. Then, of course, the injured party is the public and not the company.

nomic and Social Council and other UN bodies and the OECD have condemned and proscribed corruption. From a corporate ethics point of view there can be only one clear-cut judgment on corruption: whether active or passive it is illegitimate and immoral.

4.2. There's corruption and corruption

An assessment of the various kinds of corruption that takes into account the gravity of the breach of morals involved must, in the spirit of situation ethics, examine the actual circumstances under which deviant behavior has occurred. Only after further questions have been clarified and the various pros and cons considered is it possible to arrive at a fair verdict on the degree of illegitimacy that the situation under review presents.[35]
Among the pertinent questions are these:
– Who profits directly and indirectly and how much do the actors benefit?
– Whom does the corrupt act harm? How does the harm suffered relate to the benefit realized?
– How big a sum is in play and how does it relate to the business transaction that actuated the corruption?
– Was the sum under discussion paid for a service or for information generally regarded as aboveboard, known to everyone, and in the circumstances legitimate?
– Was there another way to the same end that, although perhaps longer and more onerous, afforded the same chance of leading to success?
A circumspect appraisal of all aspects of a case results in differing conclusions regarding the seriousness of the moral trespass. It is easy to think of examples where, in my opinion, leniency would be indicated.
   Let us imagine that after driving eight hours you have already been stuck another hour in 90-degree heat in the backed-up traffic at the border of the country where you are headed on vacation. And let us further suppose that you are bringing a friend a stereo set that is sub-

---

[35] See also DeGEORGE, R.T.: *Competing with Integrity in International Business.* Oxford University Press, Oxford/New York 1993, p. 12 ff.

ject to customs duty. Now imagine that it turns 12 o'clock just as you get to customs at last, only to be informed by the officer on duty that he is now taking his three-hour midday break. Noting your expression of despair, he suggests that if you care to pay him $30 for overtime (actually two minutes) he will settle the formalities during his break. A clear case of "speed-up payment".

Or imagine that at the airport in an African vacation-land you are told that your long-booked and confirmed domestic flight is now, surprisingly, overbooked. It looks like the dream you have nurtured for years of visiting a wildlife park near Kilimanjaro stands no chance of coming true. Unless, that is, you pay an "administrative fee" sufficient to elicit the discovery that your name was "erroneously" deleted from the confirmed passengers list.

If you pay the sum demanded, both times it is clearly an instance of corruption and unfair to those who are unable to come up with the bribe. Yet as I see it cases of this sort have to be judged differently from more serious ones – for example, paying an official a much bigger bribe to make him forget about a correctly completed customs declaration or even to clear the way for importing toxic waste, drugs or weapons. Neither kind of bribe is legitimate, and on general principle one must always try everything possible to get through without resort to a corrupt act. Plainly, however, there are qualitative differences in the gravity of the offense committed.

4.3. Cases of clear-cut corruption

Certain kinds of corruption leave no doubt as to how they should be adjudged. Where corruption is practiced as a means of gaining unlawful advantage, judgment can be pronounced unequivocally and without undue cerebration: the practice is unlawful and therefore cannot be considered legitimate under any circumstances. Business institutions are thus well-advised to make it known publicly that they do not tolerate the practice – not even when it might be commercially expedient and would quite probably go undetected. Employees who contravene this unambiguous declaration of corporate policy should not only be sacked but also reported.

Arriving at a verdict on large-scale corruption is also fairly easy to do. Wherever companies stoop to pushing lavish purchase decisions at odds with local realities whetting officialdom's appetite for outsized, technically over-complex or otherwise ill-suited goods and services either by offering "commissions" or knuckling under when they are demanded, their conduct is illegal – and in acting thus they become accomplices to the damage inflicted upon the commonweal.

4.4. Grey zones of evaluation

Where "expediting contributions" or gifts have the effect of prompting an official to do something that he would be duty-bound to do in any case and to do it adequately and within a reasonable period – in other words, where the sole object of the bribe is to provoke the actual carrying out of an act that is perfectly legal as such – I see no great moral problem. There is one, to be sure, in that someone who can afford to pay for speeded-up attention to his business enjoys an illegitimate edge over those unable to do so. Even if rewarding an official for seeing to a legitimate piece of business without delay may in certain circumstances be the "lesser" evil, an evil it remains nevertheless. For this reason a company and its employees in positions of responsibility should never under any circumstances have recourse to corruption as the means to an end, whatever this may be.

Where someone is at the receiving end of an extortionate demand, passing judgment on the ethics of the situation can prove difficult. This is particularly the case when the outcome effectuated with the aid of corruption not only does not harm the public interest but even turns out to have positive ripples.

How does one decide when government employees insist on their "commission" and make it clear that a job just won't get done without it? If a person is being blackmailed and submits, could we not say that he has acted in self-defense[36] and is therefore not morally culpable? In the ethical perspective, what is the "lesser evil" in the following case:

---

[36] Carl A. Kotchian, former head of Lockheed Corporation, argued along these lines. He gave way to a demand by government officials for a bribe in connection with the planned sale of TriStar aircraft. Later, when the payment became publicly known, he had to resign. See KOTCHIAN, C.A.: *The Payoff: Lockheed's 70-Day Mission to Tokyo*. In: Saturday Review, 9 Jul 1977, pp. 7-12.

In the course of fully legal sales negotiations having to do with a legitimate order of business – this in a milieu well-known to be corrupt – a demand for graft is insinuated, rejection of which would result in the loss of many company jobs. In weighing every aspect of the situation must we not also take into account the palpable privations that, say, a steelworker in the Ruhr area or a Lockheed aircraft employee might suffer from the loss of his job because his company refuses to pay the "locally customary" bribes in certain developing countries as the price of landing major orders?

On the basis of corporate ethics theory it is easy to respond to questions of this sort, for heroic moralism has only one thing to say to corruption of any and every kind: *no*. The practical value of the *no* is slight, however. "White sheep" companies that consistently conduct themselves morally cannot, it is obvious, survive in a herd of black sheep. Approaches to solutions must, to have a chance of lasting success, not only tackle the problem on the corporate playing field. They must be more complex in conception, include various levels, and take hold as a concerted plan of action.

5. Starting Points Toward Solutions

5.1. The level of governance

Virtually every theoretical discussion on the subject of corruption sees a close tie to poor governance. People with uncontrolled power misuse their decision-making authority to corrupt ends. They are able to do this because it is impossible to see into how decisions are arrived at and accountability is obfuscated. The same political groups are in a position to obstruct changes in the conditions that make it possible for them to line their pockets illicitly. Although corruption or other unethical conduct cannot be excused by pointing to the irresponsible conduct of governments and their bureaucracies, it would be naive to suppose that problems which can develop only in tandem with flawed governance could be solved by applying the maxims of corporate ethics.

Good governance is undoubtedly the most fundamental condition of a country's political development. It is manifested when the activity of the state serves to bring the people security, prosperity, order and continuity because an environment has been created in which everyone can unfold their productive, political and cultural abilities. Notably where the state regulates economic life excessively, where a surfeit of laws and enforcement agencies chokes every display of private initiative, and where officeholders deliberately drag their feet and operate destructively in order to foster a "market" for inducements – in such a tangle precious little can be achieved with mere moral appeals prescribed by business ethics.

So without better governance the problem of corruption is insolvable.[37] The most relevant shortcomings in the context of fighting corruption are these:
- Lack of a clear distinction between what is to be considered "public" and what "private", leaving the door open to appropriating public resources for private advantage;
- Lack of transparency in the handling of public finances, lack of independent control agencies, and thus hindrance of presentation of concrete proof;
- Absence of dependable legal machinery for preventing arbitrary application of regulations and laws;
- Weak public institutions, no free press;
- Over-regulation, as evidenced by an unwarranted number of regulations, permit requirements and laws;
- Unclear decision-making procedures hinging on very close personal connections plus capricious interventions by those who hold political power and their abuse of it for their own enrichment.

By and large one can say that the more inefficient a government is and the more "powerful" its bureaucracy, the bigger the corruption problem. When the omnipresence of imprecise or contradictory laws and regulations, the obscurity of the criteria and channels governing decisions, the lack of accountability and democratically sanctioned political controls, all in conjunction with an underpaid and corrupt officialdom, leave a firm otherwise beyond reproach no alternative but to either join the circle of corruption or else withdraw completely from

---

[37] For a detailed discussion of this subject see LEISINGER, K.M. / HÖSLE, V: *Entwicklung mit menschlichem Antlitz.* Beck Verlag, Munich 1995, pp. 114-172; see also World Bank: Governance: *The World Bank's Experience.* Washington, D.C., November 1993.

the country, then whichever it decides to do, little has been gained in the direction of improving the country's political status quo.

A will to work for better governance and concrete political action to this end are imperative for both sustainable development and the wiping out (or at least minimization) of corruption. This means:

- Dismantling over-regulation, for the overload of discretionary administrative rules and regulations provides officialdom at every level with the opportunity to exercise its authority not on the basis of objective requirements but rather in the specific interests of those (low-paid) officeholders empowered to decide.
- Reform of the public service with a view to abolishing ponderous and nebulous ways of doing and deciding things. In their place introduce more precise and intelligible statutory and administrative regulations together with more efficient information flows; then translate them into real-life jurisprudence and practice. Further, effective superintendance and accountability required of everyone holding an official position, and irregular personnel rotations in especially susceptible positions, though not at the price of impairing competence. Finally, effective, and justly enforced disciplinary and punitive measures against corrupt officials and employees.
- Revised hiring and employment conditions in the civil service, e.g. more competition for posts, better remuneration, ombudsmen, plus reduction of arbitrarily exercised decision-making authority.
- Public invitation of tenders for government and agency contracts and all planning and procurement or public purchasing contracts above a certain amount. Documentation to be made obligatory; public and open evaluation of all bids and justification of the decision taken. Because corruption can only thrive in the dark, greater transparency is absolutely essential to overcoming it. Blacklisting businesses that have been found guilty of corruption and refusing to consider them for government contracts for a certain period – until they have mended their ways – can also be a useful tactic.
- Build-up or improvement of internal audits and controls by higher authority, applicable to both officialdom and the business sector.
- Creation of independent commissions along the Hong Kong model and protection of freedom of the press. Even in industrial countries big cases of corruption have finally been brought to light only thanks to free and independent media.

All of the foregoing measures are aimed at reducing the motivation and the opportunity to indulge in corrupt behavior. One could furthermore conceive of disincentives to corruption, for example, an achievement-based scheme in which public servants would receive a share of the fees and levies they collect.[38]

Over the past 35 years Singapore has shown what can be accomplished in a political and institutional environment of good governance and incorruptible leadership. Comparable national initiatives elsewhere are deserving of every possible kind of international support. The opposite pattern of behavior should be penalized, for example, by cutting back on international development assistance.

5.2. Broad coalitions

As is the case with any endeavor to bring about constructive social change, joint effort undertaken in concert stands a greater chance of succeeding than does single-handed action. In the confrontation with corruption the situation is comparable to the "prisoners' dilemma", i.e. cooperating in good faith is more likely to produce results than a lone wolf effort.

If whole sectors, or at least the market leaders in a sector, were prepared to renounce corruption in any form as a marketing instrument, the pledging companies would strengthen their own security. More, the show of solidarity would be more effective than solo efforts in reaching the goal envisaged.

Disinterested outside institutions, first and foremost Transparency International,[39] could not only help to initiate and co-ordinate; through their published reports they would also have the means of arousing public opinion and with it the political pressure needed to combat and at least reduce corruption.

---

[38] KLITGAARD, R.: Vorbeugen ist besser als Strafen. In: Galtung, F. (Ed.): *Zum Beispiel Korruption*. Lamuv Verlag, Göttingen, December 1994, p. 82 ff.

[39] Cf. Transparency International, The Coalition against Corruption in International Business Transactions (Ed.): TI Newsletter, address noted in footnote 8.

5.3.   Corporate ethics

The long history of corruption and the fact that even making it a capital offense in some countries has not resulted in its elimination show that stricter laws, stepped-up institutional controls and an improved political framework do not of themselves suffice to master the problem. And as for moral outcries against corruption, these amount to no more than idealistic quixotry. What is needed for a solution with teeth in it is a unified exertion on all fronts, including the business front.

To put it in plainly: in the end companies are not going to be able to shirk doing their bit in the fight against corruption. True, during the past thirty-odd years it has spread like a malignant tumor, so that in many countries today it is almost impossible to do business without greasing palms. It is also true that sometimes a virtual state of blackmail exists that one must go along with in self-defense in order to stay in business. All this notwithstanding, it is neither seemly nor ethically acceptable simply to call attention to the problem and give voice to one's disquiet while shifting the responsibility for doing something about it onto others.

If one does not want to look on passively while morals collapse, and implicate oneself by doing nothing, then one must take an opposing stand. A suitable way to start opposing would be to protect from temptation employees whose work might bring them into the danger zone of active or passive corruption. Prevention begins where the problem can and does arise, namely with human beings. Proceeding from there, the Working Group for Security in Industry and Commerce (Germany) has drawn up *Ten Rules*[40] :

–   Set a good example. Avoid anything that could lead your employees to conclude that corrupt practices – even including active ones – might find favour or be tolerated in your company.
–   Secure a written commitment from your employees to abide by guidelines expressly forbidding active and passive corruption. Make it clear to them that infractions will have actionable consequences.

---

40 Cf. KARKOWSKY, J: *Vor der Versuchung schützen*. In: Wirtschaft im Südwesten. Zeitschrift der Industrie- und Handelskammern Hochrhein-Bodensee, No. 12 (December) 1995, p. 5 ff.

- Let it be explicitly known whether and to what upper limits presents, invitations and other favours may be accepted.
- Require full disclosure from employees in strategic positions of their financial or other connections to suppliers and customers.
- Hold training courses for employees on the dangers of corruption and how to recognize them.
- Appoint a contact person in your company to whom employees can turn for binding advice on what criminal law and the company's own prohibitions entail.
- Appoint one or more persons in your company to whom observations relating to corruption can be reported direct. Make it clear that this will have no negative consequences for the reporting employee.
- To the extent feasible, institute the "four eyes principle"[41] and, insofar as necessary, job rotation. Require detailed records of all operations.
- Inform business partners of the regulations in force in your company. Ask them to establish corresponding safeguards.
- Reinforce internal controls by upgrading the auditing job's professionalism and prestige and expanding the scope of its authority. In case of doubt bring in outside examiners or experts. Report violations of the law to the police and see to it that legal proceedings are instituted.

As a minimal strategy Moody-Stuart recommends, among other things, that companies which do business in developing countries and are approached by top officials for "commissions" refrain from taking part in sales transactions or projects that in the company's judgment are disadvantageous for the buyer or interested authority, respectively. Further, no compromising of the company's standards should be entertained, even when the customer appears to be "magnanimous".[42]

Every positive social change has to be set in motion by someone somewhere. Through a strict corporate policy every company, and through the exercise of responsible judgment every individual, has leave to practice conduct unsmirched by corruption. This means not

---

[41] Meaning: inclusion of a second person in handling sensitive business matters.

[42] MOODY-STUART, G.: *Schwere Korruption in der Dritten Welt*. In: Kursbuch. Rowohlt Verlag, Berlin 1995, Issue 120, p. 127.

only refusing to cave in beforehand but also standing one's ground when the pressure is turned on. The morality of such a stance is beyond doubt: corruption is bad for the people involved, for the company involved, and for the society it impacts upon.

Here as anywhere else, of course, there is no free lunch. Repudiating corruption can prove costly. If a company not only makes up its mind not to grease anyone's palm under any circumstances but to forswear corruption as an access route to the market, no matter how persistently pressed from whatever quarter, it is certain to lose market share in some countries. In a global market this can be painful, and especially so if the countries in question are very affluent markets or very profitable niche markets and competitors are without scruples.

For the moment all one would have to offset the tangible operating loss is the idealistic satisfaction of having remained true to one's standards and the hope of a political change for the better. Individual corporate action can alter a corrupt climate only marginally at the most. There is also the hope that in time the word about the correct stand the company has taken will get around, making it immune to undue expectations and coercion. In the longer term there is the further hope that when the social "cleansing" comes to pass people will remember those who refrained from joining in the merry cosi fan tutte roundelay. At the same time, though, it would be unrealistic to expect that every "new broom" government swept into office on a platform of virtuousness will in the event turn out to be so much better than the *ancien régime* it castigated and replaced.

Short-term, the repudiation of corruption in very many cases has to be juxtaposed against the appreciable price of abridged entrepreneurial success. This fact in no way detracts from the ethical argument for proscribing corruption unreservedly – but it does lessen the probability that the precepts constituting the argument will be honored in practice.

Over against the costs are the returns, admittedly much less readily quantifiable. To its own employees and its social environment the company presents a credible demonstration of its creed: this company does not just talk about values, it lives up to them. The positive example set by an internationally reputable company and made plain for all to see can encourage others to go and do likewise, thus getting a positive, cumulative upward trend off the ground.

Corruption as a Threat to the United Nations

Karl Theodor Paschke

1. Specific Problems of the UN as a Multilateral Organization

For a number of years, the U.S. Congress (or more precisely: a vociferous majority of Congress members) has grown accustomed to vilifying the United Nations Organization as a pool of waste, fraud, corruption and mismanagement.

U.S. newspaper articles over the years have gone to great pains to substantiate this image by citing hair-raising examples of UN officials stealing or embezzling funds, taking bribes and kickbacks, tampering with procurement contracts, etc. Most of these cases were reported over and over again, so that, while the substance may be uncontested, one gets the impression that the dimension of these cases has been blown out of proportion, just because they fitted into the cliché of a corrupt, bloated, wasteful UN.

After doing oversight work in the world organization for almost two years, I tend to believe that the UN may not be worse in this regard than many national administrations of comparable size. But, that is bad enough, and it is sufficient reason to be worried. I want to discuss some of the pertinent factors which are specific to this multilateral organization.

(1) First of all, the United Nations is a *multi-cultural organization*. Its staff comes from more than 150 countries. People from Europe, Africa, Asia, the Americas, bring the most diverse perceptions of "public service" to their workplace. This does not only apply to administrative practice, but impacts on their behaviour towards colleagues and superiors, even on their attitude towards handling official funds. Of course, all staff members are bound by the same rules and regulations, but, as we all know, a *"management culture"* does not rest enti-

141

H. Lange et al., Working Across Cultures, 141–145.

rely on rules and regulations, it also grows on shared beliefs and principles which do not exist in such a diverse body.

One would assume that, in the absence of universal beliefs and management principles, the organization might have developed an elaborated *code of conduct*. However, the UN Charter is not particularly outspoken in this respect. Art. 101 only talks about "the necessity of securing the highest standards of efficiency, competence and integrity". But where are these standards to be found? Who defines them? Where is the blueprint on which a world-wide consensus could be formed?

(2) Another deficiency of the UN in this field is the lack of an adequate *iudiciary svstem* which would provide a deterrent against blatant disregard of or tampering with rules and regulations. As a matter of fact, the so-called Administrative Tribunal does not hear cases where the UN administration complains about an employee, only cases where an employee has a grievance against the administration.

Even the *disciplinary system* of the UN used to be lackadaisical until recently. The creation of the "Office of Internal Oversight Services" is a significant step towards remedying this situation. I shall come back to this later.

(3) In the ongoing efforts inside the UN to improve its managerial performance and bring about reform, the Department of Administration and Management has launched a drive to increase the awareness of UN managers for *"responsibility and accountability"*. A very laudable exercise indeed in an organization which has a long and unfortunate tradition of employees shunning and blurring responsibility through opaque structures and procedures.

But, one of the difficulties which this drive faces, has to do with language: How do you adequately translate "responsibility and accountability" into the other official UN languages? I am told that the term "accountability" cannot be precisely interpreted in French and Spanish, let alone in Arabic, Russian or Chinese.

(4) Which leads me to yet another phenomenon that has relevance in the context of this EBEN Conference: the overwhelming dominance of the *English language* in international communication. I submit that this dominance goes way beyond linguistics. It influences negotiating procedures, business practice, administrative routine, human resource management; in short: it influences perceptions, intellectual processes,

thinking. Are we, then, inextricably bound to adopt Anglo-Saxon perception of what corruption means, and obligated to follow Anglo-Saxon, i.e. American, practices in battling corruption?

2. The Office of Internal Oversight Services (OIOS)

I will try to answer this question implicitly by telling you some more about the creation of my office, the *Office of Internal Oversight Services* in the UN.

The United States was instrumental in this. The U.S. delegation to the UN, backed by several initiatives in the U.S. Congress, demanded that the position of an "Inspector General" be created in the world body. In their negotiations with the other Member States, the Americans propagated their Inspector General concept in great detail. Not all these features made their way into the final GA Resolution which established OIOS in the fall of 1994. But one did which, as I have found out in the meantime, is typically American and viewed with scepticism and apprehension by a great majority of the other delegations: the *"whistle-blower" arrangement*.

The Investigations Section of my office runs a so-called *"hotline"* which invites UN staff to give us information about corruption, waste and abuse within the organization. We will take this information and deal with it seriously and responsibly, even if the input has been made anonymously. I must admit that I find it difficult to encourage anonymous allegations and I know that most UN staff members feel uneasy about it, because it can poison the management atmosphere in an organization, but here the American thinking has clearly prevailed.

For the sake of our discussion later on, may I mention another American practice that comes into play quite frequently in the international battle against corruption although it is certainly not accepted world-wide: the so-called *"sting operations"*.

Speaking of "language" and cultural diversity, I have the relate to you yet another experience I had in establishing OIOS. Coming from a statutory law background, I considered it imperative to define immediately the terms of reference for the Investigations Section of this new office, in order to secure due process and transparency for every staff member who would become actively or passively involved in an investigation. In the UN where the Anglo-Saxon case-law approach seems to be prevalent, my initiative to write definitions for "Mismanagement, Misconduct, Waste of Resources and Abuse of Authority" caused a major stir among the legal and administrative experts. After months of back and forth, a document was agreed upon which stopped short of definitions, but instead provided practical examples of what actions or non-actions would constitute such wrongdoings.

The reason which I was given for this reluctant attitude was: we cannot interfere with the legislative authority of the General Assembly, and that is what we would be doing if we tried to lay down definitions. The General Assembly, on the other hand, would never be able to agree on such definitions, at least not without years and years of complicated negotiations. I am asking myself: What about a world-wide accepted, uncontested definition of the word *"corruption"*? Probably there would be the same complexity.

To come back to United Nations specificities in our subject field, the world organization is involved in many activities which are "high risk" by their very nature or by the environment in which they occur, for example: peace-keeping, humanitarian affairs, and procurement in general.

(1) The number of *peace-keeping missions* has skyrocketed in the last few years. Somalia, the former Yugoslavia and Rwanda come to mind. In these operations, the UN has to provide elaborate and costly infrastructure, both military and civilian, under extreme time pressure and mostly in areas were civil, economic and administrative structures have broken down. How do you observe rigid bidding requirements and stringent internal controls under such conditions? How do you prevent blue helmet soldiers from getting involved in black-market schemes in a situation where everybody else steals, robs and kills just to survive?

(2) Similar conditions exist in many of the *humanitarian missions* which the UN undertakes. It is extremely difficult to uphold sound administrative practices under such circumstances and not take recourse to cutting corners.

(3) As in any public administration, the area of *procurement in general* poses a specific risk for corruption. This area should be organized with particular care, clear segregation of duties, strict internal controls, and complete transparency. Unfortunately, it has not been so

in the United Nations for a long time. Therefore, I have declared procurement matters along with peace-keeping and humanitarian affairs, the highest priorities of our oversight work. Many of our current oversight activities focus on these priorities.

* We are doing *audits* of procurement which include recommendations on how to reform respective procedures.
* We are doing in-depth *evaluations* of peace-keeping and humanitarian affairs.
* I do ad-hoc *inspections* to peace-keeping missions in the field.
* My *investigators* have zeroed in on a number of corruption cases in these areas.

Our approach is always both proactive and deterrent. OIOS sees itself as a partner of management in analyzing procedures and suggesting improvements. We also try to convey to management that oversight, i.e. internal controls, the monitoring of ongoing operations for their fiscal soundness and their congruence with the principal aims of the organization, is not just a task for the inspectors, but first and foremost a *managerial duty* which every manager must embrace him/herself.

At the same time, we recognize the preventive and deterrent character of our work. Joseph Stalin's old word "trust is good, control is better" may not be valid any more, but there was always a grain of truth in it in the sense that some element of control, of oversight, should be in place to keep your business tidy. And this is certainly true in an international organization which, as I have tried to show, is particularly vulnerable for certain irregularities.

I believe that *continuous, effective oversight* does more to decrease corruption, fraud and mismanagement in the UN than the spectacular revealing of one or two high-profile cases. I would like to think that, because we have been able to establish a credible and visible system of Internal Oversight in the United Nations, the UN already today is a better organization than what it was until 1994.

PART III

Values and Ethics in the Corporate Transformation Process

Restructuring and Mental Change

Heiko Lange

The air traffic industry was plunged into deep crisis in the early Nineties. The world's airlines lost as much money in fours years as they had earned in their previous history. Well might the situation have merited headlines such as:
– "More and more people can afford to fly – but not the airlines." Because:
– "Fewer and fewer people are paying more. More and more people are paying less."

Other factors were also troubling the airline industry:
– Increasing excess capacities
– Growing difficulties in product differentiation – declining customer loyalty
– Higher airport and air traffic control charges
– Deregulation
  Increased customer price-sensitivity
  Lufthansa was faced by fiercer competition from rival airlines in its home market in Germany
– Substitutional competitors (new media)
– Worldwide recession and its depressing effect on business travel
– Weak bargaining position for acquisition of airline-related commodities (aircraft, fuel, personnel)

H. Lange et al., Working Across Cultures, 149–159.

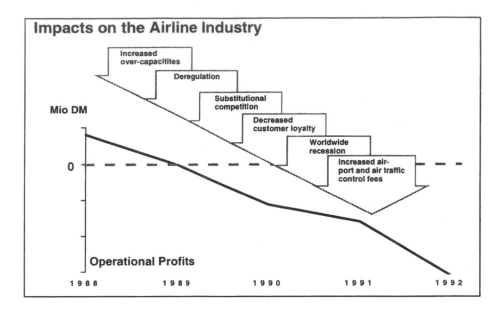

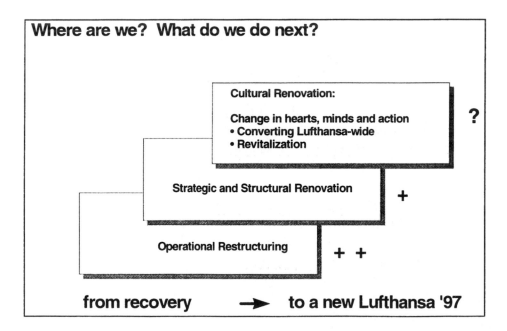

Lufthansa itself was plunged into the worst crisis in its history, ending 1992 with a massive deficit of more than 1 billion DM in 1992. The Lufthansa Board embarked on a threefold recovery plan entailing reduction, restructuring and re-organization – and soon to be followed by a campaign aimed at initiating mental change at the airline.

Barely were the decisions announced, when a divisive mood on management level spread through the company. The dilemma: Management says "be innovative and entrepreneurial" – hoping the message would get through without causing turmoil, they encountered a host of objections i.e.:

- too much talk, too little action
- requires too much coordination

- no change
- lack of risk acceptance and flexibility

- homogeneity perceived by customer
- top-heavy management
- unclear competence boundaries

- alienation from the company

- high controlling expenditures
- additional cost from duplication

- shirking of responsibility
- too slow information flow
- lack of expertise
- working against each other
- fear of responsibility
- lack of employee willingness
- no management cuts
- good intentions become lost

- difficult communications
- overview becomes diffused
- loss of synergy
- constant reorganization
- loss of quality
- no change in management
- no economic advantages
- available systems not adequately used

Any change in an organization creates resentment, anxieties and concern. The majority may see themselves as spectators with a wait-and-see-mentality. A small group of others take on the role of missionaries, believers, or trend-setters. Others will be out-and-out opponents. You have the innovators and the opinion makers. In fact, three groups can be identified: those who make things happen, those who watch things happen and those who wonder what happens.

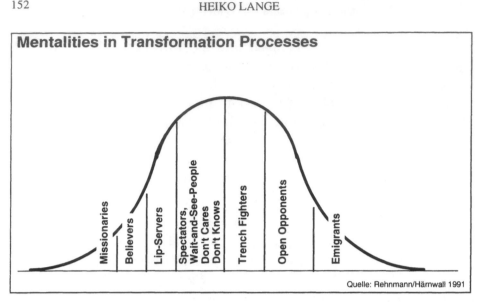

Mentalities in Transformation Processes

Missionaries · Believers · Lip-Servers · Spectators, Wait-and-See-People, Don't Cares, Don't Knows · Trench Fighters · Open Opponents · Emigrants

Quelle: Rehnmann/Härnwall 1991

After years of job security in a company making healthy profits, the employees were shocked at seeing the airline close to disaster. In pondering a remedy, all future actions had to take into consideration that, in such cases, a denial phase and a depression phase precede an acceptance and later a cooperation or learning phase.

So the task forces to be set up immediately had to be planned carefully and – with additional professional expertise and support from outside consultants. It was essential to involve managerial staff from the outset in order to gain their acceptance and cooperation.

In February 1992, Lufthansa began a special management training course by INSEAD, directed at "Management of Change". This was followed by a workshop on change processes for the Lufthansa Board of Management run by Prof. Thanheiser from INSEAD. In April 1992, a team was set up to prepare a "Management of Change" workshop for Lufthansa management. In June and July, a series of turnaround workshops started for the entire Lufthansa top-management team. The idea was that managers – without the initial participation of the Executive Board – should frame strategies and actions for the turnaround process, with the Board only later being able to make additions while not rejecting any management recommendations. A total 131 action points were defined and a steering committee – reporting direct to the Board – was formed to implement them in "Program '93".

Three targets were formulated:
- reduce manpower costs by 500 million DM
- reduce other costs by 500 million DM
- increase revenues by 500 million DM

Once the targets had been set, management involved and the steering committee established, further steps were decided on:
- operational restructuring
- strategic and structural renewal
- cultural renovation (changing hearts, minds, and actions)

The next major step was to involve the employees and the employees' representatives. Codetermination, and the rights of employees and unions in Germany, as far as information, consultation and a co-determination are concerned are manifold. But in critical situations like Lufthansa's at the time, communication and cooperation are all the more important and need to be put on an even higher plane.

Reducing labor costs by 500 million DM could only be realized by shedding 8000 jobs and obtaining significant concessions in collective wage agreements. Without the co-operation of the unions this would have been impossible. So, an intensive information program had to be started: A number of staff assemblies were held and wage negotiations conducted. It took six months before a significant agreement was reached. The unions declared their willingness to cooperate with the restructuring program, and management agreed that the employees' representatives should get a seat in the so-called "Structure-Groups" (similar to steering committees) together with management representatives in order to be kept informed about all actions for a period of three years.

Job cuts, as well as changing work practices and processes, can trigger upsets and grievances which – in a service company especially – can all too easily erode quality. To avoid any of those effects Lufthansa initiated 110 seminars, each lasting two days for an average of 80 employees at a time, in order to improve service efficiency and to discuss weak points within the processes. Each of those seminars was attended at least for some of the time by a Board Member to give the participants the opportunity to speak their minds. The "Customer Service Index" later showed that service quality did not decline during the restructuring period.

Last but not least the cooperation and communication process in the company created the basis for beginning a "Total Quality Management" program which allowed even greater employee involvement, and yielded a lot more innovation and ideas for further improvement.

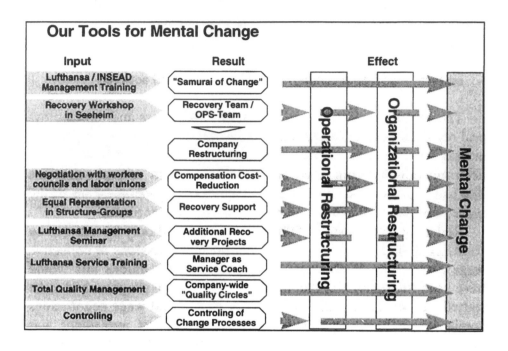

Some of the most important characteristics of the change process may be summarized as follows:
—   change comes from within and cascades downwards and upwards
—   change cannot be delegated
—   everybody sees on-going learning as essential
—   most of the competitive advantages are not created by top management, they are worked out by all employees
—   most employees are personally committed to keeping Lufthansa competitive
—   employee commitment presupposes empowerment and downward elegation of responsibility for their own decisions
—   trust, discipline, openness, mutual support instead of mistrust
—   information and open communications

Our strategic renewal hinged essentially on the forging of alliances with other leading airlines. We entered into partnerships with United Airlines, SAS, THAI, VARIG, South African Airways and Air Canada. Besides the logistics challenge arising from these tie-ups, it is highly important to harmonize their corporate cultures and the attitudes of their staff. To that end, a variety of workshops were organized to improve communications and encourage mutual trust and confidence. A "Partner Forum" was held to allow diverse groups of staff from all the airline partners to debate "human resource and cultural issues". Those points are now being discussed in greater detail by various working groups:

human resource and *cultural issues:*
- building up mutual trust, culture and synergy on all levels,
- crossborder know-how transfer,
- establishing cross-cultural teams,
- involving unions,
- communicating the joint vision top down,
- cross-border information,
- involving the management team / the key people,
- listening to early warning signals,
- building up human resources for alliances.

Operative recovery – an aim achieved by Lufthansa with positive results in 1994 – was one of the major prerequisites for Lufthansa's privatization and reorganization. Again, one of the top priorities was to dispel the existential worries among the staff and map out prospects for their future. Extensive negotiations had to be conducted with the trade unions on the collective wage agreements required to flank the new decentralized organization operating with different business areas as independent legal entities, and convince the staff that no disadvantages would ensue from replacing the previous state-run pension fund by a private pension plan. Additional effort had to be invested – at a number of staff meetings and assemblies – to ensure that the new subsidiaries acquired their own identity without shedding their identification with the Lufthansa Group.

Another major step – after Lufthansa had emerged from its crisis – and become a privatized company with a new structure was to communicate its visions and objectives, priorities and perspectives in-house and externally. Lufthansa is an airline with a remarkable history, and retaining pride in its traditions is important. As one of the world's major airlines in the largest global airline alliance, it has equipped itself for the future and has a responsibility towards the staff, customers and the public which must be made known. Customers, too, must be proud of their Lufthansa.

It was to that end that we launched our "Balance" campaign. The idea behind the campaign is to communicate the beliefs and principles guiding the Lufthansa Group into the future. Sensible entrepreneurial activities can only be based on balanced aims: Pursuing egoistic interests at the expense of others will only boomerang to one's own disadvantage in the long term. Our corporate stance seeks a balance between economical and ecological interests. But that is only one of our aims. The balance between man and technology – especially at an airline – is no less important. As is the balance between financial and social objectives – in a word, between shareholders and staff. A company must also balance constancy and change – never resting against the competition while avoiding the harm that can result from excessive activism.

Constancy and Change, Stability and Instability, Order and Chaos, Structure and Process are not contradictions. They do not contradict but complement each other.

A communications campaign gives center-stage to the attitude and responsibilities of the Lufthansa Group. It backs up a series of other programs like TQM, the Lufthansa punctuality offensive or service offensive ("We want to serve").

Mental change is a lengthy process. Tireless effort is required to ensure its lasting success – and perspectives are essential as well. Shareholders, analysts, customers and staff share a common desire for long-term success for the company and themselves. There is no way of achieving that without the staff – the task resembles the challenge of an iceberg.

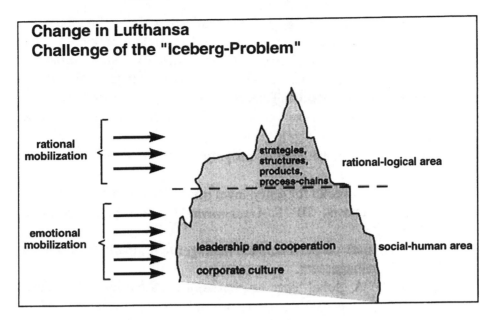

All the measures taken to engineer a company's recovery, most of the daily management decisions, are directed at the rational part – the hard factors of the iceberg tip above the water's surface, like strategies, structures, products, processes and costs. But all that will serve no purpose, if the soft factors – of emotional mobilization – are not taken into consideration. Leadership and communication, motivation and personal advancement, team spirit, morale and identification, trust, confidence and enthusiasm are productive factors, which reward the effort put into them far more than preoccupation with cost reduction and structural change.

Future prospects for the staff are essential. And, for that reason, we attached paramount importance to personal development. Three years ago, we mapped out a pyramid of activities and programs – at the time with a number of "empty boxes". In the meantime almost all the measures have been implemented, the program is very much alive, the opportunities are transparent and many of the staff have attended diverse types of seminars.

Top management courses were organized with leading business schools (London Business School, Insead, Cranfield etc), each time in partnership with four or five other companies like Shell, Standard Chartered Bank, SKF, Westinghouse, ABN Amro, Industrial Bank of Japan, Matsushita and British Telecom:

- Cross-divisional *rotation* program (integrated training & career counseling)
- 3C-Initiative: Change agents program integrated with real-time change projects
- *F-Course*: Four weeks for entry-level middle manager.
- Potential Diagnosis: 10-15 *Assessment Centers* yearly with 10 participants.
- FS 1-3: Seminars on performance management, team development & financial management.
- Explorers 21: A global learning network (210 participants): Three QSH-platforms, project-assignments and training modules.
- 14 different out-of-hour 2-day seminars (yearly 3000-4000 participants) e.g.: presentation, communication, stress management, time management.
- Apprenticeship and trainee programs.

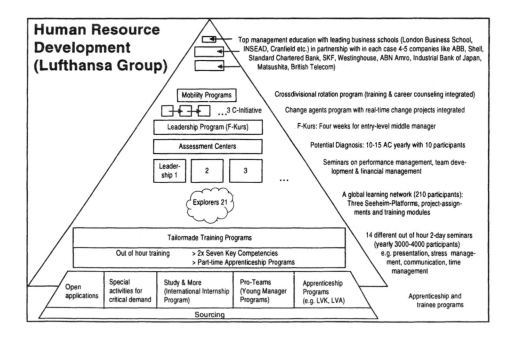

The pyramid indicates the major emphasis on management education. Middle-management are the mediators between top management and the "front-line or shop-floor": Mental change must begin at the bottom but, equally and simultaneously, it must be encouraged and practiced at the top.

New managers are in demand. But they must meet entirely new requirements. The leader of the future will no longer be a mere boss, but is likely to be far more. Within lean organizations, good performance can be rewarded less and less by promotion into higher positions; authority must be based on personality – not on a person's position.

The best specialist is no longer automatically the best manager. The manager of the future won't just be the manager of single functions and actions, but a manager of permanently flowing processes. He/she will be a moderator of group-dynamic processes, a moderator of self-organized groups, a manager of variety. He/she has to find a balance between demands and encouragement, between control and support. The new leader will create a working environment that enables employees and groups of employees to do their work on their own. Social competence and commonsense are more important than expertise.

Our operative gains in recent years are self-evident. Mental change is progressing well, but there is still a long haul ahead. Competition and other external factors trigger uncertainty (insecurity) and confusion. Economic recessions intensify the struggle for market share. The way in which the soft factors are handled (pyramid) is of overriding importance for the company's future.

The Role of Values in Corporate Transformation

The merger between ÅSV and Hydro's Aluminium Division in 1986

Bjørn Erik Dahlberg

I would like to invite you to take a look at the process of the merger that took place in 1986 between Årdal and Sunndal Verk (ÅSV) and the Aluminium Division of Norsk Hydro.

To change a company's values and culture takes time. Today, 10 years later, I hope we can evaluate some of the results of the process that was initiated at that time. I invite you to look at it from both a distance and from "close up". To illustrate my points more vividly, I will use one of our production sites as an example of this transformation process.

Let us travel along the world's longest and deepest fjord, the Sognefjord, on the western coast of Norway. The scenery here is both dramatic and impressive. However, it is not only beautiful, but also tough and demanding. It is interesting that you can take almost any criteria on health and happiness, and you will find that this county of Norway is in the forefront of most others, even though there are rather few people taking part in this welfare .

Two of our aluminium reduction plants are located along this fjord, at Høyanger and Årdal. At the head of this fjord and surrounded by mountains 3-4000 feet high, we find the municipality of Årdal, with a population of about 7000 people. Down the mountain sides, impressive waterfalls can be seen and they are the reason why energy intensive industry was chosen to be placed in such remote areas as this. About two thousand people live here, at Årdalstangen, where we produce the carbon anodes for the electrolytic reduction process. This is where the shipments of black and white raw materials, i.e. carbon

H. Lange et al., Working Across Cultures, 161–168.

and aluminium oxide, are unloaded. This is also where the finished aluminium products are shipped from.

13 km further up the valley, at the other end of the Årdal lake, we find the other half of the municipality, Øvre Årdal, with about 5000 people. Here we find the power station and the pot rooms, where the electrolytic reduction process takes place. The potrooms have an impressive length of 500 meters, and are rather dominating in the middle of this settlement. The wildest and deepest valley of Norway, the Utla valley, starts here, and ends up in the fiercest mountain area in the centre of Norway. It goes without saying that, due to extremely difficult and complex air turbulances, this site is a challenge for any industry with emissions to air.

In 1986, ÅSV, which the Årdal plant was part of, and Hydro were merged into one company. The new company became one of the larger aluminium companies in the world, with 12,000 employees and at that time, activities in 12 countries and in the USA. As production increased over the years, and hence emissions, the effects on nature became more and more obvious and damaging.

It is important to bear in mind that the people in this place found themselves in a dilemma: On the one hand, they were of course critical of the emissions from the plant, on the other hand, this industry was their livelihood. And like most people, they were proud of their municipality and defended it zealously, especially when the place became known as the "smoke hole".

This was a dilemma of choosing among and giving priority to different values. We see it time and time again, the dilemma having no geographical, social or political borders. Shall people choose clean air, which means no industry and no jobs, which in turn means poverty, or shall they accept pollution and for that have work and food?

When the question is asked like that, the answer can seem too easy. The question should be a different one and industry should address it. So let us look into the challenges the new company had to deal with:
– Profitability had to be improved;
– Operations had to be brought to a higher standard;
– There were far too many people employed;
– And we had an unsatisfactory situation with the neighbours with regard to emissions.

As soon as the new company was formed, we started a process to establish what our *vision* should be, what *philosophy* we should base this organization on, and what *values* we wanted to focus on. We engaged ourselves in a process, where we, as management, had a responsibility to lead the way, by starting the process of *naming* the vision, goals and values. We referred to this as a "top-down" and "bottom-up process".

Characteristic for such a process is communication, communication, and communication. In form of dialogue and in form of participation. These things have to fit in with people's perception of *why* they are here, what they want to work for, their motivation, ethical standards and their culture. The purpose is to focus, to build identity and to motivate. Such processes should support cohesion and build teams. At the end of the day, everyone wants to be part of a winning team. The process must, on the one hand, be such that management share what they *believe in* and *identify with*, and on the other hand, it has to be a true invitation to the organization to *respond*, *involve* themselves and *participate* in the process. This has to be an interactive process running back and forth, changing and formulating the visions and values.

The circle we thereby enter should be a period of high creativity and innovation. And there must be an expressed appreciation for the responses. This period went on for about 1 1/2 years before we ended up putting the result into a written text in a small booklet. The important thing in this period was the *quality of the dialogue* we were able to establish, thus having a circular and repeated dialogue where new ideas and necessary corrections always were welcome.

Looking back on the process today, this is where I have learnt that we could have put even more emphasis on dialogue than we did at the time. The better this dialogue is, the more people you are able to invite and involve in the process, the better the result will be, providing cohesion, identity and motivation.

We said we wanted to become a leading aluminium company in Europe, and one of the leading companies in the world. But at the same time, we also said that *quality* is more important than *quantity*. So leading did by no means solely mean the largest. Our philosophy was that we should achieve our goal through *cooperation and participation in a decentralized organization*.

All these statements can too easily become just words – empty words and lip service. It is not the statements themselves that are unique and valuable. It is the conversation about them, what we mean by them, that is unique for our own organization and that no one else can copy. You can hardly have any ownership to such a booklet alone. What you do have ownership to is the conversation you are part of.

Having been used to working in a rather centralized organization, the change to what we meant with a decentralized organization was dramatic. Even for management. You are more on your own in a decentralized organization. After having agreed to goals, strategy and budgets, it is up to you and your organization to realize the goals. This can mean a lot more fun and be very challenging, but it will also be more demanding with such a degree of freedom. Especially if you do not meet expecations.

One of the very first *values* we chose, was *respect*: to show respect for one another when we create a working environment which meets our demands regarding health and safety. But also:
– when we see the unique personality and abilities of the other
– when we invite participation and foster cooperation
– when we expect outstanding performance from each other
– and when we give others the respect we want them to give us.

Another value we found appropriate in our culture was to develop *flexibility*. We had become far too rigid and conceited with the way we were. We believe the best way to meet the challenging competitive situation is to be an organization *responsive to change*, to
– adapt to new situations
– adjust to market demands
– make organizational changes
– be innovative
– solve problems in creative ways.

So with the big challenges we had, such as improving profitability, improving operations, reducing the number of employees, fighting neighbours because of emissions - we went out and asked the organization:
– how can we reduce work accidents?
– how can you make your workplace tidier?
– how can we reduce the emissions?

And the main question became: how can *you* contribute with the way you *think* and *act* to achieve these goals? We started out by emphasizing another value we had expressed, namely *quality*. We wanted to reach our goal by being excellent within quality, precision and service.

At this point we spent money on new locker and shower room facilities, painted the plant facilities both inside and out, and cleaned up the work place to demonstrate respect for human resources, and thus set a standard for quality.

Parallell to this we started to address the question of excessive manning. Within a two year period, we had reduced the number of employees by as much as 25%. No one was laid off or made redundant. The older people were offered different types of early retirement pensions, that is from the age of 63 instead of 67, which is the age of retirement in Norway. This offer became very popular, and almost all people who were offered this, accepted. At first glance, it seems a rather expensive solution for the company. But it is impossible to reorganize and start working differently as long as there is a large excess of people in the organization. Very soon we earned back the costs this meant for the company.

I think we soon experienced that by putting very high demands on the leaders and subsequently on the organization within environment, health and safety, and on quality, order and cleanliness, we gained results within several other and different areas as well. Over the first four years we achieved improved results within the following areas:
- Lost time injuries rate fell by 75 %
- Sickness rate fell by 50 %
- Energy consumption fell by 10 %
- Emissions fell by almost 70 %
- Productivity was increased by more than 30%

By creating higher expectations to our own standards, be it within environment, safety, quality or service, we started to behave differently, and slowly we changed our *identity*. This became part of our thinking and way of doing things.

One thing I can mention, is that "ecology" became a new term in the company's vocabulary. We brought ecology in as a value we should work for, and it was given staff capacity. Soon it became an important part of our strategy. And we found ourselves becoming proactive within this area. We admitted that our relations to our surroundings include not only our products but also our *by-products* such as emissions and waste. Our attitude to emissions had changed. Our relationships with neighbours and government had changed. We started to cooperate with our customers about these items, which has proven to be very valuable.

We arrived at a point where a restructuring of the plants became necessary. These plants were integrated in the sense that a lot of different activities were mixed together on the same site. The result was that it was difficult to get a thorough understanding of the results from the different activities. People also had a certain difficulty in developing an identity and the feeling of belonging to the unit where their commitment actually meant something.

In order to get the involvement, participation and identity we were working for, we started a process of looking into the many different activities we had. The ultimate goal was to develop an appreciation of the nature of the activity in order to develop the *competence* necessary to compete among the best.

The Årdal plant, once one large plant, was split into six new units. Activities that used to be "secondary" in relation to the primary activity of producing aluminium, were now lifted out and made new "primary activities". They had their own visions, goals and strategies, and developed an identity of their own, always within the larger frame of Hydro Aluminium and Norsk Hydro. We all appreciate operating within a framework that gives us the necessary references in order to understand. References that we share, and that create *cohesion* in the organization, like mission, vision, goals, values and identity.

This is fundamental for the process of developing the competence necessary to achieve our goals. So we asked the question: what is our *core competence*, a necessity for us to have to be able to compete? And what is our *distinct competence* that gives us a competitive advantage and makes us different from our competitors? And what is our *routine competence*? And are we the best to take care of and develop that, or should we leave that to others and contract it?

We talk about the *competency organization*, our common competence, as one of our most important values. We discuss how we structurally shall organize ourselves in order to make use of the competence we have in the best way. Maybe that is our biggest challenge: how to make use of the competency that we have already got in the organization?

Often we get so eager to get hold of the newest and latest competence that we forget to appreciate what we already have. And what do we gain by bringing even more competency into the organization if we are structured in such a way that we are not able to draw upon what we already have?

When I look back on the process today, I remember we were often warned right at the start: be careful not to commit yourselves to too many written statements with high ethical values. They will be used against you every time you are perceived to break them, regardless of whether you do or not. We discussed this quite a lot in the management group and ended up saying: if that is so, maybe that is what we need: To be confronted openly every time we either break our own expressed intentions or when we are perceived to break them. That should at least give us a fine opportunity for a dialogue about leadership, values, etc. They proved to be right: we were confronted.

But we also proved to be right: it gave rise to many good discussions on our values, what did we mean by them and how to practice them. It helped to keep us on our toes. Could we defend what we were doing? That is in itself most important - that people know where they have got management. What you have expressed about values and that you are willing to defend. I think it is both true and important that *to lead is to model good leadership*. We must lead by example. To lead "anonymously" is impossible. If you don't want to share with people the values you find worth while fighting for, people will make up their own minds about who you are, and the values they address to you. Which is not necessarily a good situation.

I do not see it as a question of whether we want to lead by values or not. Our actions will always be guided by certain values. It is more a question of whether we admit the strength and importance of values. And whether we consciously want to make use of that in developing the cohesion of the organization. And with hindsight, I think the most important thing in this process is to secure a good dialogue in the organization.

I believe it can be dangerous, and thus a millstone around your neck, to make values, or strategies or goals to something that is "nondebatable". The need for flexibility and for organizations to adapt to new situations should welcome a *continuous dialogue* about these things in the organization. To share a strong and clear outcome is for the organization in itself a guiding value. Values change over time within every one of us, due to age, family situation, where we live, our surroundings, etc. The same goes for organizations.

Another thing is that we have to choose a few values to focus on at a time, or the process will be far too complicated to communicate. As the organization is developing and improving, we want to put emphasis on new values. It is important to communicate that these values, of course, do not cover the whole complexity we are relating to. New situations could call for new values to highlight.

Values can be a fantastic glue for the organization, securing the cohesion that we all are working for. That is why we should have values on the agenda all the time. This is also a way to share the same appreciation of the development and the results. And it is a good way to develop a *common language in* the organization. And we can always remind ourselves of the fact that in order to change a system you must operate from within. So what I have learned is that rather than to look for the perfect values to present for your organization, get started on the dialogue. The organization will help us with the rest if our invitation is real. That is if *trust* is present. Which was another of our values, reminding ourselves that trust is not something we can demand, but something we must deserve.

A Model in an Economic Upheaval – Questioning of Values in the Market Economy?

Decision Making and Leadership in the Transformation Process of an East German Company

Gerrit Popkes & Kati Rieger

1. Challenges Facing Managerial Cultures in the "Transformation Process"

Reunification of the once divided Germany demanded the immediate adoption of a system which was largely unfamiliar to the citizens and institutions of the former GDR. Instead of a gradual, longterm adaptation process, the market economy was abruptly and radically introduced. It was believed that the conversion of the state socialist market economy into a democratic and pluralistic market economy could be achieved merely through the introduction of appropriate public policies and the transfer of institutions. The underlying conviction was that the "beneficial dynamic of the economic interests of the private subject"[1] would enable this. The leading actors of individual companies were, however, forced to hastily adjust to completely new conditions without first undertaking a civilizing, democratization, modernization and rationalization process.[2] The system transformation made it necessary to adapt to heterogeneous norms and conditions as well as to

---

[1] Schmidt 1993, p.11, attributes this to the normative (ordo-liberal) orientation of political decision-makers. The purified adaptation and integration process (following the West German model which through the collapse of the oppositional system claimed an undisputed legitimacy) ignored the exceptional challenges in transforming a society (ibid., p.10ff). In this context, the predicted "flowering countrysides" becomes understandable.

[2] Cf. Aderhold et al 1994, p.17.

H. Lange et al., Working Across Cultures, 169–190.

adopt strongly diverse coping policies to face the changes in values, beliefs, attitudes, interests and negotiation strategies.[3] As a result, traditional worldviews fell apart. "People's adaptation to these new conditions, the tranformation in people's mindsets belong to the manifold painful realities of every day life with which very few had reckoned."[4] For many companies, this brought either economic ruin or newly discovered opportunities for growth and development whereas for workers this meant either longterm unemployment or unexpected freedom."Leaders in a transformation process must not only recognize the market's opportunities and risks on the basis of available resources in order to develop appropriate strategies, but they must also manage a 'psyche in crisis' and on top of this an organisational development process."[5]

Hence, the following problems and questions arise: Which changes in values are demanded of decision-makers in order to survive in a market system? How does one deal with the positive as well as the negative effects of the planned economy and market system? "Even if the old system was not loved, are there not traces in thinking and behavioural patterns which will only be overcome in the longterm and from which some employees and managers would not necessarily want to separate themselves."[6] The complex behavioural patterns leftover from the GDR society should have been replaced by a synthethis of old and new.[7] The transformation process not only demands new types of qualifications of the planned economy, but also of the relatively stable market economy.[8]

What type of leadership models, i.e. which underlying principles and decision making processes have been developed in companies faced with different decision-making parameters over the last six years? Is it true that a fundamental departure from conceptions, values, and accumulated experience must be achieved in order to be success-ful in a market economy?[9] *Aderhold et al* emphasize the devaluation,

---

[3] Cf. Ladensack 1994, p.40, and Marz 1993, p.73ff.
[4] Rosenstiel 1994, p.6.
[5] Marr 1994, p.53.
[6] Ladensack 1994. p.18.
[7] Cf. Ladensack 1994, p.35.
[8] Cf. Marr 1994, p.58ff.
[9] Cf. Rosenstiel 1994, p.6f.

i.e. the re-evaluation of previous types of capabilities, understanding of competence and behavioural patterns: "At the management level, the continuous negotiation of supplies, investment opportunities, production planning, and the same level of work performance are no longer required. Instead, the economic organisation of their areas of responsibilities is now the primary concern. The maintaining of deadlines, quantity production and quality control standards, ensuring the proper flow of information and materials to other departments, as well as motivating and training of workers have become more important for the middle and lower management levels than the fulfillment of informal planning deals in contrast to the irrationalities set by the leading planning officials of the former system."[10]

To which extent, however, is a fundamental structural change necessary in a company which is ensuring its own commercial viability? In the overall scheme of the company's structure, the individual should not be reduced purely to the level of a mere factor in production, as is stipulated in "classic" business administration doctrine.[11] An important goal is that new agreements should be developed to allow for the possibility of fundamentally changed values, behavioural norms and a new conception of work.[12] The challenge which ultimately must be faced is that deficiencies in the area of managerial thinking, behavioural conduct, methodological and social qualifications are far more difficult to overcome than any shortcomings at the level of professional qualifications.[13]

---

[10] Aderhold et al 1994, p.12.

[11] Cf. Rosenstiel 1992, p.14.

[12] The goal is not to put forth a "culture of success" (Rosenstiel 1992, p.20), but instead to present normative models which can also have a basis in a market economy.

[13] Ladensack 1994, p.33ff.; Marr 1994, p.56f.; and Schultz-Gambard 1994, p.183f., also support this argument and base themselves on the model of normative management. (Ulrich/Fluri 1995, p.17ff., speak of a development of a corporate-political rapprochement, credibility as a basis for the building of a "leading negotiation-oriented value system of management".) This must of course distinguish itself from the overall forcebly normative-ideological integration of the personnel in the sense of a marxist-leninist perspective.

2. Model of a Successful Company in the Transformation Process

Using a case study of a medium-sized cosmetics producer in Saxony, we would henceforth like to describe the individual factors which shape the above-mentioned challenges in the transformation process. In the following report, we will attempt to identify a "community of values and concepts"[14] and we will focus on the negotiating principles (i.e. successful strategic factors) which arose for the most part out of an analysis of the system. We chose a traditional, highly respected company which has until now managed to assert itself in a competitive market and has kept an almost intact management during reunification and which in addition has been "spared" from West German decision-making influences. We are hoping that this will lead to portraying "microcosm" which could act as a source of orientation for the necessary managerial adaptation process, i.e. under the conditions of an (unfriendly) take-over of a social and economic system.

3. Interview Process and Research Methods

In the context of a qualitative study, the interviews of management teams (managing director, departmental head and workers representatives) took place in five stages. The first stage sought to determine the biographical histories of the company's decision-makers: origins, education, types of social commitment, significant transitions in professional life and personal experience after reunification. The second stage concerned itself with a subjective description and evaluation of overall socio-economic and company-specific transformation processes. Questions also revolved inquiries about the fundamental features of planned and market economies, characteristics of the transformation process and an analysis of the company's specific success factors. The third stage of the interview focused on issues of personal and corporate ethics, leadership models, and finally conflict resolution mechanisms. The fourth stage concerned itself with one specific decision-making process. Using the actual event of "mass lay-

---

[14] Rosenstiel 1992, p.19. A company is not only the mechanical end result of technical-managerial factors. It is also the product of interpretations of those individuals involved.

offs" from the company's past, questions were formulated to determine levels of participation and communication, reactions, conflict resolution methods and an assessment of the learning processes which were undertaken.[15] The fifth and last stage of the interviews dealt with leadership models: attitudes about work, leisure time, family, motivational factors at work and the change in personal values due to the transformation process. A self-evaluation in terms of both an idealistic and realistic self-portrait of management accompanied by an assessment of leadership concepts and motivational factors were central to this section of the interview process.

This project's research method follows the principles inherent in qualitative social research.[16] The research was carried out with the help of case studies of individual managers in the company. In those times when it appeared necessary, an analysis of written sources complemented the information compilation. The approach remained inductive. A flexible analysis of the scholarly field of research was a primary goal and was followed up with a gradual collection and examination of data. The characteristics of the individual elements and the links to one another began to crystallize at first slowly and through a continuous reflexive relationship to the applied methods.[17] The research results were also the result of open, semi-structured, so-called problem-centric interviews. The questions were based on research conducted by *Ulrich/Thielemann*[18], *Aderhold et al*[19] and *Deller/ Jepsen*[20]. The answers were expressed freely without pre-prepared multiple choice answers which allowed for spontaneous questions to arise. Intermediate results were worked out during group discussions.

The project is not completed yet. In the near future the data collected at management level will be compared to another set of evaluations made by workers and employees on the basis of a qualitative research study. On the basis of the comprehensive qualitative analysis research results, a company philosophy will be developed.

---

[15] Aderhold et al 1994, p.126f., speak of a "point of crystallization" in the changed relationships between management and workers.

[16] Cf. Mayring 1990, p.27ff.

[17] Cf. Witzel 1992, p.72.

[18] Cf. Ulrich/Thielemann 1992.

[19] Cf. Aderhold et al 1994. p.193ff.

[20] Cf. Deller/Jepsen 1996.

4. Description of a Company-Specific Transformation Process

The company was founded in the mid-nineteenth century whereas the brandname was created seventy-five years ago. As part of a GDR industrial combine, the company had a turnover of M 350 million before 1989 and employed approximately 700 people. The product portfolio was relatively undifferentiated whereas the equipment production facilities were with few exceptions geared only for relatively inflexible mass production. Reunification put an end to this type of production.[21] The company was soon released from the industrual combine and thereafter applied, but was rejected for a management buy-out (MBO). With economic and currency union, the export market collapsed (previously 60 % of total sales) and the company's share in the domestic market, of which it once commanded 95 per cent of national sales, fell to 2 per cent. Sales dropped to DM 25 million in 1992 with dramatic losses. Management launched a classic catalogue of restructuring measures: the work force was reduced to 150 members, the organisational structure leveled, the range of products improved, a marketing infrastructure was created, and the manufacturing capacity was reduced whereas information processing and production were concentrated in one location. During this period of upheaval, the intensive collaboration with two West-German competitors who had been helpful in the marketing and distribution sector was introduced. As a result of pressure by the staff and the workers' representative council, at the beginning of 1992 the three top managers went through a management buy-out at contractual conditions harsher than those companies sold to West German investors.[22] Even in the face of high interest payments on loans, sales have been increasing yearly by 20 % since 1993. The number of workers has stabilized at 200. The company now owns 15 % of the market. In some product areas the company has even managed to become the leading producer in the new

---

[21] Aderhold et al 1994, p.45: "The company was once in a planned economy situated at the last rung of the planned bureaucracy. It now finds itself from a legal and economic perspective as an autonomous operating company which must try to find its place in market-structuring environment."

[22] The new owners thus paid a high purchasing price in spite of poor conditions. They were responsible for paying old debts despite a great need for high levels of new investment and also committed themselves to what would amount for this production sector as highly penalizing workers' guarantees.

federal states. The level of investment guaranteed in the MBO contract
has been surpassed threefold whereas the number of workers by 20 %.
The company was also the first in its line of production to receive
ISO-9000 certification and is presently participating in the European
Union's Eco-Audit programme. Management occupies leading positions in many associations and has also been rewarded with several
distinctions, such as the manager prize for the "Aufschwung Ost"
programme.

5. Analysis of the Economic System from a Managerial Perspective

5.1.   The innovative character of the transformation process

Describing the economic and social structures of an East German
company, one must take into account the specificities inherent in two
oppositional systems. Characteristics of both systems will in a period
of transformation run into one another and will allow those concerned
in the process an immediate comparison with the important criteria
inherent in both systems. This phase of the transformation offers an
opportunity for intense reflection about goals, careful consideration of
alternatives, planning for new business relation structures, and the
establishment of new concepts and strategies.

"Naturally, the transformation process has the advantage for all
East Germans concerned to get to know two systems very intensively.
Namely, on the one hand the planned economy and on the other hand
also the market economy. And now one can take the positive aspects
of the planned economy and transfer them into the new one [economic
system]." (Interview partner No. 2)

It is hardly possible to experiment with options in the face of the
rapid and partially negative impacts of this process.[23] Nevertheless, the
transformation process includes a potential for success with a proper
analysis of two economic and social "sources". Thus, with all the
unpleasant consequences[24] of the transformation process, its innova-

---

[23] In the sense of "trial and error".

[24] Breaking away from markets, market access barriers, preferences for West German investors, decision-makers, mass unemployment, "robber baron" mentality.

tive character also reveals itself. Through immediate confrontation, factors are developed which are either judged worth-while or obsolete, i.e. necessary to reject. The fundamental question is which criteria lead to rejection or acceptance when evaluating both systems in this company case study.

5.2.   Perceived Advantages and Disadvantages of Planned and Market Economies

Social security, full employment and highly prioritized human togetherness offered by a planned economy were perceived as positive. As a cultural institution, a socialist company not only had the task of producing goods and guaranteeing revenue, but also of conveying a sense of social security.[25] The break with this function was viewed negatively:

"Somehow people are no longer at the center... All human relations have suffered a great deal in the past five years. Material things are the only things which still count in life." (Interview partner No. 7)

This assessment should be seen as belonging to the negative aspects of a market economy, such as unemployment, reduced solidarity and the loss of security. The "elbowing principle" requires constant effort, mistrust and competition among individuals in the market economy.[26] Society is restricted to a strictly personal 'Me' and the non-existence of fair competing conditions, the fundamental significance of existing relationship-networks[27], a partial (largely material) sense of inequality, the primacy of money as a central factor and the cumbersome nature of the West German bureaucratic system.[28] The affirmation of preferences and desirable aspects of the

---

[25] Cf. Richter 1990.

[26] Homann 1992, p.20: "It makes little sense to deny the hardships which come as a price of the market economy. A market economy and competition lead to considerable uncertainties, lay-off and unemployment during structural transformation."

[27] The significance of contacts and relationships could nearly be said to be even greater than during the GDR-regime.

[28] Even university graduates in the new German regions hold predominantly negative views concerning the market economy. (cf. Rappensberger / v. Rosenstiel / Zwarg 1994, p.194ff., from a pred. qualitative study in 1991). In their opinion,

old system stems from the extreme array of criticism expressed towards the new system and partially imply quite nostalgic impulses:

"I believed that socialism was a system which could provide human beings with something. I also lived accordingly [...] And this sense of togetherness, of being able to speak with one another, about problems was, I believe, very pronounced back then. [...] That is still something I see very positively." (Interview partner No. 3)

The total collapse of the previous economic order occurred hand-in-hand with the collapse of the previously normative superstructure. Individual value systems, however, remained in principal intact and could now be measured against the values put forth as exemplary by the market economy.[29] According to this constellation, for example, "togetherness" will be missed in an increasingly colder society. This ignores the fact that this positive trait was a reaction to a deficiency in the planned economy.[30] The desired return of job security also expressed a rather ambivalent reaction because it had either failed to provide or only insufficiently provided employee motivation which had proved to be existentially important in times of drastic change or probation.

The mourning of such losses is contrasted with negative characteristics of the planned economy whose loss is in no way regretted; the lacking efficiency of the GDR's economy, for example. In it, goods were produced independently of the people's needs, resources were

---

the declaration of maximized profit that they saw as a business' primary goal in a market economy carried negative connotations, even though its system-defined "forcefulness" also is seen as a proposable goal. This negative attitude must have been met with misgivings by Homann/Blome Drees 1992 for they thought the enterprise "*should* strive to create profit" (ibid. p. 24). This would, in the end, lead to innovation, investment, growth and therefore to the extraordinary increase in the general welfare (cf. ibid. p.26). The maximization of profit (and not relative or typical profits) as the central basis of the market economy becomes the "*customary obligation of the enterprises*" (ibid. p.51).

[29] In this way, Srubar 1991, p.415, stresses that the "normative expectations and its corresponding patterns of action outlast the collapse of political and/or economical order and are only subjected to a gradual evolution".

[30] Aderhold et al 1994, p.34: "In comparison (to the modern western industrial societies; ed.,) the GDR Mark's loss of function limited individual freedom necessitated mutual and intimate dependencies. Belonging to social networks was an unavoidable compensation for provisional dry spells and poor working conditions, and so could not be terminated or switched easily."

wasted and a sense of false reality was upheld through the announce-
ment of successfully achieved plans which ultimately contributed to
the failure of industry. This experience encourages the desire to distance oneself from the denial of environmental problems and one's
dependency on a political system culminating with absolute transparency in the department of national security, the "Staatssicherheit". One
reacted with the development of a "double language", using multiple
meanings adapted to the situation in which it was expressed:
"political", business or family life. Determinism dominated the work
world; self-sufficiency was only encouraged to a degree. The lack of
performance-based rewards had a levelling effect on society.

"The disadvantages as a company were the chains that were constantly there [...], on the one hand because of the materials, and then
also the political chains." (Interview partner No. 2)

In contrast, the advantage of the market economy was that it
offered the individual a chance to show initiative and independence.
The new societal order is noticeable for an increase in (an at least
material) quality of life. Factors such as the promotion of competition
and reward based upon performance are seen as positive. As an
expression of the lasting appreciation of security, the maintenance of a
social network that guarantees at least minimum rights is likewise seen
as positive. A feeling of absolute freedom is present, yet it is called
into question at the same time:

"The market economy is an illusion. [...] You can do everything,
but you're restrained by personal circumstances. And as a result, you
chase after illusions." (Interview partner No. 3)

"I had an idealized image of the market economy. [...] I only saw
the dazzling face of this society—all glitter. [...] Now five years later I
know what a market economy means. And I also understand now, in
1996, what a planned economy was." (Interview partner No. 4)

It is not clear how impressions of the transformation process are to
be categorized, although they partially overlap evaluations of the
market economy. This challenge required that market-economical
skills should be developed from scratch. All continued education and
training measures had to be introduced parallel to day-to-day work
experiences.[31] The transitional period was seen as a chance for
individual re-orientation arising from the euphoria of self-initiative

---

[31] And not just as "learning by doing".

during a time of (professional) new beginnings and the greatly increased domain of responsibility:

"We have to take the bull by the horns and have to try and make the best of it." (Interview partner No. 4)

The hardships of the process became evident alongside the new-won freedoms: unemployment was not just a statistic but a neighbor or former colleague.

"You had to fire people with whom you sat next to day in day out. [...] There were among them good friends whom you could not protect." (Interview partner No. 1)

"This came suddenly. It used to be they could never get enough work done and suddenly they were no longer needed." (Interview partner No. 2)

A further impressive experience was the support of competitors which broke through the basic principles of the market economy as they had been experienced.[32] The goodwill[33] that was shown by clearly superior competitors in favor of the smaller East German newcomers would become a formative experience of how the market economy might operate beyond the principal pursuit of maximized profit.[34] At the same time, a partner's "sudden death" through the sale to a larger company left its mark. The extent of tensions which these events created gave occasion to evaluate one's own existence, the existence of the company and of the system in general.

"We couldn't believe it. After we'd gotten to know the company, the workers, the products, we knew what kind of environment existed. [It] was probably the first time we found how the market economy works, how quickly something like that can happen. You've got a great company which makes profits and where everything according to us was in good shape. From one day to the next there was nothing left, and suddenly [...] 50 jobs are gone in H. and a piece of industrial real estate gets cannibalized." (Interview partner No. 5)

---

[32] Their assistance was of greater use (i.e. in winning the trust of banks, access to markets and the transfer of know-how in many areas through intensive coaching) than its "costs" (in terms of revenue production and mutual distribution teams with lesser personnel drain).

[33] These actions were partially inspired by the euphoria induced by Germany's re-unification.

[34] As these events are often held in connection with individual persons, one can speak of "in person value instances"; see Seifert/Heyse 1994, p.82.

6. Leadership Induced Success Factors in The Company During The Process of Transformation

6.1. Basic concepts

In addition to factors such as brand-name recognition, efficient distribution, modern, flexible equipment facilities, certification, etc. (referred to as the factual strengths of a company), "soft factors"[35] play an important role in a company's success according to management. They form the basis of executive decision-making and coordination. A company's underlying principles of management which will be roughly outlined here, can be viewed as the result of a process of new social creation.

"[We tried] to take into consideration the essential human factor, [...] and not just profit-making as the measure of all things. We do, however, know that we cannot exist without being profit-oriented." (Interview partner No.2)

"Even if the GDR's working traditions are consciously used as a model [...] the current conditions are so radically different that the incorporation of these 'traditions' is more the result of a collective re-interpretation of one's own experiences than an actual continuation of the previous model of relations. The social structure of a new work culture will assuredly be just as influenced by past experiences as through present needs to reassure and delineate oneself."[36]

We are knowingly placing our research results in the context of existing (transformation-)literature.

6.2. Relative continuity in the values of East German leadership personnel

Studies in the differences between East and West German management generally conclude that East German leadership shows a stronger orientation towards collective and feminine values such as the impor-

---

[35] The "skills" referred to by Peters/Waterman 1982.

[36] Aderhold et al 1994, p.13. They expect, however (ibid., p.47), that the existing networks will dissolve because the affiliation with these informal social groups is no longer of elementary importance.

tance of family, society and job security.[37] *Lang* emphasizes that a far-reaching stability exists in the East German value orientation. This is particularly the case in regard to assignment-oriented values and social-cooperation.[38] Is there, then, a consistency in the leadership, personnel's understanding of values or should one subscribe to *Klages* implied model of evolving values in East Germany? He proposed that there was a compatible process taking place parallel to the evolution of values in West Germany, particularly among the youth, which encouraged values of self-development. At the same time, it determined the development of value orientations in the GDR populace to a very large degree with system-typical influences.[39]

The company's leadership personnel could be classified as "active realists"[40]: In this term, they see the positive potential of combining values of self-development with responsibility and acceptance consciousness and are thus as capable of discipline as they are adaptable and open to constructive criticism. A considerable interest in meaningful work is paired with a remarkable willingness to perform as well as to show initiative in day-to-day business activity. A balanced orientation between family, free time and career thereby becomes a goal. Assuming there is sufficient space to maneuver, one is willing to accept responsibilities.[41] The conscious desire to live up to the company's reputation in the region also plays an important role.

---

[37] Cf. Lang 1992, p.136f. It may be assumed that the differences in regard to the significance of job security in the context of current job-market developments have now stabilized throughout re-united Germany. Work-relevant values shown by leadership personnel in both east and west reveal principally similar patterns. (cf. Lang 1994, p.155). This claim is supported by Schnabel/Baumert/ Roeder 1994, p.83ff., who, within the context of ALLBUS 91, indeed show a higher percentage of materialists among adult high school graduates in the west as in the east along with other differences, but generally reveal obvious parallels in the tested value patterns.

[38] Cf. Lang 1994, p.156f. He bases his position on a series of empirical findings from research conducted between 1988-1992.

[39] Cf. Klages 1993, p.220ff.

[40] Klages 1993, p.34.

[41] Klages 1993, p.178: "Should they enter into the process of transformation prepared to engage crisis, to remain flexible and maintain performance motivation, [...] they'll have helped to make it a smoother and more rapid transformation."

"Others would have here[42] just laid off people! We didn't do that. We didn't do it for reasons of image and out of a sense of responsibility towards the region and its people." (Interview partner No. 4)

In the company, the prevailing belief is that no change in value orientations has taken place[43] and that individual and economic maneuverability were common also to the GDR[44] and that because of constant changes in organization and policy, they had been pressured to conform to the socialist combine as well. Therefore, one already had the flexibility from going through the process of transformation, and one did not wish to surrender one's socially-oriented values:

"And that I [...] even then had to help rebuild a company. That's the way we called it in the GDR. That means, we had to completely turn it around, restructure and re-organize. [...] I had to do it again in the 1980s when two companies had to be merged. Everything had to be re-organized. It took a long time to organize the people and bring them together. [...] And then suddenly in the 1990s, everything had to be re-organized again and in such a way so that it could be privatized. When privatization actually happened it had to be done again. So, I've constantly had to re-organize a company and participate in it." (Interview partner No. 3)

6.3.   Cooperative, participatory styles of leadership

The competence shown by the company's leadership is measured by its ability to activate and coordinate its members' self-initiative to act according to their respective levels of responsibility. In this way, responsibility is delegated to appropriate offices, wherein goals are formulated, and do not become assignment-oriented instructions.[45]

---

[42] Despite the cancellation of large scale production for a competitor, the company did not by the beginning of 1996 lay-off any workers due to its expecting product-sales compensation.

[43] This opinion cannot be interpreted as objective due to its reliance upon retroactive observance.

[44] Personnel with leading functions were also dismissed in the GDR (a member of the current manager crew, for example) because of non-conformist behavior (dismissal from the Party etc.) had no chance of finding a position with another company.

[45] Ulrich/Fluri 1995, p.229: "He no longer demands that he himself make all deci-

Communication between members of leadership personnel and other colleagues is institutionalized through discussions, different types of events and periodical meetings. In addition, the basic comprehension of decisions and the ability to interpret information is considered desirable.[46]

"From the start we tried above all as executive managers to tell workers in middle management how important they are, how much they are needed. and how much the company's fate is dependent on them." (Interview partner No. 1)

"We are transparent. We inform the workers, the executive management, and the middle management. We have staff meetings. [We believe] everyone should be informed about everything that goes on in this company."(Interview partner No. 4)

The appropriateness of participative (or open) decision-making structures in the company can be explained by values comparable to post-materialist basic assumptions observed in West German companies, enhanced only here and there by specific East German socialization.[47] The result, however, is not a mingling of East and West German patterns, but a new creation brought about by the process of transformation.

6.4.   The factor of a "Solidarity Community"

The deficiencies of the planned economy produced "need" or "solidarity communities" which disappeared under changing conditions such as the subjective pressure of increasingly noticeable job insecurity or employee competitiveness.[48] On the other hand it is "hard to imagine that someone in a situation of intensive existential uncertainty would be willing to call old, trusted role patterns [...] in ques-

---

sions, because he sees his function less in decision-making, organization and control as in integrating the group and making it functional."

[46] Colleagues are in principle encouraged to assume a partnership relationship. (cf. Criteria of cooperative Leadership styles at Klages 1993, p.178).

[47] Aderhold et al 1994, p.116: "The shared experience of a serious crisis, drastic lay-off and the company's thorough restructuring will favor more cooperative, more strongly 'community-oriented' styles of leadership."

[48] Cf. Schramm 1994, p.109ff.; Lang 1992, p.135, speaks of a "de-solidarity" in this context.

tion."[49] In particular, the groups of employees who had already been
working together for some time and so had been able to form relationships proved largely resistant to behavioral changes.[50] Does this
explain the phenomena that such solidarity communities having lived
through the shortfalls of the market economy and the company's continued existence, are experiencing a renaissance and a kind of "Yes,
but ..." attitude?[51] In our opinion, this extends beyond a functionally
rational interest in the company's continued existence and the regulation of individual performance as reflected in mutually observed rules
and expected limits of tolerance.[52] And this is not just to be seen
against the "backdrop of latent competition (over employment, wage
or career)"[53].

"Human values also count and people are thankful about that. And
it's a good feeling that one can say that the people are thankful that we
haven't shoved them to the side." (Interview partner No. 4)

Even if objections to the idea that new social ideologies had
mutated into the organization's official self-presentation and legitimi-
zation, they may not be overruled.[54]

7. The Necessity of Creating a Company Model

According to a normative management's point of view, it is necessary
that employees identify with the company's value system. This is an
important pre-requisite to the realization of company goals and

---

[49] Schultz-Gambard 1994, p.184.

[50] Cf. Weiß et al 1993, p.75, and Ladensack 1994, p.43f.

[51] Aderhold et al 1994, p.52ff., speaks of the transition from solidarity to profes-
sionally sober relations in which a work-related collegiality dominated, as
opposed to the previous cohesion in work and in family.

[52] Alongside the human-relations and communication structures in our model company, there also exists extra social rewards, such as recognition of workers'
longterm activity in the company, gifts handed out for weddings, attainment of
retirement age, departure from the company due to mass lay-offs, social events
for retired employees.

[53] Aderhold et al 1994, p.53; Homann 1994 would speak here of the effects of
"economic imperialism." All decisions made under conditions of scarcity follow
the laws of economy. An economy freed of all monetary principles would
become a "general theory of human behavior." (ibid., p.123).

[54] Cf. Aderhold et al 1994, p.85.

employee understanding of managerial decision-making. As such, the formulation of a concretely defined company model based on altered economical and social conditions is crucial.[55] Its meaning can only be understood in the context of the strong ideological-normative orientation inherent in the planned economy of which its thinking processes must still be reflected upon. In the company studied, the formulation of this model has only partially and rudimentarily taken place.[56]

8. The Transformation Process' Challenge to Economic and Corporate Ethics

Reliability and the objective of achieving satisfying levels at the level of action are conditions which create a necessity to alter modes of behavior or behavior-affected patterns such as attitudes, thoughts and values. Established patterns of behavior remain as a result stable. Steps to alter these phenomena are only taken when established patterns of behavior are no longer sufficient to achieve desired goals.[57] In the case of the company in question, this means that the up-dating of one's orientation is only actively pursued when the results of the drastic changes which occurred begin to be perceived as an existential threat.[58] Should the decision-makers be offered stabilizing factors which allow for the controlling of living or working space[59], the perception of an optimistic future develops, and as a consequence tends to stabilize these same value systems. Opportunities for development and improvement are made available by which the company can turn to human/social needs and values, taking advantage of the energy potential that this releases.

---

[55] Cf. Ulrich/Fluri 1995, p.53f.; Marr 1994, p.62: "Because of the uncertainty created by the process of transformation in all its complexity, the employees of a company experience a greater need for orientation, that is, visions, ideals and goals on the one hand, and transparency and communication on the other."

[56] As previously mentioned, the collective formulation of a company philosophy will be undertaken with a follow-up study on this theme.

[57] Cf. Fietkau 1982, p.20.

[58] The two-fold dependency on values and action, in which values act as reason for action and vice versa, assumes a range between re-incorporation and updating/ adaptation of old world views; cf. Fietkau 1982, p.20.

[59] i.e. rally signals such as increases in turn-over, staff or positive results.

In the model company described, one is aware of the great creative
opportunities through the newly acquired freedom of the market
system. At the same time, a new "solidarity community" has formed
itself in this company through the social transformation and a successful adaptation to the new system in the face of the failure of other
market participants in the new federal states. This is in its general lines
comparable to the community of necessity present in the former GDR.
Human relations are allocated great importance and become through
this an important source of legitimacy for a company's business transactions. Given this context, it's no wonder that a cooperative-participa-
tory management style developed itself. The collective survival of the
crisis, the common experience of living through a planned as well as a
market economy and the relative stability in the composition of the
management team favored this community-oriented leadership style.
Its corporate success thus far seems to support its legitimacy.[60]

For many individuals, the market economy brings about "a permanently high demand of adaptability."[61] In extreme cases, many individuals no longer see any transcendental of moral basis for their
actions and things which had previously been taken for granted, such
as rights, culture, customs and conventions, have lost their validity.[62]
The results are "enormous difficulties in finding orientation". Does
this dominance of functional economical imperatives over individual
social relationships as in *Habermas'* "colonization of our living
sphere"[63] have to be accepted as "the price of the market economy" or
are there other solutions? From the experiences gathered during the
process of transformation, the necessity of a standardized basis for
business decision-making again becomes clear; especially during a
take-over by a business or a system with different cultural backgrounds.[64] A similarly oriented corporate code of ethics on the basis of
a participatory and therefore communicative set of basic values must
therefore go beyond a mere reinforcement of the market economy's

---

[60] Cf. Aderhold et al 1994, p.146.

[61] The following terms are taken from Homann/Blome-Drees 1992, p.77ff.

[62] Cf. Homann/Blome-Drees 1992 , p.79.

[63] Habermas 1981, vol. 2, p.522.

[64] Dunbar/Bresser 1995, p.34: "Despite all historically defined similarities the
German re-unification was and is the integration of two states with two differing
cultures."

"classical" ethical doctrine[65] and the responsibilities which ensue.[66] A "corporate code of ethics should take advantage of the freedom in the market economy's search for profit to make use of a social compatibility".[67]

A satisfying framework for the common good capable of counteracting the negative (free-rider) impressions of business trade will never exist.[68] Should the "goal of peace"[69] further be taken as the foundation of society, pure structural theory of economic and business ethics should therefore be enhanced not just by formal theories, but individual (and therefore value-oriented) ethical extensions. It must, however, also avoid the slide into "moral heroism"[70]. The ultimate goal is the creation of new value patterns undertaken by active individuals who function as role-models and agents of integration, and who thus would contribute to change at an institutional level.[71]

---

[65] This is "atrophying" in a stylization of the ethical content of structural-theoretical paradigms.

[66] In contrast to Homann/Blome-Drees 1992, p.169ff., his participatory attitude was supposed to result not only in institutional measures, but individual levels of responsibility, for example in management as well.

[67] Steinmann/Löhr 1994, p.148.

[68] Following the globalization of economic processes, this framework would best be implemented at an international level. Such a network remains, however positive it may be, a utopia. "For pragmatic and system-oriented reasons, the conditions necessary for a successful framework has never existed." (Homann/ Blome-Drees 1992, p.114). To formulate this criteria as a basis of corporate operations (It will only be considered as a moral imperitive and in this sense obligatory for individual managers and companies when it becomes a widerang-ing enforceable sanction. ("Only after it has been recognized as universally binding and sufficiently enforceable, [...] can we also consider it morally 'valid' in the sense that it obliges the individual company and its managers."; ibid., p.46) draws out the implementation of ethical standards in corporate descision making ad infinitum.

[69] Lorenzen 1991, p.58.

[70] Homann/Blome-Drees 1992, p.173.

[71] Particularly in view of the economic and social changes within the "old" industrial societies through the internationalization of economical interconnectedness of central importance.

References

Aderhold, J. et al (1994): *Von der Betriebs- zur Zweckgemeinschaft*. Ostdeutsche Arbeits- und Managementkulturen im Transformationsprozeß, Berlin.

Deller, J. / Jepsen, S. (1995): Verantwortungs- und Wertbewußtsein bei Führungsnachwuchskräften. Eine empirische Erhebung, in: *Die Unternehmung, Journal 3*.

Dunbar, L.M. / Bresser, R. (1995): Integrations-Zirkel, in: *Personalwirtschaft*, No. 10/95, S. 34-40.

Fietkau, H.-J. (1982): *Neue Werte aus handlungstheoretischer Sicht*, Berlin.

Habermas, J. (1981): *Theorie des kommunikativen Handelns*, 2 Bde., Frankfurt.

Heidenreich, M. (1991): Zur Doppelstruktur planwirtschaftlichen Handelns in der DDR, Zeitschrift für Soziologie, Nr. 20, S. 411-429.

Homann, K. (1994): Marktwirtschaft und Unternehmensethik, in: Blasche, S. et al (ed.): *Markt und Moral. Die Diskussion um die Unternehmensethik*, Bern/Stuttgart/Wien, S. 109-130.

Homann, K. (1992): *Marktwirtschaft und Probleme der Ethik*, Erlangen-Nürnberg.

Homann, K. / Blome-Drees, F. (1992): *Wirtschafts- und Unternehmensethik*, Göttingen.

Klages, H. (1993): *Traditionsbruch als Herausforderung. Perspektiven der Wertewandelgesellschaft*, Frankfurt/New York.

Ladensack, K. (1994): Führung im Wandel: Prozesse und Probleme bei der gesellschaftlichen Transformation, in: Rosenstiel, Lutz v. (ed.): *Führung im Systemwandel. Untersuchungen zum Führungsverhalten beim Übergang von der Plan- in die Marktwirtschaft*, München/Mering, S. 13-48.

Lang, R. (1994): Wertorientierungen und Organisationsverständnis ostdeutscher Führungskräfte im Wandel, in: Rosenstiel, L. v. (ed.): *Führung im Systemwandel. Untersuchungen zum Führungsverhalten beim Übergang von der Plan- in die Marktwirtschaft*, München/Mering, S. 141-168.

Lang, R. (1992): Sozialisation und Wertorientierungen ostdeutscher Führungskräfte, in: Heidenreich, Martin (Hrsg.): *Krisen, Kader, Kombinate. Kontinuität und Wandel in ostdeutschen Betrieben*, Berlin, S. 125-142.

Lorenzen, P. (1991): Pholosophische Fundierungsprobleme einer Wirtschafts- und Unternehmensethik, in: Steinmann, H. / Löhr, A. (ed.): *Unternehmensethik*, 2nd revised and expanded Edition, Stuttgart, S. 35-67.

Marr, R. (1994): Die Rolle der Führungskräfte im Prozeß der Transformation einer Wirtschaftssystem von der Plan- in die Marktwirtschaft, in: Rosenstiel, L. v. (ed.): *Führung im Systemwandel. Untersuchungen zum Führungsverhalten beim Übergang von der Plan- in die Marktwirtschaft*, München/Mering, S. 49-65.

Marz, L. (1993): System-Zeit und Entökonomisierung. Zu Zeit/Macht-Dispositiven und mentalen Dispositionen in realsozialistischen Wirtschaften, in: Schmidt, R. (ed.): *Zwischenbilanz. Analysen zum Transformationsprozeß der ostdeutschen Industrie*, Berlin ; S. 73-108.

Mayring, P. (1990): *Einführung in die qualitative Sozialforschung. Eine Anleitung zu qualitativem Denken*, München.

Peters, T.J. / Waterman, R.H. jun (1982): *In Search of Exceellence. Lessons from America's Best-Run Companies*, New York.

Rappensperger, G. / Rosenstiel, L. v. / Zwarg, I. (1994): Erwartungen an die berufliche Tätigkeit bei Hochschulabsolventen aus den neuen Bundesländern, in: Trommsdorff, G. (ed.): *Psychologische Aspekte des sozio-politischen Wandels in Ostdeutschland*, Berlin/New York, S. 183-199.

Richter, K. (1990): Gesellschaftliche Rahmenbedingungen für das Personalmanagement im Umbruch. Ausgewählte Aspekte, in: Pieper, R. (ed.): *Personalmanagement. Von der Plan- in die Marktwirtschaft*, Wiesbaden, S. 61-70.

Rosenstiel, L. v. (1994): Zur Einführung, in: Rosenstiel, Lutz v. (ed.): *Führung im Systemwandel. Untersuchungen zum Führungsverhalten beim Übergang von der Plan- in die Marktwirtschaft*, München/Mering, S. 5-11.

Rosenstiel, L. v. (1992): Unternehmenskultur – einige einführende Anmerkungen, in: Dierkes, M. / Rosenstiel, L. v. / Steger, U. (ed.): *Unternehmenskultur in Theorie und Praxis. Konzepte aus Ökonomie, Psychologie und Ethnologie*, Frankfurt/New York, S. 8-22.

Schmidt, R. (1993): Einleitung, in: Schmidt, R. (ed.): *Zwischenbilanz. Analysen zum Transformationsprozeß der ostdeutschen Industrie*, Berlin, S. 7-25.

Schnabel, K. / Baumert, J. / Roeder, P. M. (1994): Wertewandel in Ost und West – Ein Vergleich von Jugendlichen und Erwachsenen in den neuen und alten Bundesländern, in: Trommsdorff, G. (ed.): *Psychologische Aspekte des sozio-politischen Wandels in Ostdeutschland*, Berlin/New York, S. 77-93.

Schramm, F. (1994): Welche Rolle spielt die Arbeitsunsicherheit in der Transformation, in: Rosenstiel, L. v. (ed.): *Führung im Systemwandel. Untersuchungen zum Führungsverhalten beim Übergang von der Plan- in die Marktwirtschaft*, München/Mering, S. 99-119.

Schultz-Gambard, J. (1994): Führungsstile im Ost-West-Vergleich. Ergebnisse und Implikationen für Personalentwicklungsmaßnahmen, in: Rosenstiel, L. v. (ed.): *Führung im Systemwandel. Untersuchungen zum Führungsverhalten beim Übergang von der Plan- in die Marktwirtschaft*, München/Mering, S. 169-190.

Seifert, P. / Heyse, V. (1994): Sozialisation- und konfliktbedingte Unterschiede im Verhalten von ost- und westdeutschen Führungskräften in ostdeutschen Unternehmen, in: Heyse, V. / Erpenbeck, J.: *Management und Wertewandel im Übergang. Voraussetzungen, Chancen und Grenzen betrieblicher Weiterbildung im Transformationsprozeß*, Münster/New York, S. 67-110.

Srubar, I. (1991): War der reale Sozialismus modern? Versuch einer strukturellen Bestimmung, in: *Kölner Zeitschrift für Soziologie und Sozialpsychologie 43*, S. 415-432.

Steinmann, H. / Löhr, A. (1994): Unternehmensethik – Ein republikanisches Programm in der Kritik, in: Blasche, S. et al (ed.): *Markt und Moral. Die Diskussion um die Unternehmensethik*, Bern/Stuttgart/ Wien, S. 145-180.

Ulrich, P. / Fluri, E. (1995): *Management: Eine konzentrierte Einführung*, 7th Edition, Bern/Stuttgart/Wien.

Ulrich, P. / Thielemann, U. (1992): *Ethik und Erfolg. Unternehmensethische Denkmuster von Führungskräften – eine empirische Studie*, Bern/ Stuttgart.

Weiß, R. et al (1993): Innerbetriebliche Möglichkeiten zur Qualifizierung aus Unternehmenssicht, in: *Qualifikations-Entwicklungs-Management, Journal 7/I*, Berlin.

Witzel, A. (1982): *Verfahren der qualitativen Sozialforschung: Überblick und Alternativen*, Frankfurt.

Unemployment and Experienced Injustices: The Social Responsibility of the Organization for Cushioning the Process of Downsizing

Thomas Kieselbach

1. Future Trends of Occupational Transitions

Mass unemployment will clearly be an issue of major political relevance in future, and political parties will be assessed in terms of how they propose and actually succeed in solving labour market problems. Social discourse on the subject of unemployment obtains central importance, also with respect to the assessment of solutions to mass unemployment and the attribution of individual and social responsibility (Kieselbach 1987).

During the last years a worldwide debate has emerged among social scientists and economists whether we are entering a "post-job era", reaching "the end of work" (Rifkin 1995) or – to quote another title – whether we have to face "a jobless future" (Aronowitz & DiFazio 1994). What all these prognoses of the labour market development in the highly industrialized countries have in common, is that they try to delineate a common perspective for the future of the labour markets. Their starting point lies in the fact that since the beginning of the eighties in most of the western, especially in the European countries, the increase of the unemployment rates has reached a higher plateau after every economic recovery despite a general increase in the number of employees. On the other hand you find prevailing tendencies of deregulation and flexibilization in many countries which lead to the precarisation of the labour market.

Psychological unemployment research has up to now focused on the individual effects of the exclusion from the labour market and differential attempts at coping with job loss and continuous marginali-

H. Lange et al., Working Across Cultures, 191–210.
© 1998 *Kluwer Academic Publishers. Printed in the Netherlands.*

zation by unemployment. In my presentation I will try to make a preliminary approach – in the direction of the debate which takes into consideration the factual normalization of temporary exclusion from paid work for an increasing number of people capable and willing to work – to formulate future responses from social institutions, companies as well as individuals confronted with such a rapidly changing social reality. In doing this I will start to look at the psychological problem of unemployment from a more salutogenetic perspective, trying to find out which should be the societal prerequisites that enable the individual to cope with future trends of a precarious labour market as well as with a growing number of occupational transitions the individual will have to face.

Occupational transitions which are associated with passing from one occupational position to the other have already increased and will do so even more in future. They tend to replace the normative perspective of an ideal type of a lifelong relationship to a certain company – although this was not the concrete reality for the majority of the employees in the past, not even in Europe – against a patchwork biography of different phases within, between and out of employment.

Occupational transitions may lead to personal experiences of distress exceeding personal and social resources necessary for adequate attempts at coping with the requirements of these new situations. The future perspectives of the labour market will impose rather different demands on those who have to respond to these rapid changes regarding occupational qualifications as well as the increasing probability of job transitions in the course of one`s own occupational biography.

If these tendencies of the labour market shall be met adequately, it is not justified to expect the adaptation only from the part of the individual concerned but to develop concepts instead which might be appropriate to accompany the invidual during these transitory phases on a societal level.

The answers will vary from one societal context to the other: the North American solutions tend to expect the relevant contributions from the part of the individual affected. The European context of the social discourse on individual vs. social responsibility, however, offers the opportunity to develop solutions which will not impose the responsibility merely on the individual.

2. Unemployment and Victimization

Losing the job in a labour society in which individual development is linked in many ways with occupational position is a major personal insult, bearing the risk that long-term psychosocial damage can develop as unemployment continues *(primary victimization)*. Ample empirical evidence has been provided for this (see Kieselbach 1991; Catalano 1993). One of the main moderating variables for coping with unemployment that has been identified in various studies is the attribution of the causes of job loss and of unemployment (Kieselbach 1991). Internal attribution – blaming oneself for becoming/remaining unemployed – leads to greater psychosocial problems than if external factors (e.g. society) are made responsible (Frese 1985). Attribution to internal causes is associated with higher depression rates, but also with greater efforts to find work (Feather & Barber 1983).

The social construction of unemployment in terms of the individualization of unemployment as a critical event in one's life is a major factor in the way how individuals cope with unemployment (Kieselbach 1994). When the cause of job loss and continuous unemployment are assigned in social discourse, at least for sub-groups of the unemployed, to the individuals actually affected, the latter are burdened with having to legitimate themselves as not belonging to those sub-groups of the unemployed who have only themselves to blame for their situation. The stigma thus attached to unemployment then generates a *secondary victimization* of those concerned.

The third level of victimization lies in the selective evaluation of the unemployed by their social surroundings. On the one hand, those not coping adequately with respect to their job search attitudes and their attitude towards their own labour market options are held responsible for the psychosocial damages resulting from such behaviour. On the other hand, one special feature of the unemployment experience is that the environment usually exercises a very precise control to ensure that positive self-evaluation does not violate a specific boundary – the positive boundary of continued capacity for action on the labour market. A satisfied acceptance of one's own unemployment ("proactivity" in the sense used by Fryer & Payne 1984) is negatively assessed by the social network as an exploitation of the social insurance system, and is subjected as a result to massive stigmatization *(tertiary victimization)*.

3. The Victims of Downsizing Processes

3.1.   The dismissed employees

The experience of being the direct victim of a downsizing decision within the company creates, without any doubt, high levels of distress among those being affected. Starting with the distress of anticipation especially the experience of long-term unemployment which is much more prevailing in the European countries than in the United States (between 30 and 40% in different European countries) causes psycho-social problems which for their part create relevant barriers to overcoming unemployment. Therefore especially the European countries should develop more sophisticated measures which prevent the emergence of very-long-term-unemployment as it can actually be observed.

3.2.   The management responsible for downsizing decisions

Managers being responsible for industrial restructuring on a company level are often held causally, and often also morally, responsible for the creation of unemployment. Although there are no systematic studies available on the reactions of the management, there is a rather anecdotic or journalistic evidence for the stress of those being responsible for dismissals (Lerner 1996).

   We can assume that those persons being responsible for the planning, decision, implementation, execution of and communication about dismissals often morally blame themselves and therefore experience considerable levels of distress associated with phases of industrial restructuring. Often they can only accept their own position as a tragic choice between their obligations towards the shareholders on the one hand and their subordinates on the other hand, which they have to pay for with feelings of guilt, depression and reduced productivity. These feeelings are often not anticipated by themselves. They generate psychological costs on the individual`s part as well as productivity costs on the part of the company. The dismissal of long-term co-workers may be experienced in some cases as a traumatic event which in the long run may lead to a loss of flexibility and vigour among managers.

3.3. The survivors-of-layoffs

The experience of layoffs gives rise to a crucial problem for organizations – the impact of major layoffs on those employees who remain in
the enterprise (Kieselbach 1997b). Employees very precisely register
the behaviour of those within the company who are involved in such a
process. Conclusions are drawn regarding values, norms and attitudes,
as well as the basic principles implicitly applied by the company. If
staff come to the conclusion that the individual employee is of no
value for the organization despite his or her performance, this will
affect the behaviour of those employees who remain.

Layoffs that are viewed by those unaffected as unjust or unnecessary often lead to demoralization and cynicism among such survivors
of layoffs. These attitudes, in turn, cause substantial reductions in
productivity, with the result that managements are now developing an
interest in establishing some form of consensus when redundancies
prove necessary.

In one longitudinal study concerning employees who survived
layoffs, the data obtained one month before and three months after a
wave of redundancies show that subjectively perceived justice in the
reasons given for layoffs, and for the job security of those who were
not laid off, had a direct impact on job satisfaction among the latter.
There was a negative correlation between perceived injustice and the
degree of involvement for the company, and a positive correlation
with inner withdrawal tendencies (Davy, Kinicki & Scheck 1991).

An attempt was made to investigate the inequity of redundancies
from the perspective of the survivors in terms of the procedural and
distributive justice dimensions (Brockner 1990, see also Brockner et
al. 1987). The results show that the perception of layoffs as unfair
depends on how the victims are assessed regarding their personal
affinity to the survivors, as well as in terms of relevant job-related
attitudes (interpreted as the "scope of justice"). An individual redundancy was seen as unjust particularly when, firstly, insufficient reasons
were given by the management regarding the necessity of layoffs in
general, and the selection of the individual in question; secondly,
when the organization had not taken steps to care for those laid off
following their departure from the organization (e.g. by looking for
other jobs in the same company, providing outplacement guidance, or

additional financial settlements). Survivors displayed much less identification with the company when they viewed the layoff strategies of
the management as unfair, identifying instead with the victims as
members of the same moral community (ibid, p.100).

Strategies geared to selective redundancies based on individual
shortcomings imply the notion of equity to the extent that they signify
an attempt to present particular dismissals as being the just deserts of
the individuals concerned. Redundancies are related to differing
extents in different societies to the performance and the work behaviour of the individual. Social need ('double incomes', number of
dependants), seniority and the 'last hired, first fired' principle are only
some of the principles which are intended to portray the distribution of
work as equitable (see Montada 1994b on the criterion of distributive
justice applied to employment as a scarce commodity).

It is important for the work climate in a company that the survivors
of layoffs gain a substantiated impression that layoffs are decided and
executed in accordance with justice criteria, in order that they themselves do not come to the conclusion that they could just as easily have
been among those affected. Reasons for layoffs which refer to the
competitive situation on the market or other macroprocesses of
industrial restructuring are only partially adequate as a way of meeting
this requirement. The risk being entered, on the other hand, is that
individualizing explanations can improve the psychosocial situation of
survivors, while having a negative impact on the sense of psychosocial
well-being and capacity for coping among those made redundant.

At the same time, when causes are attributed to macroprocesses
that are presented as unforeseeable and uncontrollable by both
management and those directly afflicted, this then leads, even when
procedures are experienced as equitable, to reactions among survivors
that operate in effect as postponed threats to their own employment
careers. This is a contradiction that Melvin Lerner, too, has recently
dealt with, calling it the paradoxical effect on survivors of layoffs of
procedural justice without distributive justice (Lerner 1996, p.4).

If this problem is to be dealt with by society in a responsible
manner, efforts must be made to ensure that the interests not only of
survivors are taken into consideration, but that the interests of the
unemployed are prioritized.

There is a growing realization that if management wants to avoid the negative effects of layoffs among company staff, counteracting the productivity increases that are usually the reason for layoffs in the first place, they must pay much greater and closer attention to the processes of procedural, distributive and interactional justice described below.

4. Justice Dimensions of the Downsizing Process

4.1.   Distributive justice

If employment must increasingly be seen as a scarce resource, then decision-making rules for distributing this scarce resource become more important (Brockner & Greenberg 1990; Deutsch 1985, for a more general treatment). The choice can be made between two selection principles, namely one based on need and another based on efficiency. The needs-oriented selection principle, which asks who needs employment the most or who has been with the company the longest, are often applied as a result of statutory regulations, collective bargaining agreements, paternalist structures (principle of seniority) or gender-specific role allocations (e.g. identifying women as those responsible for double incomes). It often exists in stark contrast with efficiency-oriented criteria, where the issue concerns who is most likely to increase the productivity of the company on account of their previous performance, attitude to work or skills and qualifications.

4.2.   Procedural justice

The general criteria for distributive or procedural justice formulated by Leventhal (1980) have not been applied as yet to layoffs, but they lend themselves well to these and similar situations (Brockner & Greenberg 1990 being the first to apply them in this way). These criteria demand
- consistent procedures,
- executed independently of particular interests,
- on the basis of precise information,
- with the option of correcting decisions already taken,
- taking the interests of all participant parties into account
- in accordance with ethical and moral standards (Leventhal 1980).

The critical factor here is the extent of control over the decision-making process on the part of workforces. This is largely determined by statutory regulations (such as the co-determination laws in Germany) but also permits management a certain amount of scope in applying different rules for distributive justice.

4.3.   Interactional justice

This refers to the type of interpersonal treatment that is experienced by people involved in layoff decisions – those who actually lose their jobs as well as those who survive (Brockner & Greenberg 1990). The issue here is which information is communicated in what manner regarding the reasons for
- particular assessments of performance,
- selection decisions relating to the workforce,
- the acceptance or rejection of proposed alternatives in connection with layoffs.

We can confirm by way of summary that the findings of social justice research can certainly make an important contribution to the organizational cushioning of strategies for reducing workforce size. Care should be taken to ensure that the application of social-scientific knowledge benefits the victims of layoffs first and foremost, however, which means relating it to the process before, during and after redundancies are implemented, including the re-employment process. Once this is achieved, any indirect effects of layoffs on survivors which are liable to impair the productivity of organizations can then be focused on as a supplementary step.

5.   The Demand for Social Monitoring of Occupational Transition Processes

The following section contains some general remarks, in the form of theses, on the future directions and trajectories taken by occupational biographies:
- The general increase in employment transitions leads to a greater incidence of transition-related stress (*primary victimization*)

- stigmatization effects of transitional states such as unemployment reinforce the level of stress experienced by individuals, demanding greater efforts on the part of those affected in order to cope with the new situation *(secondary victimization)*
- the personal resources (individual coping repertoires) and the social resources (e.g., social support) required for coping are often undeveloped or insufficiently available; this can prevent appropriate forms of coping with employment transitions. What happens in many cases is that those who fail to cope are made responsible for their own fate *(tertiary victimization)*, another variant of victim-blaming; or that those who are considered to cope well, i.e. the proactive unemployed, are blamed for misusing the unemployment benefit system.

These factors necessitate social counselling and guidance
- to normalize and
- de-stigmatize such transitions, which may then create an essential basis for
- improving the extent to which individuals cope with employment transitions.

The key requirement for this, however, is the existence of opportunities for filling out such transition phases in an individually meaningful way, rather than having to experience them as 'empty spaces' in one's own occupational biography.

5.1.   Outplacement as transition counselling

We will describe first considerations regarding the development of an integrated approach of transition counselling which may form the central aspect of taking over social responsibility for the coping with occupational transitions whithout impeding the self-organizational process as well as the taking over of personal responsibility of persons in transition. During the last two decades the development of a wide variety of concepts for counselling and coaching members of the upper and middle management with regard to offer them professional help in the process of exiting the organization could be observed in the US. The main interest of the organization lies in smoothing the individual process, stabilizing the image of the organization as behaving responsibly in the case of necessary separations and controlling the unintended side-effects on those remaining in the company.

Outplacement counselling concepts have been restricted so far to senior and middle management, where the assumption is made that the effort and expense that detailed guidance and counselling will turn out to be a good investment. Such company-related counselling sometimes is an integral part of employment contracts, so that employees know beforehand that they will be entitled to some form of counselling and guidance in the case of separation from the organization.

If we try to assess the efficiency of outplacement counselling we have to rely on those data provided by OP agencies themselves. Up to now, systematic, especially comparative analyses, are totally lacking. Therefore the following results have to be interpreted with care. Generally outplacement counselling agencies report transition rates into re-employment of their clients of above 90%. (Mayrhofer 1989). German counsellors with an outplacement experience of about 400 clients point out a success rate of 97% (Schulz & Schuppertz 1987), Stoebe (1993) talks about 90%. There are no relevant differences between German, European and U.S. outplacement agencies. German counsellors compared to American ones, prefer a longer lasting counselling process which is more often extended to the re-employment process. The average duration varies between 4 months (Germany) and 12 months (U.S.) (Smith 1993; cf. also Monaco 1983; Lavan, Mathys & Drehmer 1983).

In contrast to these results the transition rates of intervention schemes from the part of the labour administration for unemployed with average qualifications are much lower. They vary between 10 and 40% in Germany, evaluations from the U.S. report percentages between 60% and 90% (for a review, cf. Kieselbach, Scharf & Klink 1997; Kieselbach 1996). These differences may be explained by the qualification structure of the clientele of well-paid OP counsellors, on the one hand, with higher qualifications leading to better chances of re-entering the labour market and in the selection process of the agencies themselves, on the other hand, which tend to exclude those job-seekers with specific employment barriers (e.g., old age, addiction problems, low mobility, etc.). This implies an additional creaming-off effect improving the success rates of outplacement, as well. In contrast intervention schemes often try to counteract these selection effects focusing on those groups of unemployed, instead, which seem to be incapable of finding new employment without professional help. These factors, of course, limit the possiblity of comparisons between intervention schemes and outplacement counselling.

It is more than astonishing that the development of rather sophisticated outplacement strategies for the upper and middle management did not at all have any impact on the debate on the conceiving of intervention schemes for the unemployed in general. In Germany, for example, up to now there has been no exchange of the results from these two areas of counselling and coaching. The outplacement strategies build part of a company's corporate identity and have been widely discussed in the management literature, only recently this has also happened in the area of organizational psychology (Smith 1993). The literature of psychological and sociological unemployment research, however, fully neglected the experiences and evaluations made in the area of helping managers exiting and reentering jobs by outplacement counseling.

5.2.   Broadening the perspective towards integrated outplacement/ replacement concepts

The question arises which are the features that in the past prevented the transfer from the experiences made in the outplacement area to the conceptualizing of intervention schemes for the unemployed in general. If we try to find reasons for the relative independence of approaches regarding the counselling of "normal" and highly qualified unemployed we have to take into account that outplacement counselling has been provided by professionals on an individual level with no narrow restrictions regarding the costs implied in such a time consuming process of professional help. The companies involved regarded the expenses as precalculated expenses being part of the costs of a qualified and loyal management. These approaches were highly individualized and therefore they were rather expensive. This prevented the extension of outplacement counselling to lower qualification ranks within the company. On the other hand the develoment of group counselling concepts has not yet been supported on the company level but remained under the responsibility of institutions like the labor administration or other social institutions.

In order to prevent those psychosocial damages caused or aggravated by the experience of losing one's job or being marginalized as long-term unemployed we have to think about ways of conceptualizing occupational transitions in a way that will not impose the burden of adaptation on the individual alone but also in ways which accept responsibility on a societal level.

The aim of outplacement is to develop a concept for exiting the organization in a manner seen as fair by both sides, and to facilitate the transition to new employment (see also Kieselbach 1994). Within a support framework that helps the person to cope with redundancy, on the basis of meetings with the individual, but also in conjunction with his family members, the individual's skills, abilities, competencies and weaknesses are analyzed, employment opportunities discussed and specific strategies for job applications developed. The findings of psychological research into unemployment are taken into account when devising such counselling concepts, in order to mitigate stress and thus prevent any further aggravation of the crisis being faced.

The positive aspects of existing outplacement concepts are that they represent an attempt on the part of enterprises to assume a degree of responsibility for layoffs which are otherwise seen as being inevitable, that they provide dismissed employees with the perspective of social support, and, with the help of professional counsellors, make the fullest use of the learning potential which is also inherent in such situations. However, the conflict potential that also exists as a result of the different interests at stake has so far not been put on the agenda. The dominant picture is one of harmonization, based on the assumption that the aims, interests and values in operation are essentially congruent (Mayrhofer 1987, p.164).

Thought should be given in future to the development and establishment within society of forms of group counselling which can be implemented for all levels of company hierarchy. For companies, this means creating a corporate culture that focuses on the responsibility of the company for its individual employees. However, this would require more precise analyses relating directly to the layoff process and how it is shaped (ibid., p.168), and fuller integration of the conclusions drawn from psychological research into unemployment. When shaping the counselling process within group outplacement, approaches such as the 'Job Club' could be included (for an overview, see Klink, Waldmann & Kieselbach 1995).

A significant limitation of existing concepts, however, is that they are primarily concerned with the problems that individuals face when exiting the organization. They therefore convey the impression that their main purpose is to organize job cuts in such a way that the organization does not have to sacrifice its operational efficiency. The employee who is made redundant, however, has a justified interest in re-entering the labour market, with an employment relationship of equivalent status. Counselling by institutions must therefore deal with the process of re-employment as well. An extended concept embracing the entire employment transition process could be better termed as outplacement/replacement (OP/RP), by which is meant the continuous psychosocial monitoring and guidance of job-related transitions.

6. Advantages of Integrated Outplacement / Replacement Strategies

6.1. Advantages for the unemployed

There is wide evidence that supports the assumption that the anticipation of a stressor, professional help as a form of social support during the coping process as well as the de-stigmatization of the occupational transition for the individual concerned will reduce psycho-damages associated with job loss and unemployment. The individual effects in general of the implementation of OP/RP concepts can be seen as follows:
- de-individualization of occupational transitions
- cushioning the shock which might be associated with the dismissal notification
- increased feelings of security for the occupational future by the anticipation of a social support for the transition period
- reduction of the psychosocial stress resulting from unemployment due to a competent counselling which refers to
- clarification of financial problems
- immunization against the unemployment stress by information and working through potential damages created by the unemployment experience

- analysis of resources and deficits regarding qualifications, interests, motivations etc.
- analysis of regional options regarding actual labour market requirements and future developments, qualification schemes of the labour administration etc.
- development of personal occupational plans reconciling individual and social resources and options.

OP/RP in the sense of an integrated occupational transition counselling developed above can be interpreted as a "social convoy" (Antonucci 1985) facilitating the individual coping with occupational change. The person afflicted receives in a legitimate way social resources which can enable him in a difficult personal passage to make actively use of the growth potential also inherent in occupational transitions instead of considering himself only as a social victim.

An OP/RP concept must, however, leave aside many of those aspects associated with classic outplacement counselling, which for quite a long time had the image of a better form of a funeral which only tried to reduce organizational frictions accompanying industrial downsizing.

Only if the equal interest of the individual to get an equivalent re-employment as a result of the OP/RP counselling is taken into consideration can such an instrument gain a respected image and can be applied on a consensual basis in organizational and industrial settings.

6.2.   Advantages for the Organization

What could be the reasons for an organization to apply approaches of an integrated occupational transition counselling and guidance?

Under the perspective of an advanced management philosophy the social capital of the company staff can be understood as the crucial point of high productivity. If companies offer comprehensive transition counselling, this can be considered as taking over social responsibility for necessary processes of industrial restructuring. This in return might as well lead to a higher degree of identification with the company and therefore counteract the reduction of identification resulting from the anticipatory thematizing of a possible separation from the company. It also may create a more realistic foundation of the relationship between the employee and the organization.

The anticipation of a professional and comprehensive counselling in case of an unavoidable separation from the organization may lead to a reduction of the anticipatory stress of unemployment and might as well be able to defuse the health effects of job insecurity in the long run. Being conceived as formal regulations which might themselves be incorporated in work contracts (e.g., the entitlement to receive transition counselling) they may produce feelings of mutual commitment and obligation. Thus a legitimate claim would form the basis of help. The person to be counselled must not define himself as not being capable of resolving his occupational problems on his own and therefore disclose his help-seeking as a personal deficit but can accept the counselling as a granted part of the work contract.

He therefore would no longer be an object of altruistic care - as in many aspects the participants of special intervention schemes for the unemployed are defined for various reasons – but will in contrast develop feelings of entitlement and on this basis be able to consider himself as an equal partner of a professional counselling process.

The advantages for the organization consist of
– demonstrating the taking over of social responsibility from the part of the company
– a greater transparency in the process of reducing personnel,
– the organizational buffering of downsizing,
– the reduction of legal conflicts with respect to dismissals,
– the reduction of a loss of productivity due to reactions of demotivation, lower commitment and inner withdrawal from the part of the survivors of-layoffs.

7. A Plea for a Change of Discourse Regarding Occupational Transitions

Bearing in mind what has been said so far, it is important that integrated concepts will be developed which
– systematically relate different dimensions of counselling and guidance to each other,
– conceive of employment transitions as skill- and qualification-related moratoria,
– reduce individual's anxiety about their uncertain future to such an extent that they remain capable of taking action,

-   provide them with an accepted social identity throughout the transitional period and
-   create a social framework in which the social injustice of unemployment is compensated for by visible forms of societal responsibility.

If society provided support and guidance to people going through transitions imposed on them by industrial restructuring, this could be experienced by those affected as a form of compensation for subjectively experienced inequity, as opposed to feelings of resentment and moral outrage being the dominant reactions instead. Counselling for the unemployed in the form of guidance through a transition must be freed of any stigmatizing effects in order to ensure that the inhibitory barriers among the unemployed vis-à-vis seeking or accepting help are broken down.

Defining the relationship between the unemployed and society in terms of legitimate claims would greatly alleviate the psychosocial situation of the unemployed. They would no longer be the object of altruistic care and benefits, but partners requiring counselling and guidance during a transitional phase in their employment history (see Montada 1994). A fundamental basis for their relationship to society and its institutions would be the assumption that the costs of industrial restructuring - essential for maintaining the competitiveness and long-term survival of the economy – must be borne by the community as a whole on the basis of the solidarity principle, and not thrust upon those individuals who are personally affected by such change.

From the mental health perspective, the proposed change in discourse towards a normalization of employment transitions involving temporary phases of unemployment might well produce a climate in having to cope with the potential stressor job loss causes less psychosocial damage to the individuals in question. Primary appraisal in the anticipatory phase of the threat implied by job loss could change for the better, as could the secondary appraisal of personal and social resources for coping with a stressor that has already taken effect (Lazarus & Folkman 1984). In this way, a potentially damaging situation would no longer be seen purely as a threat, whereby the focus of attention would be on the possible harmful effects, but could also be perceived as a challenge instead, the focus then being on the feeling of mastering a difficult situation or on the aspect of personal growth

(Wortman 1983). The employment transition would not appear to individuals as something that is fully controllable, but to a greater extent at least as something over which they can exert a certain influence.

The adaptation to a thoroughly changed economic reality which already has increased the frequency of individual occupational transitions – becoming even more frequent in future – should not be imposed on the individual affected in a one-sided way. The resulting individual problems of a higher degree of corporate efficiency which implies a higher flexibility with regard to the labour market should be accepted as being within the responsibility not only of the society in general, but also of the companies undergoing processes of economic restructuring which include profound changes of their workforce. Organizations have to develop environmental features which do not only emphasize efficiency criteria but are facilitating individual coping attempts to deal with these new occupational demands without exceeding individual resources. They require working conditions which try to balance occupational zones of innovation - necessary to increase the competitivity of the organization – and occupational zones of routine, which convey a sense of security to the individual (Nicholson & West 1988) in order to enable the individual as well as the organization to profit from these social changes we are already facing at present and which will be prevailing even more in future.

References

Antonucci, T.C. (1985): Social support: Theoretical advances, recent findings and pressing issues. In: J.G. Sarason & R.B. Sarason (Eds.): *Social support: Theory, research, and applications*, 21-38. Dordrecht: Martinus Nijhoff.

Aronowitz, S. & DiFazio, W. (1994): *The jobless future. Sci-Tech and the dogma of work*. Minneapolis: Univ. of Minneapolis Press.

Brockner, J., Grover, S., Reed, T., DeWitt, R. & O'Malley, M. (1987): Survivors' reactions to layoffs: We get by with a little help from our friends. *Administrative Science Qarterly*, 32, 526-541.

Brockner, J. (1990): Scope of justice in the workplace: How survivors react to co-workers' layoffs. *Journal of Social Issues*, 46 (1), 95-106.

Catalano, R.A. (1993): Gesundheitseffekte wirtschaftlicher Unsicherheit: Ein analytischer Überblick. In: Kieselbach, T. & Voigt, P. (Eds.): *Systemumbruch, Arbeitslosigkeit und individuelle Bewältigung in der Ex-DDR*, 84-94. Weinheim: Deutscher Studien Verlag.

Davy, J.A., Kinicki, A.J. & Scheck, C.L. (1991): Developing and testing a model of survivor responses to layoffs. *Journal of Vocational Behavior*, 38 (3), 302-317.

Deutsch, M. (1985): *Distributive justice: A social-psychological perspective*. New Haven, CT: Yale University Press.

Feather, N.T. & Barber, J.G. (1983). Depressive reactions and unemployment. *Journal of Abnormal Psychology*, 92, 185-195.

Frese, M. (1985): Zur Verlaufsstruktur der psychischen Auswirkungen von Arbeitslosigkeit. In T. Kieselbach & A. Wacker (Eds.), *Individuelle und gesellschaftliche Kosten der Massenarbeitslosigkeit. Psychologische Theorie und Praxis*, 224-241, Weinheim: Beltz.

Fryer, D. & Payne, R.L. (1984): Proactive behaviour in unemployment: Findings and implications. *Leisure Studies*, 3, 273-295.

Fritz, W., Schulz, D., Schuppert, D., Seiwert & Walsh, J. (1989): *Outplacement: Personalfreisetzung und Karrierestrategien*. Wiesbaden: Gabler.

Kieselbach, T. (1987): Gesellschaftliche und individuelle Bewältigung von Arbeitslosigkeit. In: H. Moser (Eds.), *Bedrohung oder Beschwichtigung. Die politische und die seelische Gestalt technischer, wirtschaftlicher und gesundheitlicher Gefährdungen*, 28-55. Weinheim: Deutscher Studien Verlag.

Kieselbach, T. (1991): Unemployment. In: R. Lerner, J. Brooks-Gunn & A. C. Petersen (Eds.): *Encyclopedia of adolescence*, 1187-1201. Philadelphia: Garland Publisher.

Kieselbach, T. (1994): Arbeitslosigkeit als psychologisches Problem – auf individueller und gesellschaftlicher Ebene. In L. Montada (Ed.): *Arbeitslosigkeit und soziale Gerechtigkeit*, 233-263. Frankfurt/M.: Campus.

Kieselbach, T. (1996): *Out- and replacement strategies – a viable tool for the amelioration of the unemployment stress? Perspectives for coping with occupational transitions*. Paper presented at the VIth International Conference on Social Stress Research, Paris, May 25-27, 1996.

Kieselbach, T. (Ed.) (1997a): *Jobloss, unemployment, and social injustices*. Social Justice Research, 10 (2).

Kieselbach, T. (1997b): Unemployment, victimization and perceived injustices: Future perspectives for coping with employment transition processes, 10 (2), 127-151.

Kieselbach, T., Scharf, G. & Klink, F. (1997): Interventionsmaßnahmen für Langzeitarbeitslose: Wiederbeschäftigungseffekte und psychosoziale Belastungsverringerung. In: H. Strasser & G. Klein (Eds.): *Schwer vermittelbar: Zur Theorie und Empirie der Langzeitarbeitslosigkeit*, 313-331. Opladen: Westdeutscher Verlag.

Klink, F., Waldmann, H. & Kieselbach, T. (1995): Interventionsmaßnahmen bei Arbeitslosen: Kurse nach § 41a AFG und `Job-Club'-Ansatz. In: T. Kieselbach & A. Wacker (Eds.): *Bewältigung von Arbeitslosigkeit im sozialen Kontext – Programme, Initiativen, Evaluationen* (Psychologie sozialer Ungleichheit, Vol. 2, 121-134). Weinheim: Deutscher Studien Verlag (2nd ed.).

Lavan, H., Mathys, N. & Drehmer, D. (1983): A look at the counseling practices of major U.S. corporations. *Personnel Administrator*, 28 (6), 76-81 & 143-146.

Lazarus, R.S. & Folkman, S. (1984): *Stress, appraisal, and coping*. New York: Springer.

Lerner, M.J. (1996): *Victims without harmdoers: Human casualties in the pursuit of corporate efficiency*. In: L. Montada & M.J. Lerner (Eds.): Current societal concerns about social justice, 155-170. New York: Plenum Press.

Leventhal, G.S. (1980): What should be done with equity theory? In: K. J. Gergen, M.S. Greenberg & R.H. Willis (Eds.): *Social exchange: Advances in theory and research*, 27-55. New York: Plenum.

Mayrhofer, W. (1987): Der gegenwärtige Stand der Outplacement-Diskussion. Darstellung, Beurteilung und Konsequenzen für die Forschung. *Zeitschrift für Personalforschung*, 1(2), 147-180.

Mayrhofer, W. (1989): Outplacement – Stand der Diskussion. *Die Betriebswirtschaft* (DBW), 49 (1), 55-68.

Monaco, D.A. (1983): Outplacement counseling: Business and profession. In: J.S.J. Manuso (Ed.): *Occupational clinical psychology*, 189-201. New York: Praeger.

Montada, L. (1994): Arbeitslosigkeit – ein Gerechtigkeitsproblem? In: L. Montada (Ed.): *Arbeitslosigkeit und soziale Gerechtigkeit*, 53-86. Frankfurt/M.: Campus.

Nicholson, N. & West, M. (1989): Transitions and the concepts of careers. In: M.B. Arthur, D.T.Hall & B.S. Lawrence (Eds.): *Handbook of career theory*, 181-201. London: Cambridge. Univ. Press.

Rifkin, J. (1995): *The end of work. The decline of the global labor force and the dawn of the post-market era*. New York: Putnam.

Schulz, D. & Schuppert, D. (1987): Outplacement - Trennen ohne Scherben. *Der Arbeitgeber*, 39 (20), 760-761.

Smith, M. (1993): Outplacement: Die menschliche Seite des Personalabbaus. *Zeitschrift für Arbeits- und Organisationspsychologie*, 37, 201-204.

Stoebe, F. (1993): *Outplacement: Manager zwischen Trennung und Neuanfang.*
    Frankfurt/M.: Campus.
Wortman, C. (1983): Coping with victimization: Conclusions and implications for
    future research. *Journal of Social Issues*, 39(2), 195-221.

PART IV

Reflections on Cross-Cultural Issues of Business Ethics

Reason and Cultures.
Life-world as the Common Ground of Ethics

Carl Friedrich Gethmann

In terms of grammar, the title of my lecture uses the word "Reason" in the singular and the word "Culture" in the plural. In this way something is already suggested which is indeed argued by the mainstream of the Western philosophy of Reason: namely, that we are faced by a contrast which is contradictory or at least composed of contraries. Accordingly, Reason (in the singular) is what all reasonable creatures have in common, one common ability to found the principles which are subject to all the perceptions and operations of the understanding. Cultures, by contrast, are variable and manifold, and because of their very plurality are unable to claim validity in themselves. In short, cultures are those ensembles whose validity claims must be tested and redeemed before the bench of singular Reason.

This project of Reason is especially precarious in the field of practical philosophy, which is to say in the field where factual directions regarding advisable or inadvisable actions are tested for their normative validity. For this is the point where the question cannot be avoided, from where the testing authorities themselves acquire their legitimisation. On this point tradition has provided a whole series of ideas regarding self and ultimate foundation; however, there is an equally long tradition which tries to demonstrate the cultural relativity of these very ideas.

Business ethics is a field where the dispute between – as we shall say, for the sake of brevity – universalism and contextualism is by no means merely an academic debate in the ivory tower, but is rather of considerable moral, economic and legal significance. Is there a universal morality which everyone can be fairly expected to observe and according to which also human rights can be insisted on, or are there

H. Lange et al., Working Across Cultures, 213–234.

different validity claims well founded depending on cultural tradition and religious belief, even though these may be incompatible in an extreme case so that we have to assume a pluralism which is ultimately impossible to overcome?

The eminently practical and political significance of this question becomes clear immediately when in the face of everyday political events the question of the right to intervene by crossing cultural boundaries is posed. What right do we have to enter into regional conflicts in order to make peace? What right do we have to sanction such 'long-standing traditional economic customs' as slavery, child labour, clearing land by fire etc.? This can only be legitimate – or so it seems – if we see ourselves as champions of the one-and-only Reason, which is binding in the same way for all persons. However, does this not mean that cultural history, and consequently economic history, is to be developed towards a one-and-only universal form of life, a one-and-only world culture and finally a one-and-only political union with one, and only one, government, as demanded by Immanuel Kant and his followers? Does this mean that the local and regional identities, the cultural contexts, the particularised economic styles are actually illegitimate conditions, which must be overcome in the name of humanity, perhaps with the healthy force of violent power? But doesn't this in its turn make it clear that acting in the name of Reason is merely a barely concealed form of terrorism, which one should oppose, like the philosophers of Postmodernism, in the name of the truly human colourful variety of forms of life?

I hope to demonstrate that this alternative is nothing more than a dummy controversy, a pseudo-problem. It is based, firstly, on the fact that the philosophy of Reason overlooks that it is actually and in any case only a plausible programme with regard to certain factual structures of the life-world. And, secondly, the contextualists overlook that it can be an immanent desideratum of particular identity to rise above the limits of the particular. Under certain conditions, Reason itself – at least as a desideratum – is a cultural fact. But this fact would perish if the culture perished. Consequently, as the later part of my lecture suggests, a common basis in the life-world is necessary for universal moral convictions to be founded. However, these can be realised in substantially different life-worlds. A uniform, universal form of life is by no means the maxim which results from the project of Reason.

1. The Western Project of Reason

To speak of a "Western project of Reason" is, of course, to make a rough generalisation, which might seem to be impermissibly superficial compared with the profound controversies, for example, between Plato and Aristotle, Leibniz and Locke or Husserl and Carnap. Like Husserl, however, I see something like a common "telos" in the development of Western philosophy and science, which passes through the modern syndrome of philosophy, enlightenment, science and humanism to lead, for the present, to the tasks involved in working on a theory of rationality in this century (Husserl 1954). These efforts and developments are especially in view as I emphasise the following features of the Western project of Reason:

1.1.   General discursivity

According to the principle of general discursivity it must be possible to redeem all validity claims in discourse; this applies both to cognitive validity claims (claims, substantiations, knowledge) and to directive ones (directions, justifications, actions). Here "actions" are to be understood both as POIESIS and as PRAXIS.

At this point, attention must be drawn to a translation difficulty. The English word "discourse" is derived from the Latin "discurrere", but today, as far as I can see, it has become a generalised word for any and every kind of linguistic interaction. In German philosophical terminology, "Diskurs" is still closely related to the Latin "discursus", which means "moving along a path step by step". Therefore, a "discursus" is a process, namely a process carried out in speech. You will remember that both Aristotle and Kant distinguish between discursive and intuitive cognition: a finite being must reach its insights by moving step by step from elementary to complex insights, as Aristotle makes clear with the example of the syllogism, while the infinite understanding recognises all truths "at a blow" (intuitus).

In the discursive debate about a validity claim typically there are two social roles to be distinguished: The role of those who make a validity claim and consequently have to redeem it (proponents), and the role of those who react to a validity claim with doubt or agreement (opponents). Now, the principle of discursivity asserts that there are principally no domains of life, whether these be domains of knowledge or of action, in which the right of opponents to doubt and the responsibility of proponents to substantiate or justify are removed a priori. Regarding ethics as a philosophical discipline, it must be pointed out above all that the principle of discursivity also covers forms of technical and practical knowledge and that, in this sense, it expresses the idea of the unity of theoretical and practical Reason.

Expressed negatively this means that validity claims are founded

- neither by the extraordinary state of the information provider (authoritative knowledge – such as revelation)
- nor by the extraordinary state of the material (elite knowledge – such as myth)
- nor by the extraordinary state of the process of acquiring knowledge (clandestine knowledge – such as oracles, mystical intuition)

but only by the *discursive process.*

1.2.   Universal discursive competence

In principle, everybody is able and entitled to take part in discourses about validity claims, either as a proponent or as an opponent. "Universality" means that whatever can be redeemed discursively applies in principle to every reasonable being (Kant: "Vernunftwesen").

It is clear that this interpretation leads to considerable practical and also emancipatory consequences, and these have indeed been sufficiently explicated by the classical philosophers of modernism. In constitutional societies the universality principle leads to a fundamental equality before the law and from a trans-cultural point of view to the idea of universal human rights. Expressed negatively, the universality principle is directed against privilege based on ancestry, religious belief, race, class, gender and so on with regard to the right or obligation to take over the role of opponent or proponent. Consequently – as Kant explicated in classical manner – political republicanism is in the tradition of universalism.

1.3.   Science and education

Competence deficits, which indeed exist to a dramatic extent, can be overcome through enlightenment and education. The historical movement of the Enlightenment, as is well known, had a decisive share in introducing universal compulsory schooling ("universal" includes girls and the children of lower social classes), in the sense of a universal educational task of the state. Here the process of education is determined neither by definite subject matter nor by short-term goals of effectiveness but is measured according to process and subjects against the ideal of generality and universality. The paradigm, the "fact of reason" ("Faktum der Vernunft": Kant) is science. Science is the aim and the subject matter of education – education is a preparation for science.

1.4.   The theory of rationality

In the twentieth century the concepts of Understanding and Reason have been replaced by the concept of Rationality. This process has liberated discussion of "Reason" from its psychological and metaphysical connotations, which still adhere to the concept, for example, in Kant. Rationality is the concept of the ability to invent processes for the discursive redemption of validity claims, to pursue them and to access them. If validity claims which have been processually redeemed are called "founded", then rationality can be concisely defined as the ability to produce well-foundedness.

"Rationality" has been a central philosophical concept only since Max Weber, who drew on the linguistic usage of "means-end-rationality" predominant in economics (Weber 1987). At the core of means-end-rationality is the strategically adroit choice of a means suited to an end; in this way the procedure of choice is shifted to the centre of interest. With this "proceduralising" of the concept of rationality an implicit ambiguity in the earlier conception of Reason is revealed: there rationality refers to an extraordinary (extra-sensory) human ability (substantial concept of rationality) and the human ability to access procedures for founding validity (procedural concept of rationality). The proceduralization of the concept of rationality is already to be found in the tendency of modern philosophy since

Descartes towards the methodology of philosophical and scientific substantiation of validity. However, because of its connection with psychological ideas and associated metaphysical and mentalistic interpretation models, modern philosophy remains more or less openly bound to the substantial concept of rationality. Under the influence of the discussion following on from Max Weber it has therefore become customary to distinguish the theory of rationality as a theory of validity-founding procedures from a "metaphysical" concept of Reason. In connection with the discussion which was initiated by Max Weber, a theory of (theoretical and practical) rationality – admittedly in a variety of forms – is seen by many twentieth century philosophers as the fundamental teaching of modern philosophy. With regard to the procedural concept of rationality, this kind of theory of rationality has succeeded to the modern philosophy of Reason, but the central elements of generality and universality have been preserved.

2. The Contextuality of Reason

The discussion about the contextuality, plurality and relativity of validity claims has accompanied the history of the Western rationality project and the process of enlightenment from the beginning. It exerted a productive urge towards the self-explication and differentiation of the standpoint of Reason and consequently to the self-limitation of exaggerated claims. Indeed, it is a matter of self-limitation of Reason itself when confronted with the cultural bonds of human beings in a context of life, a life-world. Being bound to a context has been illustrated mainly with the three bonds of the discourse to language, history and power, and these shall be briefly discussed here.

2.1.   Reason and language

Criticism of the idea of a uniform, universal rationality from the linguistic point of view had its origins with modern criticism of Kant's philosophy of Reason in Johann Georg Hamann (1967), Johann Gottfried Herder (1881) and Wilhelm von Humboldt (1848). W. v. Humboldt makes the point that language is not the work (ERGON) of some other capacity – namely Reason – but is in itself a world-constructing activity (ENERGEIA). Although Humboldt tries to demonstrate the communication of individuality and universality in the phenomenon of language, he became a forerunner of the kind of language relativism ("lingualism") which has been carried further, in particular, in the Sapir-Whorf hypothesis in the 20th century (Whorf 1956). The uniform constitution of the world (which was ascribed by Kant to a supra-individual Reason to be found in all human beings) is dissolved into a plurality of language-worlds.

Through the agency of W. Dilthey (1958), the line of tradition from Hamann through Herder to Humboldt has an influence on the debate – carried out mainly in the environment of phenomenological philosophy – about the possibility of pre-linguistic sensory experience. Taking up Husserl's anti-naturalism, M. Heidegger (1979) asserts that even so-called pre-predicative experience must be understood as linguistic activity. In this way Heidegger performs a linguistic turn against the empiricist's and Husserl's concept of the elementary perception by sensation. In the hermeneutic philosophy of H.-G. Gadamer Heidegger's linguistic turn is universalised into a linguistic ontology: "Being that can be understood is language" (Gadamer 1960, p.450).

Another attack on the idea of a context-invariant rationality begins with Ludwig Wittgenstein's pragmatic view of language in the "Philosophical Investigations". Wittgenstein (1967) begins with the language user, who carries out acts through speech in a social environment. There is no unambiguous division of the world outside the social context of action, and consequently the meaning of an expression cannot be explained by means of objective reference to corresponding single objects. For the social environment of language Wittgenstein introduces the term "language game", where the game metaphor is meant to emphasise the rule-bound character of language use.

2.2.   Reason and history

At the centre of the considerations of historical contextualization of rationality there is the individual human being interpreting himself as part of the historical context and therefore understanding this context. However this understanding does not simply occur contingently but asserts partial, context-bound validity claims.

Dilthey's essay at a "criticism of historical reason" (Dilthey 1957, p.116) does not begin with a transcendental subject as "consciousness as such" for the purpose of substantiating the binding nature of hermeneutic textual explication, but rather with a factual "universal human nature". This individual subjectivity is determined by a concept of experience which includes cognition, action and evaluation. In his philosophical hermeneutics, H.-G. Gadamer (1960) radicalised Dilthey's approach. The basis of all action, cognition and evaluation is a pre-reflective consciousness or understanding, so that every methodical cognition and every reflective consciousness can only be interpreted as a derivative of this direct understanding.

With regard to the validity of historical understanding, Michel Paul Foucault (1966) rejected the idea of rational, supra-historical criteria. Foucault's structuralism is characterised by the attempt to establish a panorama which is as precise as possible, a tableau of a time, in order to find an overall model which the individual internalises in his actions in such a way that his behaviour corresponds to this overall model, even though not consciously. From this point of view history and the actions of individual humans within it are not to be understood in narrative terms as a chain of consequences but as a constantly changing ensemble of elements whose configurations go to make up the explanatory "EPISTEME" of a time.

Similar tendencies to historicise rationality can be found in recent analytical philosophy. Beginning with Willard V. O. Quine's classical criticism of logical empiricism, Donald Davidson (1984) denies the assumption of a pre-theoretic relation between cognition and experience: instead of this, experience was always an interpretative construct of theoretical assumptions about the world. With this thesis Davidson comes close to Gadamer's hermeneutic philosophy. The world exists only as something previously understood, where "understanding" is not an improved understanding with the goal of perfect understanding, but is always merely another form of understanding. There is a great diversity of world interpretations bound only by a common horizon of history and tradition. In a similar way Richard Rorty (1989) strives for a post-metaphysical philosophy, which is to say a philosophy that deals with the radical contingency of all beginnings, positions, needs, actions and norms, or, in general, with the contingency of culture and language.

Historical contextualization is also the tenor of the discussion about the relationship of rationality and science which has been conducted following on from Thomas S. Kuhn's (1962) conception of the history of science. According to Kuhn the science's claim that it follows clear criteria of rationality cannot be proven by historically examining the process of the construction of knowledge. According to Kuhn a scientific period is to be understood in a similar manner to a period of art history. There is a quite obvious unity, but this unity cannot be reduced to a set of canonical rules. In his studies in the history of science Paul Karl Feyerabend (1975) tries to demonstrate that the criteria of rationality are not only very often breached both by scientific discoveries and by their explanatory justifications, but also that rationality criteria had to be breached in the interests of scientific progress. A similar contextualization of scientific rationality as in Kuhn and Feyerabend has been taken up by Stephen Toulmin (1972) by calling on categories of evolutionary theory. According to Toulmin's historical investigations, the idea of a methodology based solely on deduction and provability – except in a few areas such as Euclidean geometry and Cartesian physics – has always been inapplicable and virtually meaningless.

2.3.   Reason and power

The analysis of the way ideas of rationality are imbedded in human power relationships can be traced back to the examination of class consciousness by Karl Marx and Friedrich Engels (1958). For Marx and Engels the historical-practical version of rationality is characterised by a dual historicisation: on the one hand the concept of rationality is subject to natural historicisation in the sense of the temporal-processual modification of all forms of being and thought. On the other hand, what is accounted rationality is determined by a form of historicisation, in the sense of the modifications of the historical-social "substance of thought". The historicisation of rationality arises, in a co-evolutionary manner, from the evolution of the relationship between the subject and the natural world around it by the agency of the means of production. The form of rationality predominant at a given time is in both a descriptive and a prescriptive sense the basis of society's production conditions. Building on the approach of Marx and

Engels and taking up Weber's analysis of the process of rationalisation, Max Horkheimer and Theodor W. Adorno, in their "Dialectic
of the Enlightenment" (Horkheimer/Adorno 1947), emphasised a
tendency towards the power-related character of the Western concepts
of rationality.

In a similar way Jean-François Lyotard (1979) asserted the claim
of Western concepts of rationality to totality and interpreted these in
the categories of power and rule. The Western rationality programmes
are directed toward the form of an all-determining unity, which is
founded by recurring to all-embracing meta-stories. Postmodernism,
on the other hand, is characterised by making this "thought of totality"
invalid both in its subject-matter and in its form. The end of the one
meta-story makes room for a diversity, which is valued as a positive, a
diversity of limited and heterogeneous linguistic games. Rationality
and consensus (as a condition but not as a goal) exist only within the
linguistic games. For the philosophy of Postmodernism the plurality of
rationality forms is not to be interpreted as a process of separating out
various types of rationality; rather, they represent various rationality
paradigms which can no longer be traced back to a basic meaning.

3. Retorsion and Life-world

The philosophy of Reason raises one general objection to all the vari-
ants of contextualism, only a few of which could be mentioned here.
Rationality itself is a condition of possibility for speaking in a binding
manner of language, history and power. That such binding speech is
possible is a claim raised by anyone who explicates the contextuality
of speech and action and especially by anyone who criticises these
with the aim of changing actual conditions of life.

This should now be explained on the basis of recent discussions
relating to the linguistic relativity of Reason. While for Wittgenstein
the regulation of language use is always related to the context of the
linguistic game, a number of philosophers have tried to demonstrate
that the validity claim of the rules tendentially or manifestly transcends the linguistic game, thereby opening up a possibility for a
theory of rationality as part of the linguistic turn. In doing so we call in
every respect on John L. Austin's concept of speech acts (Austin
1962). In his book "Speech Acts", J. R. Searle (1969) brought out

speech acts as the basic analytical units of communication, so that mastering language ultimately consists of mastering speech acts. The semantic structure of language relies on classes of rules which form the valid conventions in a given linguistic community regarding the performance and understanding of speech acts. With this pragmatic turn there is a convergence of the analytical view of language that goes back to Gottlob Frege and the traditional view that leads to hermeneutic philosophy. Historicity and contextuality achieve a non-eliminable significance for the conception of linguistically realised rationality; at the same time the pragmatic approach makes it possible to grasp with greater clarity the basic concerns of the traditional philosophy of Reason and to combine them with the insights of analytical linguistic philosophy. In addition to the conceptions of a transcendental or universal pragmatism in Jürgen Habermas (1981) and Karl-Otto Apel (1973), above all the philosophy of Erlangen constructivism by distinguishing between speech and language (following Ferdinand de Saussure) conceived of a philosophy of rationality after the turn from consciousness to language (Lorenz/Mittelstraß 1967).

With regard to the historical relativity of Reason a number of philosophers have tried to give the idea of scientific reason a new function. For reflection on science following on from the works of Kuhn, Feyerabend and Toulmin, the task becomes not to assume the rationality structures of the sciences unquestioningly but rather to explain the possibility of their reconstruction methodically. If one is interested in a rational scientific praxis, which is to say, if one is not willing to accept that the sciences evolve like a natural growth and that their usefulness eventuates by chance, it is not possible to be satisfied with a reflection on science which, on the one hand, describes cognitive structures using a highly instrumental logic in its approach and, on the other hand, analyses science as part of a social system, without asking about the specific substantiations of the cognitive performances of this very part-system. The dichotomy of cognitive and social points of view is to be eliminated by employing the scientific communities as the analytical units in relation to whose system of argumentation and interaction the problematic structure of rationality is to be evolved. Actions of substantiation and justification in the social context are precisely the place where the points of view of cognitive validity and social acceptance come together. What is to be accepted as true or false, however, cannot be formulated independently of the rules of acceptance and rejection inside a scientific community. These rules represent a presupposition of rationality which is assumed before the creation of scientific theories by those who are willing to take part in discourses (Gethmann 1981).

With regard to the power relativity of Reason, Jürgen Habermas and others have insisted that in the interests of criticising conditions of power one must acknowledge at least a starting point for power-free rationality. Without the utopia of an ideal communication situation there is no alternative plan for tracing real power relationships by contrast, and overcoming them.

These ways of arguing have one basic structure: retorsion (from the Latin retorquere, to reverse weapons or to turn the tables). In criminal law the term retorsion is used for immediate retaliation against a libel or a physical injury by means of a commensurate libel or physical injury. In international law it refers to a response to a hostile action by one state with a commensurate action by the other. In recent years there has been a controversy about the structure of force in this pattern of retorsive argumentation. The positions taken up range from a declaration of unfitness to the force of ultimate foundation by this argumentation. Consequently we must briefly consider the analytical structure of retorsive arguments.

At its core the argumentation consists of using against a proponent the conditions of his own claim or direction. In the modern analysis of arguments a number of names are current for schemata of this kind: anti-sceptic arguments (George E. Moore and others 1939), self-refuting arguments (John L. Mackie 1964), transcendental arguments (Peter F. Strawson 1960), self-referential arguments (Frederic B. Fitch 1946). One must assume that these names are not of equal extension but rather one must note family resemblance (Eike von Savigny 1981). Loci classici of various retorsive arguments are some passages in Aristotle's Metaphysics (Book Gamma), such as the defence of the laws of non-contradiction and of the excluded middle.

The significance of retorsive argumentation is seen by some philosophers above all in its suitability for constructing philosophical knowledge. In contrast to this ascription of significance there is the deficit in explicitness with regard to the characterisation of retorsion.

Admittedly there is agreement with regard to some classic argumenta-
tions already brought forward that they are retorsive arguments, but
there are hardly any attempts to work out a scheme of argumentation
within a theory of argumentation and to distinguish it from other
schemes such as tu-quoque arguments, ad-hominem arguments and so
on. A reconstructive suggestion of analytical origins based on an Aristotelian example (someone who declares that everything is false must
also declare that his own claim is false (Metaphysics, Book Gamma,
Chapter 8), which is generally accepted as a retorsive and convincing
argument has been put forward by Jan Lukasiewicz, Mackie and
others. Characteristic of these logically perfectly correct reconstructions is the derivation of a contradiction in the propositional part by
replacing the variable with the proposition in question in the universally quantified original proposition and drawing on a material statement concerning truth.

Formal reconstructions of this kind, however, do not make the
pragmatic point intended by this type of argumentation: the intention
is not only to show that a certain assumption leads to a contradiction
but that someone who makes a certain assumption is committed to
admitting something else that is incompatible with the assumption and
should therefore give up the initial assumption. Explicit reconstructions of retorsive types of argumentation should therefore – like argu-
mentations in general – be reconstructed as sequences of speech acts
between performers of speech acts (proponents and opponents), not as
a series of propositions. On the basis of this pattern of reconstruction
the following elements must be especially emphasised:

(a) For retorsive arguments it is characteristic that the propositional
part of the initial assumption contains a predicate which can be
applied to linguistic entities and which qualifies this assumption itself
(e.g. " ... is false"). The claim that "all propositions are short" by contrast is not contradicted by the application of the predicate "is short" to
the claim. The question of which predicators are to be applied to
linguistic structures of what type is however a matter of controversy
regarding the problems of the truth-bearer.

(b) Initial assumptions of retorsive arguments cannot be only con-
stative speech acts. For a number of other types of speech acts
analogical arguments can be constructed (such as "I promise not to

enter into obligations to anyone"; "I prognosticate that prognostica-
tions will never be possible").

(c) Self-referentiality as such is a clear-cut but non-specific feature
of retorsion. Self-references can be found, for example, even in tu-
quoque arguments without being retorsive. Tu-quoque arguments are
self-referential in such a way that the propositional content refers to
the performer of a speech act and not to the speech act itself or any of
its constitutive parts. The self-reference of retorsive arguments therefore consists specifically in the reference of the propositional content
to the qualification of the speech act performed by the utterance.

(d) For retorsion a certain form of incompatibility between the
propositional content of the initial assumption and its speech-act-
specific conditions of success is characteristic. Two acts are said to be
incompatible if it is not possible to carry them out simultaneously with
regard to the realisation of a purpose. As examples at least two types
of incompatibility can be distinguished:

   – A contradiction occurs when someone claims that p and he
   claims that not-p. The two claims are incompatible because they
   offer the opponent no clear possibility for action (agreement,
   disagreement, doubt).
   – A pragmatic inconsistency (inconcinnitas) arises, for example,
   when someone claims that not-p, although p is a presupposition for
   the successful performance of a claim. In this case there is an
   incompatibility which is to be avoided relative to the aims of reliability and comprehensibility pursued with human speech.

The emphasised features of retorsion document the fact that the
argumentative force of a retorsive argumentation depends on what
proponent and opponent regard as a presupposition of a speech act.
The possibility of explicating the conditions of success of speech acts
in different ways shows that a sceptic could always object that he does
not share certain assumptions with regard to the conditions of success,
or even that he does not share the aims of linguistic communication in
general. On the other hand, if the pragmatic presuppositions are shared
within a culture of argumentation, retorsive arguments are definitely
suitable for founding knowledge and action. Retorsions secure the
bases of a language-game or of a "life-world", but they are not suitable
for a life-world-invariable and in this sense for "absolute" ultimate
foundation.

4. Reason and Centrality

An elementary chapter of the theory of rationality is concerned with the question of who, in general and in principle, can be trusted and permitted to possess the capacities of rationality. The answer that seems natural in terms of life-world, namely "the human being" proves to be inadequate for several reasons. In the first place it is not clear how the concept "human being" should be defined extensionally. Often there is an implication that a zoological term is being employed, and, according to this, human individuals could be the exemplars of the species homo sapiens. In addition to the difficulty that in this way a zoological term becomes the basis of the theory of rationality (with the associated dangers of circular argumentation), this definition strategy amounts to a form of speciesism, as Peter Singer (1979) has pointed out, especially in connection with questions of applied ethics (see also Gethmann 1997). Further difficult problems of extensional application arise. Empirically it does not seem very credible, prima facie, to grant rationality, for example, to human foetuses or extremely intellectually handicapped individuals but on the other hand to deny rationality to higher non-human species.

The modern debate (especially in rationalism, Kant and German idealism) has, in the first instance, avoided an empirical definition and has related the question of the possessor of rational capacities to the ego-subject of (theoretical and practical) judgement. At the same time it was left open whether there are beings apart from human ones (such as God, pure spirits, animals) who can also be granted to possess reason or whether some humans cannot be said to possess it.

Within a theory of rationality after the linguistic turn the problem of the carrier of rationality must be separated from the psychological connotations of modern philosophy. The performance of discursive speech acts presupposes that the performer identifies himself as the originator of the act. A distinction must be made between this self-image of the performer and the description of the act to an actor by somebody else. The performer cannot align himself totally to the perspective of the other's description because he remains the originator of the act of description at the highest level in each case. The originator of the act is therefore the centre of his performance space, even if he apparently moves to the periphery in order to observe the centre. This is why it is natural to call this feature of the performer "centrality"[1]. Consequently the capacity of rationality is to be granted to all beings that possess the performance structure of centrality, because at most these are possible originators of discursive acts. "Centrality" is the concept which replaces "subjectivity", or "personality" within a theory of rationality after the linguistic turn.

A being with the structural feature of centrality is one that can perform or not perform an action. Such a being has therefore the capacity to act with pragmatic consistence. To perform an action a minimum persistence in time is required, because the performance of an action always takes a certain amount of time. A being which lacks persistence to such a degree that it moves out of the action's context before any thinkable action is completed cannot achieve centrality. A being of the structural type of centrality must be in a position to repeat actions or to take up incomplete actions again and, in this sense, to insist on actions (insistence). The originator of an action can therefore only be said to have centrality if he is able to reveal at least a minimum of pragmatic consistence, persistence and insistence.

The presuppositions of discursive construction of opinions and intentions include, in fact, the acceptance of the capacity for possible participation in discourse. This presupposition is not convincingly fulfilled by viewing simply the exemplars of the species homo sapiens as those beings to whom capacity for discourse can be ascribed. However, in the sense of ethical universalism it is possible to demand that precisely those beings which have centrality are to be recognised as having the capacity for discourse. It is a non-trivial, theoretical and practical task to define precisely the extension of the concept of centrality in empirical terms. However, the questions associated with this cannot be pursued in the present context.

---

[1]   It seems worth mentioning that the way I use the central-peripheral metaphor is rather opposite to Quine's in his "Two Dogmas of Empiricism". Quine argues against the analytic-synthetic dichotomy in favour of the holistic view that all statements are positioned more or less central in the same epistemic net – that is to say, are in principle of the same kind. My point is, by contrast, that there is a radical difference between the perspectives mentioned.

5. Global Game and Universal Form of Life

"Globalisation" is a much-used catchword these days. What it means in the first instance is that the partners of economic interaction, enemies and friends, are to be found increasingly all over the globe. Regions are losing their importance as economic units, among other reasons but above all because distance in space offers less and less protection from competition – at most in the form of admittedly variable transport costs. The economic effects, such as the growing intensity of competition, are perfectly clear and can, so to speak, be experienced by everyone.

From the point of view of ethics, this development is interesting, because it raises the question whether the process of economic globalisation could be the vehicle which could help to establish ethical universalism. What has not been achieved by the powers of argumentation to convince – consider Kant's plea for a world civilisation and a world government as well as the many experiments in this century from the idea of a League of Nations to the huge UNO conferences – namely, the establishment of world-wide domestic politics ("Weltinnenpolitik"), could, perhaps, be realised by the laws of economic activities. Exchange with everyone who has a human face, for example as a contractual partner, could be imagined as a practical philosophical basis for a universalistic form of mutual acceptance. It would signify the end of any discrimination based on marginal differences (according to group membership, religious belief, class, gender and so on).

Such a process would also be highly significant for business ethics because it would result in an international alignment of moral ideas in business units and the gradual disappearance of the customary cultural differences. A fundamental problem of business ethics, namely the problem of competitive disadvantage because of the observance of moral standards, could at least gradually disappear at international level. Is ethical universalism cutting a path for itself in business ethics through globalisation?

Whether economic globalisation is a catalyst promoting ethical universalism and consequently practical reason must nonetheless be doubted. This doubt is given support when one asks whether the most important expression of practical reason and consequently its most important indicator, the recognition and observance of universal human rights, is increasing in weight and significance during the process of globalisation. Looking at day-to-day political events one will not be able to assert that this is the case. Rather, from an ethical point of view, there seems to be a kind of counter-movement to globalisation: a cultural and political regionalisation. It seems that regional identities are gaining significance in the same proportion as, on an economic and political level, the dynamic forces driving towards globalisation are gaining strength.

This phenomenon must give rise to the question of whether globalisation really represents an increasing power of conviction for ethical universalism. Speaking abstractly, this would mean that the conceptual differences between ethical universalism and particularism coincide precisely with those between cultural internationalism and regionalism. Clearly, however, these differences are at odds with each other. The universalist conviction that every actor of the structural type of centrality is to be respected as a moral subject can well be reconciled with the factual embodiment of cultural life in a regional context. Conversely, a world wide cultural exchange in certain dimensions of action, such as business, can easily be compatible with particularist convictions. The fact that I maintain business relationships with a human being of a different cultural identity, taking him seriously as a partner or a competitor, clearly does not imply that I accept him as a person in the sense of a moral subject. Rather, the loosening of the bonds that hinder me within my own group from exploiting my partner to the limit might be the very reason for me to take them into account no longer in global relationships. That this is indeed the case can be seen in our Western attitudes to phenomena in the Third World such as child labour or totally inadequate labour laws – phenomena which we strongly disapprove of in our own parish.

The process of globalisation not only brings no automatic support for ethical universalism, it even seems that the reverse phenomena of cultural regionalisation and differentiation support ethical particularism. Many phenomena, such as the regional conflicts, which are increasing in number and militancy, because of religious and other cultural diversity, or the increase in sects of a fundamentalist kind inside Western civilisation, which are determined to do anything to push through their convictions, cause one to fear not only that the dynamics of globalisation do not promote universalism but even that the dialectical counter-movement of regionalisation, on the contrary, strengthens ethical particularism. This movement, by the way, intrudes into philosophy as the agent of practical reason: the post-modern scepticism about the capacity of human beings to justify and establish universalistic principles takes the form of a reminder of differences and "small identities".

The actual cultural dynamics, and post-modern philosophy as a reflex to them, give rise to the question of whether the ideas of Kant and his followers regarding a universal form of life are realistic. Even more important, however, is the question of whether it is even convincing and whether it should be accepted as a vision directing one towards action. Does it definitely follow from ethical universalism that it can only manifest itself in a universal form of life? In what follows the intention is to argue in favour of the idea of separating ethical universalism from the culture-theoretical idea of a uniform world culture. For ethical universalism it is enough to secure some central values such as human dignity as norms. Apart from that, cultural diversity in all conceivable variations can be accepted. This does not exclude the idea of a world culture or a world society; it may be left to other than ethical considerations to decide whether that is even desirable.

Since Socrates it has been one of the tasks of philosophy not only to reconstruct the rules for the creation of universal opinions and intentions and to explicate the presuppositions of corresponding discourses, but also to conceive a form of life in which the rules of the universal creation of opinions and intentions are at the same time the rules of human communication and co-operation. According to this programme, universality is not only a feature of certain discourses, nor a disposition of certain human beings, but the basis of a form of life. This universalism confronts particularism, according to which the basic rules for living together are specific to the group in each case. With Max Weber's analysis of rationalisation as a basic model for constructing Western societies, the suspicion has been supported that universality as a form of life could itself be a (sophisticated) form of particularism. Beginning with Max Weber, therefore, universality has become a topic for cultural anthropology. The programme of universality as a form of life is suspected of European ethnocentrism in this connection, and a demand arises for relativizing the universality claim.

For the universality claim of the one reason as opposed to the pluralistic conceptions of rationality it has to be conceded that the cultural life-worlds are pervaded by local and particular orientations of activity which possess a considerable capacity for achievement. Against this background rules of universal reason are only justified if they are granted functions not achieved by these particular rules.

These functions, however, make themselves felt under the conditions of conflict. Local and situation-oriented potentials for solving conflicts do not in fact guarantee that they will be sufficient for all conditions relevant to the reality of the action. Life-world potentials for solving conflicts are fundamentally subject to disturbance without regard for their limited capacity for achievement, because, as a result of the local orientation they are ambiguous, irregular and related to a limited area. Many tasks can be carried out in many ways which are often not compatible with each other; many tasks have never been required before; many solutions to problems depend on substantial premises which are no longer shared by participants in new situations. The life-world routine of peacableness is not reliable, in spite of its relatively high potential for achievement, and it is not an instrument which is always available for removing or avoiding conflicts. If the disturbances to life-world potentials for conflict solutions are sufficiently large their capacity for achievement is correspondingly small. Consequently the search for universal rules is a dynamic force contained within the tendency to life-world conflict management.

Therefore it is admittedly a non-plausible idealisation if one wants to define the rational form of life, but universality is more or less a utopian horizon which acts as the point of orientation for sketching all particular validity claims. Universal validity claims have a place in every life, which means that their functions are rooted in situative problems of human communication and co-operation. Consequently the need for universality, understood as the capacity to redeem validity claims discoursively, is a fact of the life-world. Reason is a fact in every culture, at least as a need and a claim – if that were not the case, it would have no chance at all.

References

Apel, K.-O. (1973): *Transformation der Philosophie* (2 vols.), Frankfurt (Main) 1973 (partial tr.: *Towards a Transformation of Philosophy*, London 1980).

Austin, J.L. (1962): *How to do Things with Words*, Oxford.

Davidson, D. (1984): *Inquiries into Truth and Interpretation*, Oxford.

Dilthey, W. (1958): *Der Aufbau der geschichtlichen Welt in den Geisteswissenschaften* (Gesammelte Schriften VII), Stuttgart/Göttingen (partial tr.: *Pattern and Meaning in History*. Thoughts on History and Society, London 1961).

Dilthey, W. (1957): *Einleitung in die Geisteswissenschaften*. Versuch einer Grundlegung für das Studium der Gesellschaft und der Geschichte. Erster Band (Gesammelte Schriften I), Stuttgart/Göttingen (tr.: *Introduction to the Human Sciences*. Detroit 1988).

Feyerabend, P.K. (1975): *Against Method*. Outline of an Anarchistic Theory of Knowledge, London 1975, rev. 1988.

Fitch, F.B. (1946): "Self-Reference in Philosophy", in: *Mind* 55, pp. 64-73.

Foucault, M. (1966): *Les mots et les choses*. Une archéologie des sciences humaines, Paris (tr.: *The Order of Things*. New York 1970).

Gadamer, H.-G. (1960): *Wahrheit und Methode*. Grundzüge einer philosophischen Hermeneutik, Tübingen [1]1960, [6]1990 (tr.: *Truth and Method*, London 1975).

Gethmann, C.F. (1997): "Praktische Subjektivität und Spezies", in: W. Hogrebe (ed.): *Subjektivität*, Paderborn (forthcoming).

Gethmann, C.F. (1981): "Wissenschaftsforschung? Zur philosophischen Kritik der nachkuhnschen Reflexionswissenschaften", in: P. Janich (ed.): *Wissenschaftstheorie und Wissenschaftsforschung*, Munich, S. 9-38.

Habermas, J. (1981): *Theorie des kommunikativen Handelns* (2 vols.), Frankfurt (Main) (tr.: *The Theory of Communicative Action*, Boston 1984 and 1989).

Hamann, J. G. (1967): *Schriften zur Sprache*, ed. J. Simon, Frankfurt (Main).

Heidegger, M. (1979): *Sein und Zeit*, Tübingen [15]1979, [1]1927 (tr.: *Being and Time*, Oxford 1962).

Herder, J. G. (1881): *Verstand und Erfahrung*. Eine Metakritik zur Kritik der reinen Vernunft. Erster Teil (Sämtliche Werke XXI), Berlin.

Horkheimer, M./Adorno, Th. W. (1947): *Dialektik der Aufklärung*. Philosophische Fragmente. Amsterdam (tr.: *Dialectic of the Enlightenment*, New York 1972).

Humboldt, W. v. (1848): *Über die Verschiedenheit des menschlichen Sprachbaues und ihren Einfluß auf die geistige Entwickelung des Menschengeschlechts* (Gesammelte Werke VI), Berlin (tr.: *On Language*. The Diversity of Human Language-Structure and its Influence on the Mental Development of Mankind, Cambridge 1988).

Husserl, E. (1954): *Die Krisis der europäischen Wissenschaften und die transzendentale Phänomenologie. Eine Einleitung in die phänomenologische Philosophie*, The Hague (tr.: *The Crisis of European Sciences and Transcendental Phenomenology*. An Introduction to Phenomenological Philosophy, Chicago 1962 (rev. 1970).

Kuhn, Th. S. (1962): *The Structure of Scientific Revolutions*, Chicago (rev. 1970).

Lorenz, K./Mittelstraß, J. (1967): "Die Hintergehbarkeit der Sprache", in: *Kant-Studien* 58, pp. 187-208.

Lyotard, J.-F. (1979): *La condition postmoderne*. Rapport sur le savoir, Paris (tr.: *The Postmodern Condition*. A Report on Knowledge, Minneapolis 1983).

Mackie, J. L. (1964): "Self-Refutation. A Formal Analysis", in: *Philosophical Quarterly* 14, pp. 193-203.

Marx, K./Engels, F. (1958): *Die deutsche Ideologie*. Kritik der neuesten deutschen Philosophie in ihren Repräsentanten Feuerbach, B. Bauer und Stirner, und des deutschen Sozialismus in seinen verschiedenen Propheten (Werke III), Berlin 1958 (tr.: *The German Ideology*, New York 1933).

Mittelstraß, J. (1974): "Prolegomena zu einer konstruktiven Theorie der Wissenschaftsgeschichte", in: J. Mittelstraß: *Die Möglichkeit von Wissenschaft*, Frankfurt (Main), S. 106-144, S. 234-244.

Moore, G. E. (1939): "Proof of an External World", in: *Proceedings of the British Academy* 25, pp. 273-300.

Rorty, R. (1989): *Contingency, Irony and Solidarity*, Cambridge etc.

Savigny, E. v. (1981): "Das sogenannte 'Paradigm-Case-Argument'. Eine Familie von anti-skeptischen Argumentationsstrategien", in: *Grazer philosophische Studien* 14, S. 37-72.

Searle, J. R. (1969): *Speech Acts*. An Essay in the Philosophy of Language, London/ Cambridge.

Singer, P. (1979): *Practical Ethics*, Cambridge (2nd ed. 1993).

Strawson, P. F. (1960): *The Bounds of Sense*. An Essay on Kant's Critique of Pure Reason, London.

Toulmin, S. (1972): *Human Understanding*. The Collective Use and Evolution of Concepts, Princeton/Oxford.

Weber, M. (1987): "Soziologische Grundbegriffe", in: *Gesammelte Aufsätze zur Wissenschaftslehre*, ed. J. Winckelmann, Tübingen, S. 541-581.

Whorf, B. L. (1956): *Language, Thought, and Reality*. Selected Writings, Cambridge (Mass.).

Wittgenstein, L. (1967): *Philosophische Untersuchungen*, Frankfurt (tr.: *Philosophical Investigations*, Oxford 1953).

Business Ethics in Three European Countries: A Comparative Approach

Fred Seidel, Hans-Jörg Schlierer & Ian Tovey

A number of academics have already tried to compare the approach to business ethics in different countries. Amongst others, we might refer to D. Vogel (1992) who while insisting on the "distinct" nature of business ethics in America sought to "identify" an ethics gap between this country and the rest of the world. More recently, G. Enderle (1996) has set about a comparison of the theory and practice of business ethics in North America and (continental) Europe. Meticulously eschewing any kind of value judgement regarding the moral quality of business life in these different parts of the world, he thus avoids the very trap that Vogel fell into, i.e. that of raising the American model to a universal norm. Enderle demonstrates that many differences exist in the meaning of business ethics and not just in its theory and practice. Nevertheless, we are obliged to recognise that serious problems arise when comparing the United States with Europe: whereas the former remain relatively homogenous on a political, economic and socio-cultural level, the extreme diversity of Europe is a phenomenon whose importance can hardly be overstated.

First of all, there is always a danger that an analysis of Europe will be limited to a part of Europe only and that those regions most familiar to the author or those which have already been treated in a descriptive or theoretical work will serve as the empirical basis for a "European approach" to ethics. In the article published by Enderle, the vision of Europe is heavily coloured by his familiarity with the Germanic countries in Europe, and the author himself quite frankly acknowledges that the picture he paints is "strongly influenced and limited by the author's personal experience and knowledge of subjects and languages" (Enderle 1996, p.36).

The desire to eschew value judgements that are rooted in the specific values of national culture leads one to search for criteria

235

H. Lange et al., Working Across Cultures, 235–261.
© 1998 *Kluwer Academic Publishers. Printed in the Netherlands.*

which make it possible to measure the supposedly existing differences in an objective manner. The influence of culture, however, is just as prevalent in the choice of such criteria as it is in judgements which are openly founded on the values and norms of a given society. Avoiding any such cultural influence would inevitably entail making do with a set of formal criteria with only a tenuous link to empirical reality. Two examples of the criteria identified by Enderle will suffice to illustrate this second type of difficulty which is inherent in any comparative approach.

Enderle proposes three distinct levels of analysis within the theoretical and practical field of business ethics. The "micro"-level designates the individual person, the "meso"-level corresponds to companies and all business organisations, whereas the "macro"-level refers to the economic system of a country as a whole. Such a distinction can be helpful when applied to prospective or theoretical fields of action; it becomes problematical when, as in this article (Enderle 1996, p.34), it is applied to real-life actors within the system. The actions or decisions of an employer or a consumer are, of course, analysed as belonging to the "micro"-level. This nevertheless seems to neglect the fact that such individuals, far from being totally distinct entities, also belong to social categories which act and react within the constraints and objectives of a "meso"- (the company) or "macro"-level.

Enderle then puts forward three aspects of business ethics that are designed to characterise the specific approach of a given country: the semantics of business ethics (i.e. speaking about business ethics), the practice (acting ethically in business), and lastly, the theory (thinking about ethics). He goes on essentially to analyse any intercultural differences that may emerge from the point of view of semantics: "talk about morality and business is deeply culture-bound and language dependent" (ibid., p.36).

This, of course, can give the impression that the other two aspects, practice and theory, are much less influenced by these differences. Yet, the theoretical output that exists in the field of business ethics inevitably bears the seal of the institutional structure and academic traditions in which it has evolved. The pragmatic qualities of the American approach effectively owe as much to the management style and objectives of most American business schools as the highly theoretical approach of the Germans does to the academic and scientific (*wissenschaftlich*) demands intrinsic to *Betriebswirtschaftslehre* as it is fostered in German Universities.

Our opinion is that such "universal" criteria as those previously mentioned can be useful in revealing or briefly describing cultural differences within the field of business ethics. They are, however totally unsuited to any attempt to explain such differences. This is due, above all, to their purely formal and timeless quality. And yet, any comparative approach to business ethics cannot afford to neglect two established facts that are clearly empirical in their nature.

For the last twenty years now, companies in most industrialised countries have been implicated in affairs and corruption scandals that have shaken public opinion and of which we need no reminding here. The impression given is that the crisis we are witnessing has indeed become generalised. Whether it in fact results from a dramatic decline in moral standards throughout the industrialised world or whether it simply reflects a change in public opinion and a refusal to countenance practices that were once accepted is of little significance when we consider the actual extent of the problem. The swiftness with which "business ethics" has established itself within universities and the extent to which it now pervades public discourse in the majority of European countries is ample testimony to the fact that the problems it deals with are indeed "universal".

At the same time, however, we have to acknowledge that, even if such scandals are shooting up "all over the place", they do not necessarily take on the same forms or involve the same actors. In France and Italy, a large number of politicians are heavily involved in scandals that predominantly concern companies; such a phenomenon does not seem to be so common in Germany. On the other hand, and this was clearly demonstrated by the recent boycott of SHELL, the issues that are most likely to mobilise a sizeable proportion of the population in Germany are ecological ones, whereas, in France, environmental protests are very few and far between.

The difficulty of analysing this ethical issue scientifically comes from the very duality of the situation: on the one hand, an all-pervading crisis which, sooner or later, affects more or less all the countries within the old industrialised world, and on the other, the distinctly culture-bound features with which it expresses itself in different countries. In such a debate, of course, the defendants of the systemic approach will home in on the structural similarities while overlooking specific national characteristics, whereas the champions of cultural distinctiveness will emphasise the persistence of national differences while continuing to relativise the significance of a global evolution. What this seems to show is that real comparative analysis is frequently avoided, most probably because it obliges the academic to accept the above-mentioned ambivalence.

In this article, we shall attempt to lay the foundations for a comparative analysis of three leading European nations, each with its own unmistakable specific characteristics as far as the practice of business ethics is concerned.[1] Our aim is to carry out an assessment of the particular responses that are prevalent in Western societies and economies. Our method consists in analysing three different levels of discourse, which reveal the different causes a society puts forward as an explanation of "its" ethics crisis as well as the solutions it produces.

The three levels of discourse are as follows: the discourse of "public opinion" in as much as it expresses itself through the media, company discourse both in its internal and external communication, and, last but not least, the conceptual discourse as produced by those academics specialising in this area. We shall attempt to understand these different levels of discourse within the cultural context and recent evolution of each country.

Such a complete "recontextualisation" of the ethics discourse in the three countries under study would normally require a detailed analysis of a whole series of significant cases of ethical conflict. It is clear that an analysis of such scope cannot be carried out within the confines of this article. Consequently, in assessing each country, we shall limit ourselves to a brief description of the events that have triggered public debate and an account of the predominant positions and, in some cases, the measures that have been adopted by public authorities, professional associations and companies themselves.

---

[1] This diversity between countries comes out even more clearly when an attempt is made to define the specific characteristics of a European management model (as opposed to the American or Japanese models). See in particular: Calori, R./ De Woots, Ph. (eds.): A European Management Model, London 1994.

1. Companies in the Dock

In 1995, a number of corruption scandals came to the fore leading to charges against a good many companies, first in France and then in Germany. The situation in Great Britain seems to have been slightly different. The apparent lack of such scandals has allowed *The Economist* to be particularly severe in its judgement of France. In respect of the plethora of indictments against a whole horde of political and business leaders, it considers that France is presently going through a particularly severe crisis "even by Italian or Japanese standards" (January 6th 1996, p.24). That any Japanese, Italian or French nationals might be shocked at such an exhibition of a superior moral sentiment will probably surprise nobody but the (anonymous) author of the article. However, it is enough to stand back from the hubbub of current events in order to ascertain that Great Britain, like France and, more recently, Germany, has had its fair share of ethical strife in the business world.

We will not concern ourselves here with the number of corruption scandals that have emerged in each country, nor with the extent or gravity of the ethical crisis that has supposedly encouraged those practices that have now come under scrutiny. Such criteria may provide the basis for a value judgement but they are hardly relevant in the context of a comparative study.

An analysis of public opinion, on the other hand, may allow us to develop a list of criteria that can be used to account for the "moral state" of the nation and the extent of its moral collapse. This will also help us to bring to light the behavioural norms that, by general consent, should rule all business activity as well as the limits which are considered desirable in controlling the business sector.

Lastly, this should also enable us to detect traces of a conflict between traditional norms of behaviour and more recent ones. In short, we wish to take stock of the ethical situation of business and of public life as they are "produced" by each country out of its political, social and economic culture.

1.1.   France: "Big Bosses" pursued by the "good little" Magistrates

"Les grands patrons sous la pression des juges" (company bosses under pressure from the magistrates). Thus a leading French daily specialising in economic matters sums up the corruption scandals that littered France in 1995. Indeed, as many as 20 heads of major French companies and a few well-known politicians were placed under examination during the year (Les Echos, Hors série, 10th January 1996, p.19). Three former ministers were found guilty of passive corruption together with their "corrupters", all of them heads of leading companies. The chairman of one of the most important companies in France was placed under examination, suspended from the execution of his functions before being finally released from his post by the board (an extremely rare occurrence in France). Even a very popular news presenter on television was convicted of passive corruption and received a suspended prison sentence. A number of other investigations are in progress and many more convictions can be expected in the near future.

The major players in this moral drama are thus named: in the right-hand corner, "big bosses" and politicians of every hue, in the left-hand corner, the "good little" investigating magistrates. The choice of adjectives in the article previously alluded to is significant. The opposition between "bosses" and "magistrates" has the effect of personifying the growing cleft, frequently deplored by many a commentator, between those "in power" and the "people". The magistrates are thus considered to be acting as spokesmen on behalf of the people and their demands for justice against a political and business elite which holds all power and all the privileges pertaining to it.

Two factors allow us to provide logical explanations for the manner in which public opinion has reacted: on the one hand, the centralisation and personification of power that prevails in France[2] and, on the other hand, the clear primacy of the individual (as opposed to the group). We shall focus solely on the former of these factors which

---

[2]   See: *Dix Propositions pour réhabiliter l'éthique dans l'entreprise* by Cathérine Golliau and Arnaud Leparmentier (Le Nouvel Economiste, N° 963 [16/09/1994] pp. 58-63). This article primarily concerns the professional standards of business leaders who are seen as being the first to need some form of moral rehabilitation. See also a survey calling into question the power exercised by business leaders in the French newspaper, *Les Echos* (Les Echos [08/12/1994] pp. 58-59).

are more readily observable in French society and the business world. It has often been pointed out that the business and political elite in France is drawn from the rather narrow breeding ground of a few *Grandes Ecoles*. Moreover, moving from ministerial office to the control of a major French company is a common occurrence.[3] The all-prevailing role of the "président directeur général" in a French company can be attributed to the fact that he completely dominates the company's control structure as well as its management structure. He is, so to speak, the company equivalent of the French president who enjoys an omnipotent position in French political life.

1.2.   Great Britain: Ethics is just another management issue

It would be wrong to claim that corruption scandals and ethical issues do not come up regularly in the British press. The Barlow Clowes affair, implementation of fair trading at BT, and the Co-op bribes scandal provide enough evidence of the former in major British newspapers and magazines during the latter half of 1995. Nevertheless, a closer survey of relevant articles reveals a rather clear distinction between, on the one hand, articles taking the form of commentaries or analyses of business ethics as a general topic worthy of interest and, on the other hand, rather blandly informative news reports of various misdeeds in the business world. The impression given is that the perennial existence of corrupt business people is stoically accepted as such and that any new scandal should not trigger off another round of moral diatribe or renewed indictment of the moral decline of the business world. On the contrary, the subject of business ethics is simply to be considered as any other major management topic to be discussed as such in the usual management sections of relevant publications.

In this respect, *The Economist* is typical of the distinctly restrained way in which ethical conflicts are understood and treated in the British press. Indeed, it is interesting to note that the magazine is particularly scornful, not only of the "downpour" of scandals that has recently

---

3   See an extremely enlightening dossier on this subject in *Le Figaro* [5/7/95], p. 2. The nomination of the former minister for the economy, M. Alphandéry, at the head of EDF (Electricité de France) clearly demonstrates that, in spite of announcements to the contrary by the president of the French Republic, this "musical-chairs" method of recruitment still prevails.

overwhelmed France, but also of the "panic" and general willingness to mount an "anti-corruption purge" that have subsequently emerged. While it does not deny the existence of an ethics crisis, it conveys the opinion that the issue of business ethics deserves a much more serious attitude than that prevailing in a number of other countries.

This point of view is totally in keeping with *The Economist's* general reservations regarding virtue for virtue's sake or the idea of "doing good because it is right". Doing business is seen as a "confusing mix of self-interest, altruism and other influences" that all have to be considered in the decision-making and strategy development process (The Economist, June 5th 1993). This approach is backed up, in particular, by the suggestion that the present increase in corruption scandals can be attributed to current economic and managerial trends such as globalisation, downsizing and delayering rather than to a decline in morals. The argument is that the resulting destruction of traditional lines of communication and control only serves to encourage and foster unethical behaviour and its effects.

This all implies that ethical issues are, above all, managerial issues and that an ethical policy is to be treated as one would any other business tool or resource. Treating one's customers, employees and suppliers sensitively and equitably is a strategy that will lead to greater efficiency and a smoother running of the firm, while concern for general ethical issues in society at large is a marketable asset that can produce a more favourable pay-back on investment. It is recognised, of course, that such policies can backfire, as in the case of the Body Shop Ltd., if not handled carefully, but such problems are often explained away with the assertion that business ethics is simply a tool which is not yet mastered by all concerned (August 19th, 1995).

Such an attitude is more than borne out by a year's reporting of the now infamous Barings affair. Rather than even seeking to label this affair as a corruption scandal, in contrast to certain French papers that reported the case, *The Economist* underlines the fact that the collapse of the bank was due to problems of communication and an irresponsibly arm's length approach to autonomy, an incredible lack of control over reporting, an incoherent management structure, and, above all, "sheer managerial incompetence". The refrain is the same, i.e. that bad ethics is first and foremost a question of bad management, and that bad management is likely to foster a suitable terrain for bad ethics.

Surprisingly enough, the notion of "virtue" or "personal virtue" is mentioned as a response to the problem, but further reading reveals that we are dealing with an Aristotelian concept of virtue in which long-term relationships (in the form of "covenants") and concern for all the stakeholders in any firm should provide a basis for any ethical business decision.

Unlike businessmen, politicians have been the target of much moral ranting and raving concerning "sleaze" at Westminster. What is noticeable, however, is that they have rarely been involved in the type of business-related scandal that has dominated the French headlines over the last year (kickbacks on public contracts, fictitious invoices, etc.). The "Arms-to-Iraq" affair and the question of secure seats on quangos are certainly among those problems that contributed to the setting up of the Nolan Royal Commission on standards in public life, and it is clearly recognised that the public's perception of the "sleaze" factor among politicians is at a low ebb. However, this reaction to the dishonesty and corruption of certain MP's seems to be more directly linked to their status as "public servants" than to their involvement in business malpractice of the type studied above. In the few cases where some form of collusion between the worlds of business and politics does exist (e.g. the "money for questions" affair) the reaction of the press tends to consist mainly in diminishing the significance of the issue and in berating the present prime minister and MP's for handling some very real problems indecisively and for refusing to discuss them openly. Poor management and communication, once again.

"Nobody said ethics was easy", claims *The Economist* (May 16th, 1992), but it is also clear that no amount of moral indignation will solve the problem. There seems to be a fundamental belief that business ethics is a topic to be handled and integrated as intelligently and as calmly as one would any other new management tool or concept.

1.3.   Germany: Abide by the law and consider the costs

Contrary to what can be observed in France, a survey of the German press reveals that the wave of criticism directed at unethical practices in the business world does not target individuals but rather the whole business system. If, for example, one considers the spate of articles concerning the cases of passive corruption at Opel and the system of surreptitious payments by suppliers in order to obtain business, it becomes clear that this corruption scandal is treated, either explicitly or implicitly, as just one more among so many similar cases.[4] The impact of this case of passive corruption is perceived as no more than a warning signal in the general degradation of the "German model". This process of taking a single case of corruption and transforming it into a general statement on the present state of society is part and parcel of a generalising attitude which considers that the correct functioning of the economy is a direct result of the moral quality of society as a whole. We are no longer in the context of a struggle between the "good guys" and the "baddies", but rather that of an opposition between the "right" system and the "rotten" one. This attitude is predominant in recent public indignation at the "Italianisation" of German society or in one journalist's comforting reassurance that the Opel affair was "relatively tame" compared to everything that goes on in France.

In fact, from the point of view of the German press and indeed of the German public at large, the country is not going through an ethics crisis; it is simply having to face a problem of maintaining law and order. The past success of the German economy, after all, is proof enough of German moral integrity. Although many have strayed from the straight and narrow path, this moral integrity (still) exists; there is simply a greater need for laws and regulations that will better preserve it. This kind of attitude explains why *Der Spiegel* ascribes the general moral decline of the present situation to the increasingly light sentences that have been handed down for cases of corruption and business malpractice since the 1950's (sic!). This also explains why the majority of press articles contain demands for reinforcement of the relevant laws and more effective enforcement of legal investigation and bringing to trial. Thus it is only in strengthening the institutional framework that one has any hope of controlling the criminal malpractice that is infiltrating every level of society. Criticism of the Supervisory Board and the need, according to a number of economists, for greater control within companies themselves are simply the other facet of this call for reinforcement of the institutional framework.

---

[4] See Heinz Bluethmann: Schmieren statt kalkulieren. Korruption: In Amtsstuben und Firmenbüros verfallen die Sitten, in: Die ZEIT Nr. 29 vom 14. Juli 1995, S.15-16.

Another point of view that is regularly expressed in the German press could be called the "standpoint of the accountant". Illegal actions are profitable for those who perpetrate them, but they imply a high cost to society and are damaging for the national economy. Corruption should be fought because it gives rise to a calculable burden on society as a whole. This helps to explain why tax deductibility for "useful expenses", which are generally nothing more than "kickbacks" paid out in order to ensure certain lucrative markets, has been roundly denounced for the first time ever. In this respect, the government's response is particularly interesting: given that such actions are common practice in international business, forbidding them would only put German industry at a competitive disadvantage and severely restrict its ability to secure contracts and business. Such a standpoint clearly expresses the antagonism that is perceived to exist between companies and the economic system and reveals the problems that can arise when an ethical policy is applied in the context of increasing economic globalisation.

2. Companies Rising to the Challenge

The German, French or British companies that had integrated a business ethics policy into their strategies before various scandals broke out or before the fear of legal proceedings drove them to it were few and far between. Today, thanks to public opinion or a growing awareness of the real stakes on the part of each individual company, a large number of companies are beginning to react. The means and the strategies that they are likely to use in order to bring ethical standards back into the world of business are not that varied. One could expect, therefore, that the tangible measures that companies would implement in the three countries would be very similar. Nevertheless, it turns out that companies remain firmly under the influence of their home business culture when it comes to thinking up practical solutions to the ethical problems they are having to face. This serves to remind us that the field of business ethics, which is to be considered as a branch of applied ethics, must take into consideration the cultural "boundaries" that limit the range of possible solutions for any company and which render any simplistic universal approach ineffectual.

2.1.   France: Discovering codes of ethical conduct and corporate governance

When the French started to talk about business ethics in 1989, this did not hail the beginning of a real debate on the subject. A few articles alluded to the importance that the field had taken on in the United States, a few management specialists managed to put their ideas across in the specialised journals, but, on the whole, French companies maintained a cautious reserve, visibly satisfied as they were with the public esteem they had enjoyed since the mid-80's.

Since 1994 the situation has changed considerably, and the publicly expressed criticism of companies and, above all, of their directors marks a sharp contrast with the praise that had been showered on them for their command of business strategy such a short while ago and often in the same publications. Although only a handful of the 200 largest companies in France had introduced a code of ethical conduct, the impressive wave of indictments that hit company directors in 1994 and 1995 stung the government, the confederation of business leaders and certain major companies into action.

The government, for example, prohibited all company financing of political activities, thus putting an end to the type of practice that had brought many a politician into disrepute and which had involved a large number of companies working with or for local authorities. The CNPF, the national confederation of business leaders, strongly advised companies to cease contributing to the electoral campaigns of politicians. A number of commissions set up by the CNPF or other employers' associations and including the heads of some of France's leading concerns published their reflections on the role of companies in society (the Pébereau report) and on the means needed to control more effectively the exercise of power and management in companies quoted on the stock exchange (the Viénot report).

A number of major companies in the end decided to elaborate codes of ethical conduct in order to guide and control the actions of their directors, managers and employees. In general, such codes rarely resemble the Anglo-Saxon models that are now so well-established. The "stakeholder approach" has met with little favour among company directors and the normative approach which prescribes standards of behaviour is generally refused even by those companies whose early commitment to ethical policy was roundly praised. At LAFARGE, for example, it is explained that the company has no ethical charter, strictly speaking, owing to the conviction that "moral behaviour is a matter for the individual conscience".

Should the individual conscience need any guidance, then the company's "corporate culture", considered as the depository of norms and values, should be referred to. Such is the case at BOUYGUES, an enormous family enterprise where the charter, which consists of 12 commandments, bears the title "What I believe in". It represents a veritable declaration of principles by the founding chairman which are brought to the attention of all employees, in particular, during integration seminars organised by the firm. The little blue book "Ethique et Management" of the ACCOR group refers to the values shared by the different companies within the group, and even if the rules of conduct are written in the first person singular it is patently clear that these represent the personal values of the two founding chairmen.

2.2. *Great Britain: The "business community" can look after itself*

In making claims for the distinct nature of the American approach to business ethics, Vogel (1992) stresses, amongst other things, that the approach is highly "legalistic". Apart from the fact that the authors of the present article would obviously object to the way in which this quality is set up as a universal norm against which other systems are to be evaluated, a British approach might follow the thoughts of Elizabeth Vallance (1995, p.15) who considers that if some act is already deemed illegal, then there is hardly any point in calling it "unethical". "In other words, it may be best not described in ethical terms at all."

This is to some extent typical of the fact that, in spite of whatever may link these two English-speaking countries, the British approach, above all, appears to be highly anti-legalistic. Calls for more harshly restrictive measures as a response to any new financial or business scandal are rarely followed up, and one often encounters the assertion that such measures would amount to throwing the baby out with the bath water. One of the earlier papers published by the Institute of Business Ethics in London makes it clear that "rigid control can sometimes be worse than the abuse which it tries to eliminate" and that legal constraints should only be necessary if all else fails (Cooper 1989, p.6). Calls for stricter regulation of the derivatives markets, said to pose a threat to international financial stability, following the Barings scandal were not entertained for long, and *The Economist* inevitably referred its readers to the French *Crédit Lyonnais* whose losses in "boring old banking businesses such as loans and investments" (March 11th, 1995) relegated the status of the Barings case to that of a curious historical anecdote.

The journalistic recommendation is generally for "internal supervision", and this, on the whole, seems to be the credo of the business community itself. In general, individual companies in Britain seem to be adopting internal codes of ethical conduct and reflecting on their application within the firm. If a gap between British and American firms has been clearly demonstrated in the past (Schlegelmilch 1989), it can also be shown that the rate at which such codes have been developed and adopted has accelerated constantly since the mid-70's when the first major codes were introduced (Schlegelmilch 1989 & Webley 1995). According to Stanley Kiaer of the Institute of Business Ethics, the proportion of companies with a code is approaching 50% (compared to 84% in the US).

A similar approach is replicated on a national level, where the "business community", which is possibly less diverse than in the US, wants and seems to be able to look after itself. The Institute of Business Ethics itself, even though the original thrust for its foundation came from the Christian Association of Business Executives, is, to all intents and purposes, typical as a emanation of the business community designed to reflect on ethical issues for the business world at large. In the words of its chairman, Neville Cooper, the institute is "run by businessmen and is firmly based on the convictions and experience of its subscribers, which are manufacturing companies and city institutions". Interestingly enough, such issues seem to be so much the concern of the business community itself that a recent series of telephone calls to such institutions as the Confederation of British Industry or the Department of Trade and Industry on the subject of the existence and availability of codes of conduct led to quite some blankness and confusion as to what a code of conduct actually represented.

The internal workings of this approach are also evident in the work of the committee chaired by Sir Adrian Cadbury and the subsequent report published in May 1992. The aim of this committee, composed of businessmen and chaired by one of the most respected among them, was not to devise new regulations or restrictions but, above all, to cull recommendations from "best practice", i.e. to set up a list of guidelines based on the best examples of ethical policies as evidenced in major British firms. The report deliberately avoided calling for any legal back-up in the form of mandatory decisions in law. The guidelines as well as the policies were intended to be voluntary and an ideal situation that companies should aspire to or be encouraged towards. Rather than a structure of legal constraint, such encouragement should be based on example and take the form of Stock Exchange, market or peer pressure.

The business response in Britain to ethical issues and conflicts seems to be pragmatic, deductive (as opposed to absolutist) and above all anti-legalistic. The fact that British legislation is based on Case Law tends to lead the business community to eschew intervention from government for fear of the sledgehammer-style dispositions that may result. It also seeks to avoid having the agenda imposed from outside by an increasingly critical public. The best way to deal with the crisis is in looking after one's problems in an ideal context of "self-regulation".

2.3. Germany: Companies clean up their act and the law does its job

The wide belief that social institutions and the economic order are responsible for guaranteeing ethical behaviour generally signifies that, in a context of crisis, the legal framework and its unimpeded functioning are often called into doubt. Corruption and other business malpractice are the concern, not only of the "business community", but of the whole of society. The number of those in Germany calling for new measures to deal with the situation as well as stronger sentences intended to combat the deteriorating awareness of what is right or wrong is very high. Yet the laws in existence already provide the necessary legal means. According to the public prosecutor's department in Munich, the number of investigations into business corruption increased from 30 cases in 1991 to 595 in 1994. Such legal proceedings have involved managers at every level in the company structure without distinction. The investigation at OPEL, for example, rapidly extended even to the parent company in the United States and concerned 200 employees including 19 top-ranking managers. Furthermore, one of the managing directors and member of the Board of Management was immediately suspended from his functions by the company as a direct consequence of the accusations of passive corruption weighing against him. In as much as the individual is admittedly responsible for his or her own acts but is not perceived as the visible and exemplary model of moral behaviour, it is easier for "institutions" to get rid of the "trouble-makers" quickly.

The immediate and radical nature of the measures taken is often quite surprising, especially in a field that is as sensitive and as much in the public spotlight as the relationships between politicians and business people. In the 1980's, a number of scandals concerning the financing of political parties broke out. The principal fallout from these scandals was a restrictive regulatory framework and increased public "sensitivity" regarding the relations between business and the world of politics. In particular, this new attitude brought about the political downfall of Lothar Späth, the all-powerful prime minister of the State of Baden-Württemberg and one of the great hopes of the CDU to succeed Helmut Kohl. At the beginning of 1990, the press reported that he had received "gifts" from industrial representatives worth a (mere!) few thousand deutschmarks in all. Within barely 9 weeks, he was forced to resign from all his political functions.

If the law can thus be seen to be doing its job, German companies, on the other hand, are also beginning to react. Confronted with a deterioration of their image, a number of chemical firms, such as Bayer in 1986, introduced a code of ethical conduct committing the company and all its partners/employees to respecting the environment and standards of security. Most German companies, on the other hand, have gone a different route. They have introduced structural measures or set up "institutional barriers" in order to proscribe corruption and guarantee "moral rectitude" (Wirtschaftswoche vom 5.10.1995, p.132). Such measures can include an absolute ban on accepting gifts worth more than 50 marks, the removal of personal addresses on business cards, or complete transparency in sales negotiations. Amongst other things, OPEL has started to evaluate the effectiveness of continuously rotating its buyers so that it becomes impossible to take advantage of associating too frequently with subcontractors. An example of the way in which companies are held responsible for the actions of their employees and partners is given by the State of Hessen. Any company implicated in a corruption case is put on a blacklist and is consequently excluded from any public invitation to tender. It appears, therefore, that the German response to ethical issues and conflicts is to reinforce legal restrictions and improve the organisation and control structure within companies, the aim of this being to supervise each individual more effectively and prohibit illegal acts.

3. Developing a Theory of Business Ethics

In comparison to the situation in the United States, research into the field of business ethics in Europe only developed a number of years later. Within the European context, we have to recognise that the pioneers in this field were the Germanic (Switzerland, Germany, the Netherlands) and the Scandinavian countries rather than the countries in the South of Europe. From the middle of the 1980's onwards, a general debate about ethics in the business sphere developed which tended to involve various institutions affiliated to the Catholic and Protestant churches, a few professors of business administration, some philosophers and publishers, as well as a few rare company heads.

We cannot hope to provide an exhaustive presentation of European output in the field of business ethics. We shall attempt to describe the principal standpoints and situate the authors in relation to the classical approaches of business ethics. To this effect, we shall propose a framework for classification which, we think, can lay claim to certain universal applicability, even though it is essentially derived from German approaches[5] to the subject.

Essentially, any reasoned approach to business ethics must take a clear position in regard to two fundamental questions:

---

[5] The major works which have had an impact on the study of business ethics in Germany are presented by Homann, K. / Blome-Drees, F.: "Unternehmensethik - Managementethik", in: Die Betriebswirtschaft, Jg. 55 (1995), pp. 95-114. For those who speak German, this article represents a very helpful introduction to the debate on business ethics in Germany, especially as it is written by one of the leading participants in the debate. The recent synthesis proposed by Steinmann and Löhr is also very useful: Steinmann, H. / Löhr, A., "Zehn Jahre Unternehmensethik – eine Bestandsaufnahme der Kernprobleme", in: Schachtschneider, K. A. (Hrsg.), Wirtschaft, Gesellschaft und Staat im Umbruch, Berlin, Duncker & Humblot, 1995, pp. 225-241.

1. Is the question of morality primarily a function of the institutions which a society creates or is it exclusively related to the notion of the individual?
2. What is the relationship between economics and ethics?

If morals can only be said to exist in the context of individual autonomous action, then the aim of business ethics must consist in elucidating individual decisions. On the other hand, if we consider that morals are embodied in society's institutions and in the way they operate, the scope of business ethics is extended and should then in-corporate reflection on society's institutions (e.g. companies) and the moral behaviour they engender. Applying this first dimension to the development of an ethical approach would imply assigning a position between the two poles on an axis, i.e. the moral autonomy of the indi-vidual and the social/institutional determination of moral behaviour.

Depending on whether the relationship between economic impera-tive and morality is perceived as one of fundamental antithesis or whether it is seen as one which can certainly engender conflict but which is not essentially antagonistic, a different position will be assigned vis-à-vis the second important ethical dimension

Those who acknowledge an antagonistic relationship between eco-nomic activity, which asserts that self-interest is the only goal to be pursued and that battles must be fought keenly in order to glean success, and moral behaviour, whereby the interest of the greater number is to be pursued and the needs and desires of others paid heed to, must decide in what situation and to what extent they will give priority to one or the other. Apart from those rare authors who do not deal with this aspect at all, our experience shows us that the notion of antagonism is generally present in reflections of a philosophical or sociological nature, whereas the absence of a fundamental conflict (although this usually implies the primacy of economic activity over all other concerns) is a common feature in the works of economists.

A comparison of the conceptual discourse that prevails in these three countries is only possible, of course, if we emphasise the points of convergence that emerge in the various writings of each country, as opposed to the sources of divergence. We shall seek, therefore, to bring out those elements that are common to the majority of writers on the subject in each area, rather than give an account of the often subtle differences that divide them.

3.1. Germany: The primacy of the economic order

The importance given to the theoretical foundation of business ethics is surely that feature which most characterises the German approach in general in the eyes of the non-German observer. In this respect, it stands in marked contrast to the approach which prevails in Anglo-Saxon countries and which aspires above all to pragmatism. This does not imply that German contributions to the field of business ethics ignore the tangible aspects of moral behaviour in business, but that they strive first and foremost to interpret these realities with reference to a general theory of business ethics. Within the context of this attempt to construct a theoretical basis for study, contemporary German philosophers and sociologists such as Habermas, Apel, Albert, Lorenzen and Luhmann, represent fundamental references. Economics represents a second important source for the theoretical foundation of this field.

This high esteem in which theoretical conceptualisation is held can be explained fairly easily if one takes into account the major objectives of German authors. In their capacity as professors of Management Science for the most part, they seek to establish business ethics as an academic discipline that is fully acknowledged within their field. The creation of university chairs such as those at the University of Sankt-Gallen or at the University of Eichstätt represent the first step in this direction. For the necessary recognition of the university community to be obtained it is essential to demonstrate that such a discipline conforms to academic principles, and that implies the existence of a general theoretical structure.

The indispensable rigour which should underlie any theoretical edifice is also evident here in the consolidation of the terminology used. Contrary to what happens in France where the terms "morality" and "ethics" are often used in a random fashion, most German authors seem to have come to an agreement on the few terminological rules to be observed. Morality is thus distinguished from ethics in the same way that one differentiates between the economy as an observable economic activity and economic science. Morality designates the object (i.e. the rules, values and conflicts that really exist in the everyday business world) of a field of intellectual thought that we call business ethics.[6]

There is also a fairly wide consensus as far as the general business environment is concerned, that is to say, the established economic order which includes not only the traditional institutions of a liberal economy, private property and regulation of economic activity by market forces, but also the regulatory framework imposed by the state or by business protagonists themselves. Most German authors defend what could probably be termed an "institutional ethic", as opposed to a "decision-making ethic" which concentrates on autonomous decision-making process of the individual. To justify this particular approach, the essential distinction between the "rules of the game" and "tactics or strategies within the game" is called to mind. As in a game of chess, where a precise set of rules indicates the moves permitted but where each player will try to invent a winning strike, the economic environment is also subject to rules that allow certain actions and forbid others, while establishing competition as the major guiding principle.

Finally, the German specialists in business ethics generally arrive at the same empirical conclusions. They acknowledge that many a company, ipso facto, is already pursuing objectives and developing behaviours that can be deemed to reveal a clear set of ethical concerns. As to identifying what underlies this sudden surge in interest for business ethics, they are unanimous in replying that companies, when faced with global crises, have to confront the imperatives of their business environment and thus find responses to issues that are increasingly ethical in nature.

In conclusion, it is clear that German authors attach more importance to an institutional approach to business ethics. Moreover, they are quite vigorously opposed (Steinmann/Löhr 1996; Homann/Blome-Drees 1992; Ulrich 1986) as to the question of whether the relationship between ethics and contemporary economics should be considered antagonistic or as a relationship that certainly can engender conflicts but which is not essentially conflictual.

---

[6] See Homann/Blome-Drees, Op. cit. p. 98. See also Seidel F. (sous la coordination de), Guide pratique et théorique de l'éthique des affaires et de l'entreprise, Paris, ESKA, 1995, pp. 29-316. See: Pesqueux, Y./Ramananantsoa, B., La situation de l'éthique des affaires en France, in: Revue Ethique des Affaires, N°1, 1995.

3.2.   France: Between secular morality and christian tradition

The most obvious characteristic of business ethics in France is surely a lack of a specific conceptual approach. French philosophers (Etchegoyen 1991; Comte-Sponville 1995) have gained a great deal of public recognition, it is true; their publications, however, in no way aim at elaborating a theory of business ethics as a specific branch of applied ethics. Their primary concern seems to be public life in general (as opposed to the private life of the individual), which itself incorporates the economic, political and social spheres. Those authors which deal with the more specific problems pertaining to business and corporate ethics (Gélinier 1991; De La Bruslerie 1992) carefully refrain from putting forward any theoretical framework which might provide a basis for approaching both the empirical facts and the possibility of defining a theory linking economics and ethics.

As far as the empirical facts are concerned a general consensus reigns. A serious decline in moral standards in business and politics, as evidenced by the growing number of corruption scandals of all kinds, is heavily criticised by all (Gélinier 1991; Etchegoyen 1991). The link is then made to the behaviour of the various elites who can no longer stand as a model of virtuous conduct (De La Bruslerie 1991, p.20). This decline in standards among the political and business elites is, in the end, often interpreted as a result of the fact that the most highly placed deciders and executives are protected from any form of redress or sanction (Gélinier 1991, p.10). The internationalisation of the economy is cited as a second major source of present moral destitution. This reference to the global evolution of the economy occurs frequently in the works of economists and management experts (Puel 1989; Usunier/Verna 1994) but remains mainly absent from the more philosophical approaches.

As to the question of the relationship between economics and ethics most writers in this field seem to come up with the same responses. From philosophers (Etchegoyen 1991) to managers (Gélinier 1991), while not forgetting those economists with a strong Christian orientation (Puel 1989), the same requirement can be heard: economic imperatives should (in principle) be subordinated to moral order. At most, they may try to reassure companies which fear having to sacrifice profits on the altar of moral rectitude by asserting that "in the middle and long term, ethics pays" (Gélinier 1991, p.10).

It should also be noted that, for the time being, in France, no real debate is taking place between those who have published their reflections on the subject of business ethics. Most of the works that have been published strongly resemble a "pamphleteer" style of writing: they seek to convince the readers of the need to act according to the principles thus developed and only rarely accept to engage a debate about other conflicting approaches. J Moussé (1993), who, in this particular respect, represents the exception that confirms the rule, owing to his constant concern to examine the theoretical positions of others as well as their practical suggestions, confirms this analysis when he calls for an open debate among those who are intimately involved in the study of the field of business ethics.

Finally, in order to summarise this all too brief presentation of the theoretical approaches to business ethics in France, we should insist on the strong tendency in most of these approaches to generalise the observations to the whole of society. Moral behaviour is seen as the cement which binds together the edifice of society which is characterised by the firm interdependence of the economic, social and political spheres. This interdependence is made possible by the presence of the elites. Their moral destitution reflects the destitution of the French political, social, and economic model which is no longer capable of generating those moral values which ensure the cohesion of the State and French society. This, without doubt, explains why the call for action is so forceful among the majority of French authors. In the absence of a new socio-economic-political ideal that is capable of uniting the French people, many authors draw their inspiration from the French model of secular "Republican" moral behaviour or from a humanism which possesses often a strong Christian orientation.

French theoretical output is close to the pole indicating the predominance of moral behaviour and close to the pole indicating the "moral autonomy of the individual" since French authors emphasise the role of the individual and consider that moral behaviour is always embodied in individual decisions; it should, nevertheless, be stressed that the individual is rarely considered as a totally autonomous being. The individual under consideration is the social actor "taken as an individual", an individual belonging to the French elite and from whom exemplary standards are required in return for the privileges enjoyed.

3.3.   Great Britain: Pragmatism first and foremost

In Great Britain, the field of business ethics represents a clear field of study in which systematic approaches and frameworks have already been developed and in which a common language enabling exchange is emerging. Not only have regular books and articles been appearing on the subject since at least 1984, but most publications contain frequent references to other authors, thus leaving one with the impression that the debate is fully open. For British authors, business ethics is also perceived as a distinct area in the field of ethics and in particular as a branch of practical applied ethics. Elizabeth Vallance (1995), for example, sees it as separate from the classical theories of moral philosophy which are more concerned with personal ethics only.

British authors are rarely concerned with developing an all-embracing theoretical framework in order to explain the conceptual basis of their study. When a framework is mentioned, it generally refers to some form of decision-making model with which the author is intent on presenting a list of guidelines for clarifying ethical issues and adopting suitable approaches. It is interesting to note that as far back as 1987-88, one of the major topics of concern was how to teach business ethics in universities rather than what the conceptual basis might be (Mahoney 1990).

These authors generally recognise that, although open uninhibited talk about ethics in British business is still rather difficult, the British have been discussing ethical issues for a long time now. Corporate governance and treatment of employees have been major areas of debate since at least 1970 (Vallance 1995, p.5), while numerous consumer issues have inspired public concern for nearly two decades (Mahoney 1990, p.46). The difference is, of course, that they have not been talking about "ethics" but about "good management practices". There seems to be little need to develop far-reaching conceptual frameworks simply in order to talk about the smooth running of day-to-day management issues, however intrinsically ethical these may be. This, of course, relates to the fact that the British are notoriously ill at ease with huge abstract concepts and are generally reluctant to sound off and overstate such ostensibly value-based subjects. As for many authors, development of an approach is to be derived from everyday practice.

This attitude is hardly surprising when it is acknowledged that, in Britain, business and ethical concerns are certainly not antagonistic or separate in nature. However, it should also be realised that this is accepted in as much as the priority should always be given to the essential aim of business, that is to say making profit and "maximising long-term owner value" (Vallance 1995, p.38). Business should not seek to take over the ethical welfare of the whole nation and ethical results should not be the primary aim of business; "Ethics is not everything and everything is not ethics" (ibid., p.36). Business ethics represents, above all, an important "strategy" in business dealings and an important factor in establishing an explicit approach (Mahoney 1990, p.48) to clarifying and enacting business' aims.

On the whole, these writers tend to think that, in the medium or long term, ethics does pay. Nevertheless, with characteristic British realism (cynicism?), they remind us that in some cases bad ethics can also pay and that good ethics is not always a guarantee.

As we have already seen, the notion of ethical behaviour as an individual decision-making process, particularly with concern for long-term relationships with all partners, often comes to the fore. However, ethics is not just an issue for individual consideration, since the company, whose behaviour is not just the sum of individual ethical actions, is also a moral actor. On the other hand, this does not denote an institutional approach in as much as institutional intervention in the system in the form of overall restrictive rules and regulations is as a whole shunned. The company itself is perceived as an individual autonomously devising strategies and making decisions for which it is ultimately responsible, in a market which is not a "moral system" but simply a "mechanism" (Vallance 1995, p.37). Both individuals and companies have moral responsibilities, and the important thing is to get them functioning as a whole.

4. Different Responses to a Common Crisis

This unavoidably succinct analysis of the different perspectives on business ethics in three different European countries allows us to confirm the fact that we are indeed facing a generalised ethics crisis in the business world. The existence of an consistent approach to ethical issues in the three countries and in respect of the three different dimensions of our analysis is a clear indication of this. Nevertheless, we are also forced to acknowledge that the three countries, through public opinion, practical approaches and theoretical perspectives, create highly dissimilar perceptions of business ethics. We can but conclude, therefore, that any discussion between representatives of such different outlooks on the subject will necessarily be difficult.

The relatively strong coherence that is observable in the general discourse of each of the three countries seems to indicate that "national culture" plays a decisive role in the development of each country's perspective on the subject. It supplies an overall institutional framework of reference that will serve as the basis for all reflection on the area of business ethics. The French situation provides the most telling example, perhaps. Public consensus around the notion of public morality, in the absence of any dominant institutions other than the State, represents the foundation stone of a cohesive society. By virtue of this fact, any ethical problem becomes a universal problem incorporating all political, economic and social aspects, so much so that it becomes virtually inconceivable that the field of business ethics could evolve as a specific branch of general ethics.

It is obvious that the cultural determination of these different outlooks on business ethics, both on a theoretical as well as a practical level, can create problems for those ethicists concerned with elaborating an approach that might have some claim to universality. Moreover, this phenomenon can become a real hindrance when devising a strategy in an international business context. Indeed, the structure underlying the ethical discourse and its dependence on cultural determinants generally remains quite opaque for the nationals of another country. The foreign observer, on the other hand, runs the risk of misinterpreting the internal logic of the approach in as much as it does not correspond to rational and acceptable criteria as they prevail in his or her own culture. The most pressing question then is in what way the field of business ethics can preserve a universal relevance inherent in any scientific approach (and rendered all the more indispensable by the clear empirical evidence of a general ethics crisis) without sacrificing the necessary analysis of distinctive cultural identities to any form of "cultural and moral imperialism".

So that the study of business ethics in the international environment, and with regard to its theoretical and practical dimensions, may progress, we feel it is necessary to carry out as complete an analysis as possible of different "national" approaches. It should now be obvious that the aim is not to "measure" or evaluate these different approaches according to some preconceived table or benchmark, but to "reconstruct" them after having analysed the "cultural context", i.e. the interactive and institutional practices of a given culture and the mental perception one has of them. Given that this "cultural context", which is at work in our "preconscience", both shapes and restricts our intellectual horizon, it becomes essential for the researcher to "stand back" from his or her own culture. As this rarely occurs spontaneously, there is a need to create structures designed to facilitate greater understanding of these issues, and this can be achieved through the setting up of international and multi-cultural work groups.

References

Bluethmann, H. (1995): *Schmieren statt kalkulieren. Korruption: In Amtsstuben und Firmenbüros verfallen die Sitten,* in: Die ZEIT vom 14. Juli 1995, S.15-16.

Calori, R./ De Woots, Ph. (eds.) (1994): A European Management Model, London: Prentice Hall.

Comte-Sponville, A. (1995): *Petit traité des grandes vertus,* Paris, PUF.

Cooper, N. (1989): *What's all this about Business Ethics,* London, IBE.

Enderle, G. (1996): A Comparison of Business Ethics in North America and Continental Europe, in: *Business Ethics,* Vol. 5, pp. 33-46.

Etchegoyen, A. (1991): *La valse des éthiques,* Paris: Ed. F. Bourin.

Gelinier, O. (1991): *L'éthique des affaires: halte à la dérive,* Paris: Seuil.

Golliau, C. / Leparmentier, A. (1994): *Dix Propositions pour réhabiliter l'éthique dans l'entreprise* , in: Le Nouvel Economiste, N° 963 [16/09/1994] pp. 58-63.

Harvey, B.(1994): *Business Ethics. A European Approach,* London: Prentice Hall.

Homann, K. / Blome-Drees, F. (1992): *Wirtschafts- und Unternehmensethik,* Göttingen: Vandenhoeck & Ruprecht.

Homann, K. / Blome-Drees, F. (1995): Unternehmensethik - Managementethik, in: *Die Betriebswirtschaft,* Jg. 55, pp. 95-114.

La Bruslerie (De), H. (1992): *Ethique, déontologie et gestion de l'entreprise,* Paris.

Mahoney, J. (1990): *Teaching Business Ethics,* London: Athlone Press.

Moussé, J. (1993): *Ethique et Entreprise,* Paris: Vuibert.

Pesqueux, Y. / Ramananantsoa, B. (1995): La situation de l'éthique des affaires en France, in: *Revue Ethique des Affaires,* N°1, pp. 15-35.

Puel, H. (1989): *L'économie au défi de l'éthique*, Paris: Cujas.

Schlegelmilch, B. (1989): The Ethics Gap between Britain and the United States, in: *European Management Journal*, Vol. 7, N°1.

Seidel, F. (co-ordination) (1995): *Guide pratique et théorique de l'Ethique des Affaires et de l'Entreprise*, Paris: ESKA.

Steinmann, H. / Kustermann, B. (1996): Current Developments in German Business Ethics, in: *Business Ethics: A European Review*, Vol. 5, pp. 12-18.

Steinmann, H. / Löhr, A. (1995): Zehn Jahre Unternehmensethik – eine Bestandsaufnahme der Kernprobleme, in: Schachtschneider, K. A. (Hrsg.): *Wirtschaft, Gesellschaft und Staat im Umbruch,* Berlin: Duncker & Humblot, pp. 225-241.

Steinmann, H. / Löhr, A. (1996): A Republican Concept of Business Ethics, in: Urban, S. (ed.): *Europe's Challenges,* Wiesbaden :Gabler, pp. 21-60.

Vallance, E. (1995): *Business Ethics at Work*, Cambridge University Press.

Vogel, D. (1992): The Globalization of Business Ethics, in: *California Management Review*, Vol. 35, N°1, Fall.

Ulrich, P. (1986): *Transformation der ökonomischen Vernunft*, Stuttgart/Bern: Haupt.

Usunier, J.-C. / Verna, G. (1994): *La grande triche – Ethique, corruption et affaires internationales*, Paris: La Découverte.

Webley, S. (1995): *Applying Codes of Business Ethics*, London: IBE.

Discourse Instead of Recourse

Is it Worth Using a Guided Approach to Negotiation When Working Across Cultures?

Warren French & Bernd Mühlfriedel

1. Introduction

"Working Across Cultures" – what first comes to mind when reflecting on the theme of this conference are conflicts such as Japanese imports and retaliatory French tariffs or Anglo Dutch petroleum operations providing revenue to African dictators. But, we do not have to go off the continent to encounter problems that are based on cultural differences. Although Europe doubtlessly has a common cultural identity, there are disparate values, perceptions and opinions even among the European countries. Let us look at two examples that make it clear how important cultural awareness is for mutual understanding and the resolution of conflicts over business transactions.

One of the most heated discussions Europe has experienced in years is the issue of substituting national currencies with a common European currency. While the French do not object to substituting the Euro for the Franc, the Germans see the Deutsch mark as the symbol of their economic success. It is a business card for Germany that shows stability and power, and provides its holder with worldwide respect. In contrast, the French take pride in their cultural rather than economic identity and place less emphasis on currency value as a sign of worldwide respect.

A second example illustrates an ongoing cause of cultural problems with moral implications. When companies from high wage countries like Sweden or Germany build factories in countries with cheaper production cost, e.g. Greece or Czech Republic, or outsource work to partners in those countries, they are often surprised by the differences in the social and legal status of workers, as well as an

H. Lange et al., Working Across Cultures, 263–285.

apparent lack of concern over time deadlines. The resulting conflicts have a negative effect on the economic success of these ventures.

These examples are but two of many, and evidence the need for a process which can be used to resolve conflicts based on different cultural values with moral overtones. Discourse may provide that process.

2. Why Discourse Ethics?

An ongoing problem in business life is the conflict of values, whether within organizations or between companies (Steinmann/Löhr 1994, p.72). Such conflicts constitute the focal point of morality (Baier 1965). These conflicts are especially evident when we look at relationships between business people with different cultural backgrounds.

Conflict resolution can be attempted, of course, by using appealing or manipulating techniques. As there is usually no willingness to alter one's opinion, especially if grounded on different cultural values, this approach can only lead to no resolution at all, the complete resignation of one party, or, at best, a compromise. The compromise, while overtly a solution, rarely satisfies and benefits both parties.

A lasting consensus might be achieved, however, if a somewhat time consuming, but potentially successful approach is taken. The establishment of a stable relationship most likely requires a constructive, argumentative process. A successful argument would be one that ties consensually arrived at values to both parties' self-understanding of their needs and to their interest in satisfying those needs (Rehg 1994). Lueken defines "argumentation" not as an adversarial confrontation but as a "symbolic action performed to overcome a controversy and aiming at consensus" (Lueken 1991, p.246). The two parties give each other insight in their underlying reasons and thus make it possible to reach an agreement on reasons that can be acknowledged by both parties. It is important to point out that this consensus, built on justified reasons, does not exist before the argumentation and has to be constructed through the discursive process (Kamlah/Lorenzen 1973, p.45ff.). Discourse allows us to reconstruct normative claims through a cognitive process in order to arrive at that consensus (Rehg 1994).

But what are the differences between an argumentative versus an appealing process and how do we know that consensus is a more desirable state than compromise? Kambartel and Habermas listed the following four criteria which differentiate argumentation from appeal (Kambartel 1974, p.66f.; Habermas 1983, p.98ff.). First, an unprejudiced approach towards any kind of assertions, regardless of whether they affect opinions or interests. Second, non-persuasiveness, i.e. the willingness to conduct the discourse without using appeals. Third, the willingness to refrain from using sanctions for consenting or dissenting. And fourth, expertise, i.e. the capability to present one's reasons in a way that they have a good chance of being approved by the other party. Conflict resolution efforts which have those four features raise the chance of a consensus between the parties.

Take the time to construct a consensus rather than accept a compromise? The reason for this is that consensus may be the only means of resolving conflicts, which both leads to an improvement of the current situation and is not subject to arbitrary reasoning (Lorenzen 1987, p.228ff.). Consensus is not vulnerable to sudden shifts in power or interest, since it is based on the much more stable fundament of mutually accepted reasoning (Steinmann/Löhr 1994, p.154).

One might argue that the conditions for an argumentative process are too idealistic and that they do not exist in a competitive environment. With the fierce global competition in mind, is it therefore senseless to use the argumentative approach to conflict resolution when working across cultures? Does it not seem to be better to prepare oneself for the verbal fight by getting information on the other party's situation and interests in order to assess the balance of power? Drawing this conclusion would be evidence of a very short-sighted view, which aims at taking advantage of situations in which one has more power than one's counterpart. In dealing with people from different cultural backgrounds this adversarial approach can backfire, especially if long-term relations are anticipated. When the gap of cultural unfamiliarity between two parties has to be bridged, it is essential to be able to rely on a strong basis of mutual trust. This element of trust can best be built by using discourse ethics in conflict resolution. Moreover, it is vital for the parties to discuss openly any assertion in order to obtain a mutual understanding of the way people from other cultures reason. According to Habermas an appropriate solution, one that elicits a feeling of trust, hinges on truthfulness and an open presentation of pertinent facts in addition to a mutual comprehension of conflicting positions and their underlying values (Habermas 1979).

In a sense, what we need is more appropriately labeled moral discourse rather than ethical discourse. While ethical discourse exists *within* a cultural tradition, moral discourse, according to Habermas, operates across the different self-understandings of the parties involved (Rehg 1994). Moral discourse considers the interests of those indirectly as well as directly affected by the conflict and its resolution. To avoid confusion, our use of the phrase discourse ethics should be interpreted to include the focus of moral discourse so as not to be constrained by the ethical values of any one culture. Discourse ethics in this broader sense theoretically offers a feasible procedure to resolve business conflicts, especially when working across cultures.

The claim that discourse ethics assumes a utopia, because the conditions for an ideal dialogue are never fulfilled in reality, seems to be based on the misunderstanding that discourse ethics either occurs in an ideal form or not at all. The fact is that the features of a perfect argumentation are ideal goals but not absolutely necessary conditions for conducting an argumentative conflict resolution process (Steinmann/Löhr 1994, p.80f.). Nevertheless, anyone involved in a business conflict could benefit by acting in accordance with these goals in order to increase the likelihood of a mutually beneficial outcome.

The purpose of this paper is to investigate whether a guided approach to negotiation, based on the assumptions of discourse ethics, is more productive than non-guided negotiation when attempting to achieve a consensual resolution of moral conflicts.

3. Propositions

Toward this end, *two propositions* were investigated:

P1. Successful resolution of conflict over moral issues is more likely achieved by using guided negotiation rather than by non-guided negotiation.

P2. Successful resolution of conflict over moral issues is less likely achieved when the parties to the conflict are from different countries than from the same country.

The sample for the investigation included 30 subjects who were assigned to ethical negotiations as follows:

Group 1. Five pairs from the same country.
Group 2. Five pairs from different countries.
Group 3. Five individuals paired with a Habermasian Negotiator from the same country.
Group 4. Five individuals paired with a Habermasian Negotiator from a different country.

All of the subjects possessed university degrees. After experience in the workplace they had returned to a university for graduate training in business. None of the subjects had formal training in negotiation or exposure to Habermas' writings. The Habermasian Negotiator possessed university degrees in philosophy and business, and had guided similar ethical negotiations using the Kurtines-Pollard procedure prior to those described in this experiment (Kurtines/Pollard).

4. Research Method

All subjects within the four groups were presented with two moral issues framed as occurring in a mythical land so as to eliminate nationalist prejudices (Exhibit 1). The subjects were asked to choose one of two positions which described judgments on the issues. They were then asked the degree to which they supported their choices. Some of the subjects in Groups 1 and 2 were paired so that they would be expected to exhibit the same level of moral reasoning while the rest were paired so as to be likely to exhibit different levels of moral reasoning. The expected level of moral reasoning was assessed in a preexperimental administration of the Defining Issues Test.

The Defining Issues Test was created by James Rest (1979) to mirror the stages of moral reasoning which had been identified by Lawrence Kohlberg (1969). This pretest was administered to investigate a third proposition, one advanced by Habermas (1990). He claimed that a discursive resolution to moral conflicts was more likely to occur if both parties to the conflict were capable of a high (post social convention) level of moral reasoning. Habermas had quoted Kohlberg's levels of moral reasoning when advancing his proposition.

Non-guided Resolution: Groups 1 and 2

The subjects were given a tape recorder and audio tape to record their negotiations on the two moral issues about which they held different positions. They were then instructed to seclude themselves sometime in the following two weeks and attempt to negotiate a resolution between their positions. They were also told that a "no resolution" result was acceptable if the audio tape showed that they had negotiated in good faith.

Guided Resolution: Groups 3 and 4

The protocol for resolving moral conflicts through the use of discourse ethics is based on Habermas' concept of ideal communication (Habermas 1979). Kurtines and Pollard (1989) have outlined a step-wise procedure from attempting to reach a consensus through the process suggested by Habermas. That procedure, with modifications to preclude negotiatior bias, was used by the Negotiator in ten negotiations with subjects in Groups 3 and 4. The format was as follows:

Step 1. Negotiator asked the subject which of the two positions the subject had chosen after evaluating the moral issue.

Step 2. Negotiator asked the subject why that position was chosen. Only moral principles/underlying values were accepted as valid reasons by the Negotiator before the guided negotiation continued. Verbal probes were employed if underlying values were not readily offered.

Step 3. Negotiator told the subject that the Negotiator had chosen the second (other) of the two positions. Negotiator then tactfully asked if the subject could reiterate the Negotiator's position in the subject's own words.

Step 4. Negotiator asked if the subject could venture a reason why the Negotiator had chosen the opposite position. Negotiator agreed with the subject's assessment if a reasonable value, different from the subject's value (offered in Step 2), was ascribed to the Negotiator. Verbal probes were used to elicit this ascribed value, if the ascribed value was not readily forthcoming.

Step 5. Negotiator stated that there was an obvious difference in positions. Negotiator then asked the subject if there existed a third or alternative position which the subject believed that both parties could accept. Tactful probes were used to move the subject toward creating a new position and away from defending the subject's original position or attacking the Negotiator's original position. Only if the subject could arrive at a new position was the sixth and last step of discourse procedure attempted. Negotiator accepted this newly reasoned third position if it could be judged feasible, universalizable and conducive to consistency between thoughts, words, and actions.

Step 6. Negotiator asked what underlying value could justify the newly created position – a value which could be accepted not only by the two parties to the negotiation but also by the entire community. Tactful probes were used to move the subject away from paraphrases of either the original value underpinning the subject's original position or the ascribed value underpinning the Negotiator's original position.

Following the rules of the procedure presented by Kurtines and Pollard, only three requests or probes of the subject were allowed during each of the six steps. In a true to life effort to resolve moral conflicts the Negotiator could be more proactive in explaining his/her reasoning behind an expressed rather than ascribed original position as well as suggesting a new third position along with a value which would justify that alternative position. While allowing the Negotiator this leeway might have increased the probability of conflict resolution, the role of the subject as an active contributor to these discourses could have been diminished, thus undermining the rationale for the discourse process in this experiment.

5. Results

The success of the guided and non-guided negotiations is summarized in Tables 1 and 2. The details of the positions and principles adopted by each of the negotiating parties are presented in the attached Exhibits 2, 3, 4 and 5. As shown in the Tables and Exhibits, there is very strong support for Proposition 1. Guided negotiation did lead to more mutually agreed upon resolutions to the two moral issues. And, if we accept the notion put forward by Lorenzen and Habermas that a lasting resolution is suspect if resulting from compromise, then Proposition 1 looks even stronger. None of the non-guided resolutions rested on a reordering of principles. That implies compromise. In contrast, 80% of the guided negotiations resulted in new positions which were grounded on mutually agreed upon principles not present in the original presentation. That gives hope for a lasting resolution. The intensity to which an original position was held by a subject in the guided negotiation had no effect on reaching a final resolution. Nor did the differential intensity of feelings about original positions have much effect on the resolution in the non-guided negotiations.

There is mixed support for Proposition 2. From the non-guided negotiations two of the five intercultural pairs arrived at a new position while only one of the five intracultural pairs had success. The opposite was true for the guided negotiations. The five intracultural pairs ended with ten new positions, nine of which were based on new principles. In the case of the five intercultural pairs, nine of the ten issues resulted in new positions and seven of those nine resolutions were based on new principles.

The informally presented third proposition was that the ability to reason at a higher (i.e., principled or post social convention) level of moral judgment was correlated to discursive resolution of moral issues. The sample size was too low in both the guided and non-guided pairs to draw any meaningful conclusions. See Table 2. What does show up in the results is that in over half of the cases a guided resolution can produce success with those who may reason from a lower level of moral judgment.

6. Conclusions

At first glance, the two moral issues, approached under a guided negotiation format by subjects from EEC countries, seem to elicit little differences in opinion. Four of the five subjects chose to take the coins and all five then elected to punish the humanitarian thief less than the selfish thief. The similarity in positions is not surprising, since government subsidized medical care in European countries precludes such situations that lead to the question about taking the coins.

However, when delving into the reasons behind the subjects' positions differences appear. The German and British subjects based their decision on a utilitarian value. Theirs was a teleological approach to the situation. In contrast, the French subjects took a deontological approach to the issue. They saw obligation based on friendship and a "right" to health as superceding any property rights.

But, it would be a mistake to create value stereotypes for a culture based on such a small sample. Within cultures a spectrum of values can be expected to underpin moral positions. This is especially true for the U.S. subjects described in Exhibits 2 and 4. Admittedly, that may be because the U.S. is a relatively young nation populated by immigrants with different cultural values. Even then, a majority of the U.S. subjects appeared to ground their initial positions on a teleological or consequentialist perspective. This contrasts with the apparent deontological rationale expressed by the French subjects in Exhibits 3 and 5.

These differences become even more striking when looking beyond the results and analyzing the deliberative processes in the non-guided negotiations. Although the non-guided negotiation between the French and the Indian subjects led to a new position on the issue of stealing, considerable time and effort had to be spent by both parties to overcome their basic beliefs which frequently came up in the discussion process. In contrast to the French subject, who often used examples from her motherland in order to explain her position, the Indian subject often unveiled his belief in solidarity among members of a universal community. Other examples of the influence of underlying ethical values, that are coined by the cultural background, could be observed in the discursive behavior of subjects from Far Eastern countries. A common rationale behind their positions was the importance of the family and the strong ties between the members of a community. Additionally, it was expressed that even if change in societal values was necessary it should come gradually without revolutionary upheavals. Finally, we noticed that people with strong religious beliefs tended to stick to their deontological principles ("Thou shall not steal.") and applied them universally in both moral issues. Therefore, it was hard to achieve a consensus, especially if the other party was not aware of this fact.

In essence, when guiding negotiation across cultures one must not only be familiar with discourse ethics as a necessary component on the road to a consensus, but also that the probability of success will be enhanced by cultural awareness and knowledge about traits of the other negotiation party's cultural background. This is what Habermas emphasized when he stated that the highest level of communication was dependent on all the facts being laid out as well as a mutual comprehension of positions and values (Habermas 1979). Where he might have been mistaken is with his assumed relation between level of moral reasoning and level of communication (Habermas 1990).

The guided negotiation with the two subjects judged capable of high levels of moral reasoning resulted in complete resolutions of both moral issues. This was expected, given the parallel Habermas draws between discursive communication and the highest level of moral reasoning. What was not expected was the success of guided discursive reasoning with those who tested at a lower level of moral reasoning. Over 75% of the issues negotiated with those with lower level of moral reasoning also resulted in successful resolutions using the Kurtines-Pollard protocol. This raises hopes about practical feasibility of discourse ethics, especially since Rest has found that most people do not reason at the highest (post social convention) level.

In summary, whether advocates of discourse ethics follow the Erlangen school of thought expressed by Lorenzen or the Frankfurt school represented by Habermas the results of this investigation are encouraging. The procedures to operationalize the theory of discourse ethics can produce positive results.

References

Baier, K. (1965): *The moral point of view.* New York.
Habermas, J. (1979): *Communication and the evolution of society.* Boston.
Habermas, J. (1983): Diskursethik – Notizen zu einem Begründungsprogramm. In: Habermas, J. *Moralbewußtsein und kommunikatives Handeln.* Frankfurt/M., pp. 53-125.
Habermas, J. (1990): *Moral consciousness and communicative action.* Cambridge/MA.

Kambartel, F. (1974: Moralisches Argumentieren - Methodische Analysen zur Ethik. In: Kambartel, F. (Ed.): *Praktische Philosophie und konstruktive Wissenschafts-theorie*. Frankfurt/M, pp. 54-72.

Kamlah, W. / Lorenzen, P. (1973): *Logische Propädeutik. Vorschule des vernünftigen Redens. 2nd ed.*, Mannheim/Wien/Zürich.

Kohlberg, L. (1969): Stages and sequence: the cognitive developmental approach to socialization. In: Goslin, D.A. (ed.): *Handbook of socialization theory and research*. Boston.

Kurtines, W. / Pollard, S. (1989): *The Communicative Competence Scale – Critical Discussion (CCS-CD)*, Miami: Florida International University Working Paper.

Lorenzen, P. (1987): *Lehrbuch der konstruktiven Wissenschaftstheorie* (Textbook of the Constructive Philosophy of Science). Mannheim (Germany).

Lueken, G.-L. (1991): Incommensurability, Rules of Argumentation, and Anticipation. In: van Emeren, F.H. et al. (Eds.): *Proceedings of the Second International Conference on Argumentation*. Amsterdam, pp. 244-252.

Rehg, W. (1994): *Insight and solidarity: the discourse ethics of Jürgen Habermas*. Berkeley/Los Angeles.

Rest, J. (1979): *Developments in judging moral issues*. Minneapolis.

Steinmann, H. / Löhr, A. (1994): *Grundlagen der Unternehmensethik* (Foundations of Business Ethics), 2nd ed., Stuttgart.

Steinmann, H. / Löhr, A. (1995): Unternehmensethik als Ordnungselement in der Marktwirtschaft. In: *Zeitschrift für betriebswirtschaftliche Forschung 47*, pp. 143-174.

Exhibit 1a

Stealing

After they had finished their affairs with The Merchant, the Hobbits had dinner and went to bed. They got up early the next morning and began working. While the Hobbits were working in the field, a friend of Rob's came by with news of his mother. Rob's mother had the same problem with her eyesight that Dale's had. Rob did not have the money for his mother's operation either, and he had far less than Dale. He needed one hundred gold coins. Rob's friend told him that his mother's eyesight was getting worse and that she might go blind. The only one who had that much money was Mr. Maggot, a miserly old scrooge who lived on the next farm. Rob went over to ask him for the money, and Mr. Maggot turned him down. He said that he had worked and saved for a long time and that he wanted to keep his coins. Rob left Maggot's farm, but while he was leaving he saw that Mr. Maggot was going to town for the afternoon. Rob had seen where Mr. Maggot kept his gold coins and he knew that he could come back in the afternoon and steal the 100 coins. Mr. Maggot had a whole room full of gold coins and would probably never even miss one hundred. Rob knew that there was no other way for him to get that many coins. He wasn't sure about what to do so he considered his choices. On the one hand, he felt he had an obligation to respect Mr. Maggot's right to keep the coins. On the other hand, he knew that if his mother did not have an operation she would probably lose her eyesight.

If you were Rob what do you think you would do?
1) Not take the coins.
2) Take the coins.

---

* Issues taken from Kurtines and Pollard (1989).

Exhibit 1b

Punishment

Suppose that before Rob could decide what to do, Sam, who knew about Rob's mother, had already taken the money, and that he had a friend help him. Together, they had taken 200 coins. When Mr. Maggot got back from town he discovered right away that the coins were missing (since it was his peculiar habit to count them three times a day) and went immediately to Rob's farm. At the farm he asked Rob to search the house and they found the 200 coins in Sam's room where he had hidden them. Confronted with the evidence, Sam confessed that he had indeed stolen them. Since Sam and his friend came under Rob's jurisdiction, Mr. Maggot demanded that Rob punish them for stealing the coins, because Hobbits consider stealing a very severe violation of "The Rules". Rob knew the standard punishment for an offense as severe as stealing was to be sentenced to spend time locked in the pillories in the town square as a form of public humiliation. It was Rob's decision about how much time each Hobbit should spend in the pillories.

After confessing, Sam said that he took the coins to give his half to Rob for his mother's operation. Sam's friend, on the other hand, said that he took the coins so that he could use his half to take a vacation trip that he had always wanted. Rob knew that stealing was a very serious offense and had thought about how he might punish Sam and his friend. On the one hand, he felt that he had an obligation to sentence them both to the same amount of time as punishment because they had both committed the same offense. On the other hand, he could sentence Sam to less time because he had taken the money in order to try and do some good.

If you were Rob what do you think you would do?
1) Punish Sam less than his friend.
2) Punish Sam and the friend equally.

---

* Issues taken from Kurtines and Pollard (1989).

Exhibit 2: Non-Guided Negotiation: Issues – Stealing & Punishment

Group 1 Issue	Subject's Country	Moral Reasoning Level	Intensity of Position	Original Position	Final Position	Original Principle	Final Principle
Steal	S01 - US	high	high	Not take coins	Ask for loan, if no loan then steal coins	Evil outweighs good	(No new principle)
Steal	S02 - US	low	low	Take coins	Ask for loan, if no loan then steal coins	Utilitarian	(No new principle)
Steal	S03 - US	high	high	Not take coins	(No new position)	Meritarian justice, property rights	(No new principle)
Steal	S04 - US	low	low	Take coins	(No new position)	Egalitarian justice	(No new principle)
Steal	S05 - US	high	low	Take coins	(No new position)	Utilitarian	(No new principle)
Steal	S06 - US	low	high	Not take coins	Take coins	Stealing is wrong	(No new principle)
Steal	S07 - US	low	low	Take coins	Not take coins	Higher "right"	(No new principle)
Steal	S08 - US	low	medium	Not take coins	(No new position)	Meritarian property rights	(No new principle)
Steal	S09 - US	low	high	Not take coins	Take coins	Empathy, universalizability leads to chaos	(No new principle)
Steal	S10 - US	low	medium	Take coins	(No new position)	Utilitarian	(No new principle)

Group 1 Issue	Subject's Country	Moral Reasoning Level	Intensity of Position	Original Position	Final Position	Original Principle	Final Principle
Punish	S01 - US	high	high	Unequal p'ment	Equal punishment	Value of charity	(No new principle)
Punish	S02 - US	low	low	Equal p'ment	(No new position)	Equal responsibility merits equal justice	(No new principle)
Punish	S03 - US	high	low	Equal p'ment	(No new position)	Stealing is wrong	(No new principle)
Punish	S04 - US	low	low	Unequal p'ment	(No new position)	Egalitarian justice	(No new principle)
Punish	S05 - US	high	low	Unequal p'ment	Equal punishment	Unselfish intent modifies punishment	(No new principle)
Punish	S06 - US	low	high	Equal p'ment	(No new position)	Respect for societal code	(No new principle)
Punish	S07 - US	low	medium	Equal p'ment	(No new position)	Equal responsibility merits equal justice	(No new principle)
Punish	S08 - US	low	high	Unequal p'ment	(No new position)	Utilitarian, compassion	(No new principle)
Punish	S09 - US	low	low	Equal p'ment	(No new position)	Universalizability leads to chaos	(No new principle)
Punish	S10 - US	low	low	Unequal p'ment	Equal punishment	Utilitarian	(No new principle)

Exhibit 3: Non-Guided Negotiation: Issues – Stealing & Punishment

Group 2 Issue	Subject's Country	Moral Rea-soning Level	Intensity of Position	Original Position	Final Position	Original Principle	Final Principle
Steal	S11 - India	high	high	Equal p'ment	Unequal punishment	Utilitarian	(No new principle)
Steal	S12 - France	high	medium	Not take coins	Take coins after other options explored	Right of property earned by merit	(No new principle)
Steal	S13 China/ Phillip.	high	medium	Take coins	Negotiated medical fee	Utilitarian	(No new principle)
Steal	S14 - US	low	high	Not take coins	Negotiated medical fee	Family well-being	(No new principle)
Steal	S15 - US	high	low	Take coins	(No new position)	Property rights	(No new principle)
Steal	S16 - China	low	low	Not take coins	Take coins	Universalizability	(No new principle)
Steal	S17 - Korea	low	medium	Not take coins	(No new position)	Social order	(No new principle)
Steal	S18 - Bulgaria	low	high	Take coins	(No new position)	Charity outweighs law	(No new principle)
Steal	S19 - China/ Malaysia	low	medium	Not take coins	(No new position)	Situational fairness	(No new principle)
Steal	S20 - Vietnam /France	low	low	Take coins	(No new position)	Objective fairness	(No new principle)

Group 1 Issue	Subject's Country	Moral Reasoning Level	Intensity of Position	Original Position	Final Position	Original Principle	Final Principle
Punish	S11 - India	high	medium	Equal p'ment	Unequal punishment	Equal responsibility merits equal justice	(No new principle)
Punish	S12 - France	high	medium	Unequal p'ment	(No new position)	Unselfish	(No new principle)
Punish	S13 - China/ Phillip.	high	high	Equal p'ment	(No new position)	Deterrent retribution	(No new principle)
Punish	S14 - US	low	high	Unequal p'ment	(No new position)	Rehabilitation pro- portional to intention	(No new principle)
Punish	S15 - US	high	medium	Equal p'ment	(No new position)	Equal responsibility merits equal justice	(No new principle)
Punish	S16 - China	low	low	Unequal p'ment	(No new position)	Unselfish	(No new principle)
Punish	S17 - Korea	low	high	Unequal p'ment	(No new position)	Spirit of law	(No new principle)
Punish	S18 - Bulgaria	low	medium	Equal p'ment	(No new position)	Equity	(No new principle)
Punish	S19 - China/ Malaysia	low	medium	Equal p'ment	(No new position)	Stealing is wrong	(No new principle)
Punish	S20 - Vietnam/ France	low	medium	Unequal p'ment	(No new position)	Charity supercedes law	(No new principle)

Exhibit 4: Guided Negotiation: Issues – Stealing & Punishment

Group 1 Issue	Subject's Country	Moral Reasoning Level	Intensity of Position	Original Position	Final Position	Original Principle	Final Principle
Steal	S21 - US	high	high	Take coins	Loan from Maggot with interest	Personal benefits outweight cost	M. compensated and can enjoy his right to wealth
Steal	N - US	-	-	Not take coins	Loan from Maggot with interest	Dishonesty, end does not justify means	M. compensated and can enjoy his right to wealth
Steal	S22 - US	low	low	Not take coins	Sell/mortgage farm	Societal order, family well-being	Property sacrifice less than freedom sacrifice
Steal	N - US	-	-	Take coins	Sell/mortgage farm	Utilitarian	Property sacrifice less than freedom sacrifice
Steal	S23 - US	low	low	Not take coins	Community provides money	Stealing is wrong	Sets precedent for community spirit
Steal	N - US	-	-	Take coins	Community provides money	Utilitarian	Sets precedent for community spirit
Steal	S24 - US	low	medium	Take coins	Sam works for Maggot	Love	Enhance reputation of a community member
Steal	N - US	-	-	Not take coins	Sam works for Maggot	Property rights	Enhance reputation of a community member
Steal	S25 - US	low	low	Take coins	Loan worked off or a trade	Utilitarian	Generosity, reciprocity
Steal	N - US	-	-	Not take coins	Loan worked off or a trade	Respect for autonomy, property	Generosity, reciprocity

Group 1 Issue	Subject's Country	Moral Reasoning Level	Intensity of Position	Original Position	Final Position	Original Principle	Final Principle
Punish	S21 - US	high	medium	Equal p'ment	Alternative punishment for friend	Equal responsibility merits equal justice	Altruism
Punish	N - US	-	-	Unequal p'ment	Alternative punishment for friend	Unselfish	Altruism
Punish	S22 - US	low	medium	Unequal p'ment	Community service outside of stocks	Unselfish utilitarian	Time served outside of stocks benefits community
Punish	N - US	-	-	Equal p'ment	Community service outside of stocks	Non-discriminatory law	Time served outside of stocks benefits community
Punish	S23 - US	low	high	Equal p'ment	Time and place of punishment cause	Equal responsibility merits equal justice	Compassion, dignity
Punish	N - US	-	-	Unequal p'ment	Time and place of punishment cause	Higher community valued motives	Compassion, dignity
Punish	S24 - US	low	low	Unequal p'ment	Community service	Unselfish giving	Reparation
Punish	N - US	-	-	Equal p'ment	Community service	Law & order	Reparation
Punish	S25 - US	low	low	Unequal p'ment	Community service	Happiness	(No new principle)
Punish	N - US	-	-	Equal p'ment	Community service	Impersonal justice	(No new principle)

Exhibit 5: Guided Negotiation: Issues – Stealing & Punishment

Group 1 Issue	Subject's Country	Moral Reasoning Level	Intensity of Position	Original Position	Final Position	Original Principle	Final Principle
Steal	S26 - England	high	low	Take coins	Community donation	Utilitarian	Recognition, universalizability
Steal	N - US	-	-	Not take coins	Community donation	Social order	Recognition, universalizability
Steal	S27 - Germany	low	low	Not take coins	Loan from Maggot with interest	Utilitarian	(No new principle)
Steal	N - US	-	-	Take coins	Loan from Maggot with interest	Egalitarian	(No new principle)
Steal	S28 - Germany	low	low	Take coins	Loan from community	Utilitarian	Charity/universa- lizability
Steal	N - US	-	-	Not take coins	Loan from community	Property rights as part of social fabric	Charity/universa- lizability
Steal	S29 - France	low	medium	Take coins	Loan from Maggot with interest	Obligation of friendship	(No new principle)
Steal	N - US	-	-	Not take coins	Loan from Maggot with interest	Social order	(No new principle)
Steal	S30 - France	low	low	Take coins	Loan with interest from Maggot	Right to health	Equity
Steal	N - US	-	-	Not take coins	Loan with interest from Maggot	Property rights	Equity

Group 1 Issue	Subject's Country	Moral Reasoning Level	Intensity of Position	Original Position	Final Position	Original Principle	Final Principle
Punish	S26 - England	high	low	Unequal p'ment	Partial alternative punishment	Utilitarian	Autonomy valued over impersonal rule
Punish	N - US	-	-	Equal p'ment	Partial alternative punishment	Social norms for societal oder	Autonomy valued over impersonal rule
Punish	S27 - Germany	low	high	Unequal p'ment	Community Work	Aid outweighs greed	Courage/shame for greed
Punish	N - US	-	-	Equal p'ment	Community Work	Social order	Courage/shame for greed
Punish	S28 - Germany	low	low	Unequal p'ment	(No new position)	Unselfish utilitarian	(No new principle)
Punish	N - US	-	-	Equal p'ment	(No new position)	Non discrimination	(No new principle)
Punish	S29 - France	low	low	Unequal p'ment	Less pillory time, greater fine for friend	Match community order with social concern	Deterrent to others but signals social progress
Punish	N - US	-	-	Equal p'ment	Less pillory time, greater fine for friend	Social order	Deterrent to others but signals social progress
Punish	S30 - France	low	high	Unequal p'ment	Time and location different for public	Respect societal responsibility to sustain health	Societal progress based on egalitarian justice
Punish	N - US	-	-	Equal p'ment	Time and location different for public humiliation	Equal responsibility merits equal punishment	Societal progress based on egalitarian justice

Table 1

All Subjects	Non-Guided Negotiation		Guided Negotiation	
New Position	3	15%	19	95%
New Principle	0	0%	16	80%
Σ	20	100%	20	100%

Within Culture	Non-Guided Negotiation		Guided Negotiation	
New Position	1	10%	10	100%
New Principle	0	0%	9	90%
Σ	10	100%	10	100%

Between Cultures	Non-Guided Negotiation		Guided Negotiation	
New Position	2	20%	9	90%
New Principle	0	0%	7	70%
Σ	10	100%	10	100%

Table 2

Guided Negotiation

Moral Reasoning Level	Within Culture				Between Cultures			
	High		Low		High		Low	
New Position	2/2	100%	8/8	100%	2/2	100%	7/8	88%
New Principle	2/2	100%	7/8	88%	2/2	100%	5/8	63%

Non-Guided Negotiation

Moral Reasoning Level	Within Culture						Between Cultures					
	High/High		High/Low		Low/Low		High/High		High/Low		Low/Low	
New Position	-	-	1/6	17%	0/4	0%	1/2	50%	1/4	25%	0/4	0%
New Principle	-	-	0/6	0%	0/4	0%	0/2	0%	0/4	0%	0/4	0%

Culture as the Intermediate Structure of the Economy

Peter Koslowski

Business ethics has clarified the relationships between the moral norms and the individual actions of the people acting in cooperations and of the actions of cooperations themselves. Very little analysis has been done, however, on the relationship between economic culture and economic ethics or business ethics. The work on corporate culture seems to be almost unrelated to the work on business ethics. This separation of the endeavours of business ethics and of corporate culture or, more general, of economic ethics and of economic culture cannot be justified since if we look at the subject matter of the both fields, we find that the ethics and culture of the economy are closely connected.

1. Ethics as the Science About the System of Culture

When we look at the tradition of the cultural science or, in the German tradition, the *Geisteswissenschaften*, the humane sciences, we find that the distinction between normative ethics and positive cultural analysis that is quite familiar and influential today is not known to them. Wilhelm Dilthey in his famous *Einleitung in die Geisteswissenschaften. Versuch einer Grundlegung für das Studium der Gesellschaft und der Geschichte*[1]. (Introduction to the Humane Sciences. Essay on the Foundations of the Study of Society and History) of 1883

---

[1] W. DILTHEY: *Einleitung in die Geisteswissenschaften. Versuch einer Grundlegung für das Studium der Gesellschaft und der Geschichte* (1883), Vol. 1, Stuttgart (Teubner), Göttingen (Vandenhoeck & Ruprecht) 8th ed. 1979, p. 6ff. Cf. also P. KOSLOWSKI: "Ethical Economy as Synthesis of Economic and Ethical Theory", in: P. KOSLOWSKI (Ed.): *Ethics in Economics, Business, and Economic Policy*, Berlin, Heidelberg, New York, Tokyo (Springer) 1992, pp. 15-56.

H. Lange et al., Working Across Cultures, 287–304.

writes that ethics is "the science about the system of culture" From the idea that ethics is not only the science of normative morals but also the science about the entire system of culture three important insights are to be gained:

(1) The analysis of morals and of culture or ethos as the Greek said belong together. Ethics is not only the analysis of normative morals but also the analysis of the entire culture of a society. The connectedness of ethics and culture originates in the close relationship of morality and customs or in German *Sittlichkeit* and *Sitte*, the pair of opposite that Dilthey uses, or *Moralität* and *Sittlichkeit*, the distinction Hegel uses. The semantic closeness of *Sittlichkeit* and *Sitte* in the German language points to the fact that morality and morals and the other norms of convention and customs are closely related.

(2) The object of ethics and of the humane and social sciences, and therefore also of economics, is the culture of a society: its way of life and its self-interpretation of this way of life. There is no contradiction as some authors like W. Frühwald contend between *Geisteswissenschaften*, humane sciences, and *Kulturwissenschaften*, or cultural sciences. The science of the objectivations of the human spirit, of the *Geist*, is cultural science. The term "Geisteswissenschaften" emphasizes only the "mental" or "spiritual" dimension of culture. It does not, however, intend to imply that the objectivization of this spirit of a culture does not belong to the object of the cultural sciences. The objectivations of culture in institutions and texts, in rules and laws, in the symbolic objects and material objects of art and of economic production are objectivations but are *not only* objectivations. They are, at the same time, self-referential interpretations of their realm of social reality they offer to the addressee, the human subject. The objectivations of culture are never only objects but at the same time the carriers of the self-interpretion of the humans to whom they serve. In all cultural institutions and systems of rules, this element of self-reference and self-distancing of the addressee from these rules and his or her relationship to these rules can be found. The institutions of culture urge the self-conscious and self-interpreting individual to take position towards them. The individual concerned, addressed and determined by the cultural institutions must take position to the meaning of these institutions and cannot relate to them in the same way as to objects of the outer material, non-cultural world like the world of nature.

(3) In the study of the system of culture in the *Geisteswissen-schaften* or social and economic sciences, the analysis of society and history are inexorably interconnected. The object of the social sciences is historical. This means that the object of the social sciences changes, is influenced by elements of uniqueness and contingency and by multiple causation. The culture and economy are not objects like the objects in the natural sciences where the object of study can be reproduced in experiment infinitely and at any time. We skip here the problem and influence of history on the theory of the history of nature as we find it in biological evolution where the natural sciences face also the problem of history, particular in all kinds of evolution theory.

The tradition of the *Geisteswissenschaften* and of historism offers three insights for the analysis of the problems of economic culture:

(1) Ethics as the analysis of the system of culture emphasizes the positive, pre-moral cultural content of the norms of economic action against an abstract moral normativism in ethics and business ethics. Business ethics must also analyse the extra-moral forms of an ethos. This extra-moral ethos or culture can legitimately be done in this or that way. It is not morally determined that one can choose morally only one individuation or shape of, e.g., a certain corporate culture.

For the topic of the book at hand *Working Across Cultures*, the cultural sciences of *Geisteswissenschaften* demonstrate, therefore, that there are different forms of ethos, forms that are morally relevant in a strict sense and forms of ethos that are not morally relevant. Forms of economic ethos and economic culture are morally relevant in the strict sense if they touch the basic respect for the human person and human life. There are, however, also forms of ethos that are not of this kind but where the forms of economic ethos and culture are not morally relevant but still ethically interesting: e.g. how to organize social security, how to cultivate the firm and so on. It is important to distinguish business morality and business ethos for avoiding falling into abstract moralism and moral aggression. Not all cultural and ethical norms in the broader sense are morally relevant.

(2) The self-referential character of the cultural order and of its institutions as well as the cultural interpretations and making sense of these institutions is made visible by placing economics and business ethics within the context of the cultural sciences. The self-referentiality of the individual, the need and the chance of the individual to take

position towards the norms that he or she is supposed to follow is to be found in individual economic action and in the cultural institutions of the economy. This self-referentiality of the economy and of business must be emphasized against neo-classical economic theory that seems to lose sight of the symbolic, self-distancing and self-interpreting character of human economic action.

Economic agents do not only react to market signals but interprete and distance themselves from these signals at the same time as by reacting to them in their economic actions. In order to understand economic action we must understand the motives that determine the reactions of humans to market signals. These motives, however, are culturally shaped and influenced by the ethos and ethics, the customs and morals of the society and economy in question.

Working across cultures means to understand these cultural determinants of economic action.

(3) Against the timelessness and unhistorical character of neo-classical economics as well as of transcendental and discourse-theoretical theories of ethics and business ethics, the historical character of the economic systems and institutions must be remembered. The economy even in its constitution and system rules is not an unchanging market order valid for all places and all historical periods but it is an economic system that is subject to history, to historical influences stemming from the unique cultural and historical genesis of the economy in question.

To give an example: All economists warned against the common currency in the process of German unification: They did not understand the historical uniqueness of the situation which could not be measured in terms of monetary stability only but in which the political decision-maker had to take into account the unique and special character of the situation in which the economy was to be unified.

When individuals work across cultures in business and particularly when multinational firms work across cultures it is necessary to see that the acting persons in this economy must understand the history of this economy and the culture of the partners with whom the firm conducts business.

Working across cultures requires the awareness of the fact that the economic ethos and the culture in which we and our business partners live in have historically risen and are historically determined.

2. Ethical Economy as the Theory of the Morals and Ethos of the Economy

Turning to economic ethics, one must consider the two aspects of ethics, the aspect of the interpretative analysis of mores and morale, and the aspect of the theory of how one should act. This dual mode of theorising should also be applied to ethical economy as the theory of the ethos of an economy, which is simultaneously a theory of the actual ethos and the customs of the economy, and a theory of the ideal norms of morality. The term "ethical economy" is suggested as designating the theory of business ethics and ethos. On the one hand, business ethics or ethical economy as its theory is an analytic and interpretative, positive theory of the economic ethos and the economic culture and provides a descriptive theory of actual economic behaviour. On the other hand, it is also a normative theory of the ethics of economic behaviour as it relates to the moral norms of the economy. This ambiguity of ethics as cultural ethos and as a moral norm leads to the dual character of ethical economy. Ethical economy is divided into a positive, non-normative form of cultural economics and into a normative theory of economic ethics. The latter can again be divided between the formal economic ethics of the ethical coordination of the economy and the material economic ethics of the formation of preferences within the context of economic action.

Cultural-hermeneutical economics or positive ethical economy is the hermeneutics of economic action and explains how cultural factors are causal factors of economic action and economic coordination. In the cultural theory of economics the economic culture and customs of a national economy, the economic culture and customs of the other economies and of the global economy are the variables which need to be interpreted and explained. This theory presumes that the actual culture and the actual ethos causes a certain style and recurrent features of economic action in a given society. In this form of hermeneutical economics and in the cultural study of management science, in the analysis of the cultural and ethical causes of economic action, the positive, non-normative aspect is predominant. Economic phenomena like elasticities of demand are to be interpreted and explained in terms of cultural and ethical factors.

The other part of ethical economy, its normative part, looks at the methods of forming preferences and at the coordination of preferences and actions that are deemed morally acceptable in an economy. This normative part of ethical economy, normative economic ethics, is divided into a material and a formal ethical economy. Material ethics includes experiencing, judging and choosing values in an economy, while formal ethics involves the coordination of economic actions through an ethics of generalization.

3. Gustav Schmoller's Ethical or Cultural Approach to Economics, or: Economics as a Cultural Science

Gustav Schmoller and the Historical School did not isolate economic theory from other social sciences and ethics, but used the integrated concept of a national economy, which analyses ethical and cultural determining factors and integrates the methodological approaches of ethics and cultural studies into economic theory. Schmoller writes about the unity of the national economy:

Das gemeinsame, die Einzelwirtschaften eines Volkes oder Staates Verbindende, ist nicht bloß der Staat (ergänze: der Markt), sondern ist ein Tieferes: die Gemeinsamkeit der Sprache, der Geschichte, der Erinnerungen, der Sitten und Ideen (...) Es ist das gemeinsame Ethos, wie der Grieche das in Sitte und Recht krystallisierte sittlich-geistige Gemeinbewußtsein nannte, das alle Handlungen der Menschen also auch die wirtschaftlichen beeinflußt[2].

(The common element which relates each economic individual or nation together is not only the state (or the market), but is something deeper: the common language, history, memories, morals, and ideas. It is a common 'ethos', how the Greeks called it, the spiritual-moral sense of community, that is crystallized in morality and law and that influences all human actions, as well as economic actions.).

Schmoller calls his approach to the national economy "ethical"[3], thereby focusing on the ethical-cultural sense of community. As far back as 1897 he writes:

---

2   SCHMOLLER, G.: "Über einige Grundfragen des Rechts und der Volkswirtschaft. Offenes Sendschreiben an Herrn Prof. Dr. Heinrich von Treitschke", *Jahrbücher für Nationalökonomie und Statistik*, 23 (1874), pp. 225-349, and 24 (1875), pp. 81-119, here (1874), p. 254.

3   *Ibid.* (1874), p. 253.

Die heutige Volkswirtschaftslehre ist zu einer historischen und ethischen Staats- und Gesellschaftsauffassung im Gegensatz zum Rationalismus und Materialismus gekommen. Sie ist aus einer bloßen Markt- und Tauschlehre, zu einer Art Geschäftsnationalökonomie, welche zur Klassenwaffe der Besitzenden zu werden drohte, wieder eine große moralisch-politische Wissenschaft geworden, welche ne- ben der Produktion die Verteilung der Güter, neben den Werterschei- nungen die volkswirtschaftlichen Institutionen untersucht, welche statt der Güter- und Kapitalwelt wieder den Menschen in den Mittelpunkt der Wissenschaften stellt[4].

(Today's political economy represents an ethical and and historical conception of state and society rather than one determined by realism and materialism. From a pure theory of the market and of exchange, a kind of 'cash nexus economics', which was once a class weapon of the rich, economics has again become a great moral-political science. It analyses not only the production but also the distribution of goods, the value-adding processes as well as the economic institutions, and it puts man instead of goods and capital in the center of the science).

Political economy according to Schmoller is a humanistic concept, a historical and ethical science:

Die Sitten sind nicht angeboren und nicht von der Gottheit gelehrt, sie sind geworden, sind der fortwährenden Umbildung und Läuterung unterworfen; sie sind die ewig neue Offenbarung des Geistes im natürlichen Leben. Durch die Sitte baut der Mensch in die Natur eine zweite Welt, 'die Welt der Kultur' hinein. Und zu dieser Welt der Kul- tur gehört auch die Volkswirtschaft. (...) Die volks-wirtschaftliche Organisation jedes Volkes ist nichts anderes als die eben besprochene wirtschaftliche Lebensordnung, sie findet ihren wesentlichsten Aus- druck in den ethischen Regeln, in den wirtschaftlichen Sitten und in dem wirtschaftlichen Rechte jedes Volkes[5].

---

4   G. SCHMOLLER: *Wechselnde Theorien und feststehende Wahrheiten im Gebiete der Staats- und Sozialwissenschaften und die heutige deutsche Volkswirtschafts- lehre. Rede bei Antritt des Rektorats gehalten in der Aula der Königlichen Friedrich-Wilhelms-Universität am 15. Oktober 1897*, p. 26; quoted as motto to: A. SPIETHOFF (Ed.): *Gustav von Schmoller und die deutsche geschichtliche Volkswirtschaftslehre. Dem Andenken an Gustav von Schmoller, Festgabe zur hundertsten Wiederkehr seines Geburtstages 24. Juni 1938*, Berlin (Duncker & Humblot) 1938.

5   G. SCHMOLLER: *Über einige Grundfragen*, pp. 256-257.

(Mores are not innate nor taught by God; they have emerged and are subject to ongoing change and catharsis; they are the eternally renewed revelation of the spirit in natural life. Through morality man builds a second world, the world of culture, into nature. And the economy is also a part of this culture. The economic organization of all peoples (nations) is nothing more than the formerly explained economic order of life; this order finds its essential expression in the ethical rules, in the economic mores and in the economic law of each nation).

The ethical approach to economics regards the economy as a cultural sphere and economics as an ethical and cultural discipline because the economic order is built on the "ethical-mental-cultural sense of a people or nation". This notion of "people" or nation is fluid because it emerged during the historical process.

Das Wort 'Volk' ist dabei gebraucht einerseits als der Inbegriff der Vorstellungen über das, was die Glieder eines populus, einer natio eint, andererseits als der Stellvertreter für alle Arten innerer psychisch-moralischer Verbindung von Menschen[6].

(The term 'people' (nation) here is used, on the one hand, as the incarnation of all the reflections about what unifies the parts of a 'populus', a nation. On the other hand it represents all different kinds of internal psychological-moral relations between human beings)

Schmoller puts high demands on economic analysis: What is it that unites a national economy in psychological-ethical and economic terms? How do these psychological-ethical and economic forces influence, condition, and change the economic institutions and norms, especially as they relate to transactions and institutions? For Schmoller the terms "Volk" in "Volkswirtschaftslehre" or "nation" in "national economics" stand for all relations between human beings that may form a nation. This term does not designate a given and natural or *"völkische"* dimension but a spiritual and changeable form of socialization[7].

---

[6]   in: G. SCHMOLLER: *Die Volkswirtschaft, die Volkswirtschaftslehre und ihre Methode*, Frankfurt (Klostermann) (= Sozialökonomische Texte, vol. 16/17) 1949; first as article in: *Handwörterbuch der Staatswissenschaften*, 1893.

[7]   SCHMOLLER's analysis of the economy was conceived in the context of the foundation of the Second German Reich and its unification of Germany in 1870. From SCHMOLLER's analysis one can see that the unification of a nation and of

The psychological-ethical and the natural conditions of the national economy are, according to Schmoller, two independent, though closely related systems, which are to be analysed for their own individuality and for their influence on one another.

Die Welt der wirtschaftlichen Kultur dankt ihre Entstehung doch in erster Linie den geistigen Kräften der Menschen, die sie uns zunächst als Gefühle und Triebe, als Vorstellungen und Zwecke, weiter als Handlungen und habituelle Richtungen des Willens darstellen. Sofern Psychologie und Ethik das Ganze der Kräfte untersuchen und darlegen, hat man neuerdings ... öfter die Nationalökonomie eine psychologische oder auch eine ethische Wissenschaft genannt[8].

(The rise of the world of economic culture is caused first by the spiritual forces of man, which present themselves to us as emotions and impulses, as imaginations and puposes, and then as actions and as habits of the forces of the will. In light of the psychological and ethical analysis of these forces, economics has been recently thought of as a psychological or ethical science).

The ethical approach to economics recognizes not only the pursuit of self-interest as the principle of economics, but demands that all motives of action, even those beyond merely economic motivation, have to be taken into consideration in the theory of economic action[9].

Political economy, according to Schmoller, can not only analyse natural-technical conditions and the resulting prices, but it also has to examine how psychological-ethical and natural-technical causes relate to each other and influence one another.

Jede volkswirtschaftliche Organisation ist beherrscht von zwei Reihen relativ von einander unabhängiger Ursachen. Auf der einen Seite stehen die natürlich-technischen Ursachen, die die ältere Nationalökonomie ausschließlich ins Auge gefaßt hat; auf der anderen stehen die aus dem psychologisch-sittlichen Leben der Völker stam-

---

Europe cannot be reached simply by the expansion of the market. See: P. KOSLOWSKI: "Die Herstellung des europäischen Binnenmarktes 1992 und die Entstehung der 'Nation Europa'" (The Making of the European Single Market 1992 and the Rise of the 'Nation Europe'), in: P. KOSLOWSKI: *Wirtschaft als Kultur. Wirtschaftskultur und Wirtschaftsethik in der Postmoderne*, Wien (Edition Passagen) 1989, pp. 168-191.

8   SCHMOLLER, G.: *Die Volkswirtschaftslehre* , p. 52.

9   *Ibid.*, p. 53.

*menden Ursachen, die man bisher wohl ab und zu genannt, aber nicht
systematisch in ihrer Bedeutung für die Volkswirtschaft erforscht hat.
Eine Wissenschaft der Nationalökonomie wird es im strengen Sinne
des Wortes dann einmal geben, wenn nicht bloß die erste, sondern
auch die zweite Reihe der Ursachen erforscht sein wird[10].*

(Every economic organization is governed by two different kinds
of relatively independent causal factors. On the one hand, there are the
natural-technical causes, which are the only thing considered by the
old economic theory; on the other hand there are the causes that have
emerged from the psychological-moral life of the people, which have
been mentioned from time to time but have not been systematically
analysed in their importance for the economy. Economics, as a science
in the strictest sense, will exist when not only just the first, but also
the second causes are explored).

Schmoller uses the argument of completeness as a way of counter-
ing an economic theory that has been narrowed by materialistic and
naturalistic concepts. Only if ethical and cultural factors also appear
within the economic analyses, it is possible to grasp the substance of
economic theory.

Schmoller continues:

*Jene erste Reihe von (natürlich-technischen) Ursachen bildet den
natürlichen Unterbau, das Fundament der Volkswirtschaft; die aus
der anderen Quelle stammenden Ursachen erheben sich als ein viel
beweglicherer Zwischenbau auf diesem Fundament; erst beide
zusammen ergeben ein bestimmtes Resultat; erst auf beiden zusammen kann sich ein bestimmtes volkswirtschaftliches Gebäude erheben.
Ein großer Teil aller bisherigen volkswirtschaftlichen Untersuchungen litt an dem großen Fehler ... bestimmte wirtschaftliche Zustände
direkt aus jener ersten Reihe von Ursachen abzuleiten. Sie vergaßen
oder übersahen den ganzen Zwischenbau ... Sie litten stets an der
Sucht, aus technischen und natürlichen Prämissen zu erklären, was
jenseits aller Technik liegt; sie behaupten, aus bestimmten tech
nischen Tatsachen folge eine absolut notwendige bestimmte Lebensordnung und Gesetzgebung, während diese doch, wie auch die
Geschichte zeigt, sehr verschieden gestaltet sein kann. Sie verkannten
eben die Natur der Sitte und des Rechts, die Macht der sittlichen*

---

10 G. SCHMOLLER: *Über einige Grundfragen*, p. 264.

Gefühle und Kulturideen, die auch die ganze Volkswirtschaft beherr-schen[11].

(These first natural-technical causes form the natural basic struc-ture, the foundation of the economy; the second causes appear as a much more flexible intermediate structure; only when the two are combined is there a specific result; only when the two are combined a specifically emerged and constructed economic order results. A large part of all economic analyses so far has suffered from a large mistake ... to deduce certain economic situations directly from the first causes. They ignored or overlooked the whole intermediate structure ... They insisted on deducing from the technical or natural premises to find what was beyond all technology; they assert that from certain techni-cal facts, a necessary, certain order of life may be deduced, whereas – as history also shows – this order may be very different. They mis-judged the nature of morality and law, the power of moral emotions and cultural ideas all of which govern the whole economy.)

With his theory of an intermediating psychological-ethical struc-ture, Schmoller attacks two concepts he believes are erroneous: He does not believe that the natural organizational form of the national economy is absolute, and he also opposes the assumption that the eco-nomic order and institutions are determined completely by the exter-nal natural and technical conditions[12].

His term *Volkswirtschaftslehre*, economics as an ethical and cul-tural theory, is an attack on the idea of a timeless "natural" economic organization and on the idea that the economic substructure deter-mines the economic superstructure. In his view both these ideas are disproved by the existence of an economic, intermediate structure of ethics and culture which may weaken or strengthen the effects of natural conditions. Schmoller's idea of an intermediate structure is very fruitful. It is more powerful than the Marxian hypothesis that there is a reflection of the substructure in the superstructure[13] and it

---

[11] *Ibid.*; Cf. also P. Koslowski: *Gesellschaftliche Koordination. Eine kulturwissen-schaftliche und ontologische Theorie der Marktwirtschaft*, Tübingen 1991.

[12] *Ibid.*, p. 260.

[13] Comp. from the TREITSCHKE-SCHMOLLER controversy the judgement by Treitschke about Marx that there is too little scientific rigour in his work, in: H. TREITSCHKE: *Der Socialismus und seine Gönner. Nebst einem Sendschreiben an Gustav Schmoller*, Berlin (Georg Reimer) 1875, p. 81.

shows the – if not systematic then at least factual – neglect of the cultural "superstructure" in neoclassical economic theory. But Schmoller also opposes the tendency of "pure" economic theory to leave all questions about the cultural and ethical conditions of preferences, particularly those that influence the market, to an "institutional framework", so that in the end this framework is more interesting than the events in the market itself.

According to Schmoller the national economy is not only the sphere in which exchange and production occur, but is also an ethical economic order. Therefore economics does not become a science until both the natural and the psychological-ethical conditions in the economic life of different societies are explored. Economics as a science should not be restricted to an analysis of price-quantity-relationships, but should also take into account the origins of prices and values in the motives of the buyers and the institutional, ethical and cultural framework of an economy. The economic order and organization of a nation and firm is the order of everyday life[14]. This in turn means that it is part of the cultural and ethical order, and that the economy is a central aspect of the culture of a society[15].

Schmoller provides an instructive example through his discussion of elasticities of demand:

An einem Ort mit ausgebildeten Geschäftssitten ruft eine Markt-überführung sofort eine Gegenspekulation hervor, an einem anderen ohne solche führt dasselbe Überangebot zu einer langen chronischen Preisdrückung. Ein Sinken der Zuckerpreise in England bewirkt eine steigende Konsumtion, das gleiche Sinken bei uns bewirkt das nicht, weil bei uns die Sitte des Zuckerkonsums eine andere ist[16].

(Where the business customs are well developed, an oversupply leads to counter-speculative behaviour, there are other places without these customs where the same oversupply leads to a long and chronical suppression of the price. A decrease in the price of sugar in Eng-

---

[14] G. SCHMOLLER: *Über einige Grundfragen*, pp. 257 - 261.

[15] Comp. also: K.W.CHR. SCHÜZ: "Das sittliche Moment in der Volkswirthschaft", *Zeitschrift für die gesamte Staatswissenschaft*, 1 (1844), pp. 136f. - comp. also K. H. RAU: "Bemerkungen über die Volkswirthschaftslehre und ihr Verhältnis zur Sittenlehre", *Zeitschrift für die gesamte Staatswissenschaft*, 26 (1870), pp. 106-121.

[16] G. SCHMOLLER: *Über einige Grundfragen*, p. 258.

land leads to a rise in consumption, the same decrease in our country does not do the same thing because the custom of sugar consumption is different).

Elasticities of demand are influenced by ethics and culture.

Nicht Angebot und Nachfrage als Waren- und Geld- oder Kreditgrößen, sondern als Summierungen von psychischen Kräften beeinflussen den Wert. Sie wirken stets nur als Druck und Gegendruck auf den überlieferten Wert, der zunächst die Neigung hat, sich zu behaupten. Bei der Summierung dieser Kräfte sind manche scheinbar zugehörigen Elemente ohne jede Wirkung. Von einem einfachen berechenbaren Ergebnis auch der zur Wirkung kommenden Größe kann nicht die Rede sein. Die realen Änderungen der Warenmengen (Angebot) und der Geldmengen (Nachfrage) werden allerdings die Werte, wenn die dahinterstehenden psychischen und Machtverhältnisse dieselben oder ganz ähnliche bleiben, in der Regel entsprechend heben oder herabdrücken. Aber es bleibt stets fraglich, ob diese Voraussetzung zutrifft. Thut sie es nicht, ändern sich die psychischen Voraussetzungen, die gesellschaftlichen Einrichtungen und die Machtverhältnisse, so kann die gleiche Mengenveränderung sehr verschiedene Änderungen der Werte zur Folge haben[17].

(Supply or demand as summations of psychic forces, but not only as real, monetary or credit quantities influence the value. They act as pressure or counter-pressure affecting the value, particularly the first given value which asserts itself. In the summation of these forces some apparently affiliated elements do not have any effect. It is impossible to speak of a simple calculation of the effect. But the real changes in the quantities of goods (supply) and the quantities of money (demand) will normally increase or decrease the values if the underlying psychic or power relations stay the same. But it is always questionable whether this precondition exists. If not, if the psychic preconditions, the social institutions, and the power relations change, the same change in quantities can effect very different changes in values.)

---

[17] G. SCHMOLLER: *Grundriß der Allgemeinen Volkswirtschaftslehre*, part 2, Leipzig (Duncker & Humblot) 1904; reprint Düsseldorf 1989, vol. 2, pp. 113 f. SCHMOLLER gives the example of the price increase for estates in Berlin-Charlottenburg between 1864 and 1898 of the ratio 1 to 50 whereas the poulation only increased in a ratio of 1 to 13; see: *ibid.*

The effects of morals and culture on consumption, therefore, have to be introduced in an analysis of the market. The order of demand includes, as Schmoller says, the order of life, the way of life, in general[18].

In contrast to Schmoller the Austrian School of economics declares that questions about the origins of the structure of demand are outside the reach of economics. Ludwig von Mises, as a representative of the Austrian School and a critic of the Historical School, states that elasticities of demand are historical facts which should not be explored further by economic theory. He believes that these elasticities are historic facts and should be understood and described by historians but not be analysed by economists[19]. Mises follows in Rickert´s distinction between cultural science and natural science which states that cultural science and history focus on the particular whereas the natural sciences focus on the general, on general laws of causation[20].

The theory of the ethical intermediating structure in the economy mediates between the base and the superstructure of the economy and links the technical or natural sciences and the aspects of economic culture. This theory of the intermediate structure refutes the dualism between the general laws of nature and the particular traits of history and ethics. It shows that it is wrong to equate the ethical-cultural with the individual and the general with that which belongs to nature[21]. Ethical and cultural behavioural expectations, the interpretation of human existence and the order of individual and collective life, the ways in which individuals conduct their lives, are neither completely general nor completely unique. These role expectations and modes of conduct are historically developing and understandable by self-observation and empathy which is made possible through mediation between the general standards and the special circumstances as well as the individual interpretation of and coping with different situations.

---

[18] *Ibid.*, pp. 104, 109, and: *Die Volkswirtschaft*, p. 57.
[19] L. MISES: *Human Action. A Treatise on Economics*, New Haven (Yale University Press) 1949, p. 51.
[20] H. RICKERT: *Kulturwissenschaft und Naturwissenschaft*, Freiburg i. Br./Tübingen (J.C.B. Mohr) 1899, p. 38.
[21] G. SCHMOLLER: *Die Volkswirtschaft*, p. 41. He points out that history is not only individual.

Ethical economy as ethical and cultural economic theory, therefore, is an interpretative cultural and social science, which encompasses not only the commonly-held motive of striving for income[22],
but also the motives influenced by ethics and culture. Economics must
explain and understand the historical, particular "style"[23], representative of a particular period of time in cultural and ethical development,
as well as the general and timeless principles of morality.

Problems in economic theory not only involve the issue of choice,
as it pertains to utility and production theory under the assumption of
revealed preferences, but also the cultural analysis of supply and
demand in the market. A theory of the market economy must contain
both the ethical-cultural motives and the external economic causes
that determine supply and demand. Only when the interaction between
motives and revealed choices is known the elasticities of demand can
be understood, i.e. not only be taken as historical facts but also be
explained as results of regular causes that can be explained and interpreted in laws of causation. Only when all this is known would a prediction of the development of demand be possible. Because the businessmen and the politicians are not interested in historical descrip-
tions, but rather in explanations and predictions of elasticities of
demand, only then by using the ethical-psychological, interpretative
explanations of elasticities of demand can we come to a complete
description and prediction of the economic reality.

4. The Paradoxical Character of Culture as Social Totality and as a Part of Itself

In this paper the word "culture" has been used in a paradoxical way: as
the system of culture that describes the total social system, all systems
of norms and institutions, be they economic, political, juridic or artis-

---

[22] Comp. G. SCHMOLLER: *Über einige Grundfragen* ..., p. 253: The doctrine of
self-interest is only a means to circumvent psychology. On the other hand,
according to Schmoller, can the drive to gain income on a certain level of
cultural development affect certain classes in such a way that they will act as if
they are affected by mechanical process.

[23] Comp. A. SPIETHOFF: "Gustav von Schmoller und die anschauliche Theorie der
Volkswirtschaft", in: A. SPIETHOFF (Ed.): *Gustav von Schmoller und die deutsche geschichtliche Volkswirtschaftslehre*, p. 19.

tic ones, and culture and ethics as the intermediate structure between the laws of the economy and the legal norms. It is therefore necessary to distinguish between the larger and the narrower concept of culture. Culture in the narrow sense and as intermediate structure denotes the norms that have not gained the character of legal norms. Legal norms are norms that are justiciable, norms that are able to be inforced by a law suit. According to H. Kantorowicz, the law is the totality of social rules that prescribe external behaviour and are justiciable (*gerichtsfähig*). Justiciable are rules that are apt to be applied by an organ of the judiciary in due process.[24]

The narrower concept of culture as the intermediate structure between the law and the substructure of the economy is a useful analytical category for the following reasons:

(1) It makes clear that there is no solely economic causation but that the economy is influenced by the ethos of a society. The emphasis on the cultural overdeterminedness of economic causation within the economy is the argument that the concept of culture as the intermediate structure of the economy directs against the tendencies of neoclassical economic theory to conceptualize the economy as a self-sufficient entity influenced only by economic causation and being self-equilibrating in a "general market equilibrium".

(2) Against the Marxist theory of a dualism of superstructure and substructure, the concept of the economy as the intermediate structure of the society puts emphasis on the fact that the law is not a simple reflection (*Widerspiegelung*) of the economic basis but that the spontaneous forces of the market and of culture as well as of societal communication form a discourse in which the legal norms are prepared, debated and made culturally-ethically obligatory as ethical and cultural norms before they are made legal norms. The concept of culture as the intermediate structure does also justice to the fact that there are many cultural-ethical norms that are true norms but remain in the status of cultural norms and never become legal norms.

General ethics and business ethics in particular are the preparation and the inducement to the law and business law as already Plato stated it in his *Laws*. Ethics is the inducement, preparation and motivation

---

[24] H. KANTOROWICZ: *Der Begriff des Rechts*, Göttingen (Vandenhoeck & Ruprecht) 1963, p. 90. English original: *The Definition of Law*, Cambridge (Cambridge University Press) 1958.

for the free compliance with the law that has the power to compel. A good example for this fact is the legislation on insider trading. This legislation started from the more informal cultural norms of the stock exchange, was prepared by them and was then codified in legal norms justiciable in courts.

The culture of the economy is also an intermediate structure in the sense that it is a mediator between the motivation by mere economic self-interest and the motivation by the mere fear of the inforcement of the law. The ethical and the economic culture are an intermediate structure or mediator between what we want anyhow and what we are legally obliged to do. It moves us in the direction of the legal norms without already having their compulsory potential.[25]

5. Ethical Economy and the Global Economic Ethos

The task of business ethics and business culture to form an intermediate structure becomes even more relevant in the present world economy. There is a need for an intermediator between the different business cultures that the multinational firms and all acting persons in a highly integrated world market encounter. The need for intercultural mediation as well as the fact that this intercultural exchange gains an hitherto unknown intensity require the expertise to handle and analyse the intermediate structure of the culture in which he or she makes business and of the cultures influencing the world market from all "global players".

Working across cultures in a global world market also requires that we develop a joint global economic ethos for the global world market since we are already operating in one integrated global market. It is obvious that this is particularly true for the multinational firm which faces the intercultural encounter already within its corporate structure by its employees coming from different world cultures.

For the development and creation of a global economic ethos it is not sufficient to develop the formal conditions of dialogue and discourse only or to increase only our readiness to communicate with

---

[25] Cf. also P. KOSLOWSKI: *Prinzipien der Ethischen Ökonomie. Grundlegung der Wirtschaftsethik*, Tübingen (Mohr Siebeck) 1988, 2nd. ed. 1994. English translation forthcoming Dordrecht (Kluwer).

other cultures. Rather, we will have to develop a material common world economic ethos that regulates the behaviour and moral and cultural norms for the basic economic actions in the global market. There seem to be essentially four elements of a future ethos of the world economy: First the ethics of contract, second the ethics of respect for the rules of economic exchange and trade, third the readiness and accustomedness to apply fairness in pricing, fourth the will and intention to acknowledge professionality as a value and as an obligation to follow it in one's own economic actions.

The theory of the economic culture as an intermediate structure between the law and the economic causation in the market offers the theoretical tools to analyse and shape our own business culture and our encounters with the business cultures of our partners and of other world cultures.

The Ethics of Interest:
A Cultural-historical Perspective *

Luk Bouckaert

The prohibition of interest was an important element in Jewish, Islamic and Christian culture. Equally worth of notice is the almost universal agreement that a prohibition of interest would be irrational in modern society. Why did a prohibition of interest and usury occur in diverse pre-modern cultures, while it appears to be superfluous in modern society? For the French historian Jacques Le Goff the birth of capitalism is the key to understanding both the ancient passion against interest, branded as usury, and the modern matter-of-fact acceptance of interest as the reward for productive capital. In *La Bourse et la Vie* he outlines the historical significance of the moral debate on interest and usury: "In the seven centuries which separate the twelfth century from the nineteenth no other phenomenon can be found in the West in which economy, religion, the desire for money and the pursuit of eternal salvation were more remarkably intertwined than in usury ... The enormous debate which developed around usury, in a certain sense led to the birth of capitalism" (Le Goff 1987, p.9).

The absence of any moral reference in modern theories of money has not prevented a renewal of interest in the ethics of money. The first Paolo Baffi Lecture given by the well-known economist A. Sen (1991) with the title *Money and Value. On the Ethics and Economics of Finance* is an excellent example. In his lecture, Sen analyzed the pre-modern writings on interest of Kautilya (India, 4th century B.C.), Aristotle (Greece, 4th century B.C.) and the Book of Deuteronomy (written between 1000 and 500 B.C.). His intention was to show how the positions set out made a great deal of sense in their socio-cultural context, and that today, despite the different context, an ethics of finance has a rational and not a purely religio-moral basis.

---

* With thanks to Ref. Dr. Francis P. McHugh (Von Hügel Institute, Cambridge) for his remarks and stimulating comments.

H. Lange et al., Working Across Cultures, 305–320.

In this paper, I would like to outline the rise, disappearance and rebirth of the ethics of interest, which contains a logic that has been completely lost, because modern theories of interest have ignored or travestied the context, arguments and significance of the original debate. I will demonstrate that the various cultural traditions referred to were primarily concerned with the balance between the social and the capitalist economy.

The rise of the modern economy has given a central position to free-market rationality, a development described by L. Baeck in terms of the superseding of the Mediterranean by the Atlantic tradition of economic thought (Baeck 1994). The social economy – with its gifts, prohibition of interest and interest-free loans – was marginalised. The social motive did not disappear completely, but was seen as an exogenous factor. It was reduced to the role of complementing or correcting the market. In the second half of the twentieth century this correction has, in the wealthy industrialised countries, been embodied in a collective and politically regulated system of redistribution and social security.[1]

The crisis of the welfare state forces us to look for a new balance between a social-oriented economy and modern economic rationality. Ethical banking shows us that the social economy is searching for new forms and expressions. Economic problems such as environmental damage and debt overload have given new urgency to a moral theory of interest. Concepts such as time preference, liquidity preference, opportunity cost and risk cover only explain interest as a market phenomenon. New concepts with normative implications, such as sustainable development and debt forgiveness throw a completely different light on the significance of interest. It is more than a market variable: interest is also a political and moral phenomenon, an expression of deep-seated social choices.

The discussion about interest and interest prohibition is the story of the tension between a social and a capitalist economy. Naturally we can deal with only a few fragments of this cultural-historical epoch.

---

[1]   The individual was relieved of his religiously inspired duty of solidarity, which was taken over by a system of collective insurance and redistribution (de Wit / Terpstra 1991). Those entitled to welfare payments today do not pay interest any more than the medieval receiver of *mutuum*. Both cases concern economic transactions which express solidarity, although there are many points of difference between social security and the system of interest-free lending.

Although the Jewish texts are far older, we will begin with Aristotle, because his writings were used as a philosophical argument in support of interest prohibition by both Christians and Muslims. We will end with two current phenomena which call for an ethics of interest: ethical investment and current environmental problems.

1. Aristotle's Anticapitalism

The theme of the community *(koinonia)* is the key to a proper understanding of the Aristotelian interest prohibition. It is, furthermore, remarkable how interest prohibition in other cultural contexts is also closely linked to the maintenance of the community. The Aristotelian interest prohibition limits the dynamics of a capitalist economy which threatens the family, the village community and above all the polity.

Aristotle's principal concern is with the division between the economy of the natural community and the economy of monetary gain, types of economy which are mutually exclusive and cannot be reconciled. The community economy functions to fulfil natural needs, which are finite. They are limited to a fixed end which is integrated in the social order of values and norms. Education internalises the right order of values, aims, functions and relationships and makes human beings social and political animals. The division of labour, social hierarchy and social institutions, including exchange and money, must be subject to this natural and social teleology. Relationships of exchange and the price of goods must reflect the natural priority of needs and the concomitant hierarchy of social functions. In this community economy, money is purely functional, a unit of reckoning and a means of exchange. It cannot and must not be used to produce value of itself. The community alone, in fulfilling its natural and ordered structure of needs, creates economic value, real wealth. The Aristotelian economy aims for a complete equality of market exchange value and social usefulness.[2]

---

2   Social use value must be distinguished from subjective use value, which refers to the individual preferences of the consumer. For Aristotle, the use value expressed by the social structure of needs and teleology is the origin and measure of individual preferences.

Against the natural community economy stands the economy of monetary gain – called *chrématistikè technè* by Aristotle (in its narrow sense). The underlying dynamic is the accumulation of money, the archetype of unrestrained capitalism. Money and the exchange of money, rather than the social and natural use value of things, become the source of surplus value. For this reason Aristotle sees profit from trade in which one only buys and sells goods, without creating any social use value, as outside the community economy. Interest for money lent is the most flagrant attack on the Aristotelian concept of the community economy, since it involves a double reversal of values. Money itself is given a use value with its own finality instead of fulfilling its purely functional role as a means of exchange. But worse yet: the natural and social use value of things becomes a means to achieve exchange value on the market. In his criticism of the economy of monetary gain Aristotle seeks to show how political and moral values are instrumentalised in the process of capital accumulation which knows no end or boundary.

According to Koslowski (1994, p. 55), Aristotle's anti-capitalism is not only principled and philosophical but also practical. After the flourishing of Athens, the military, political and economic dismantling of the Greek *polis* set in from the second half of the fourth century. The Greek cities were increasingly integrated into the Macedonian empire, independent agriculturalist families lost their land, export-production in the Greek cities was in difficulties, the period 331-324 B.C. was characterised by famine. Aristotle's argument for the autarchy of the *polis*, the revaluing of agriculture and the strengthening of the household economy can be viewed as a conservative alternative to the political and economic crisis of his time.

2. Credit Provision as a Religious and Ethical Duty

Jewish communities have for various reasons been intensely occupied with money and trade. In Islam, trade and the development of the money economy is a recognised form of activity. Reading the Christian moral-philosophical treatises on interest prohibition will reveal the skilfullness of the compromise between a principled Aristotelian rejection of interest and economic necessity. One form of capitalism or another is, at least, accepted and tolerated in each of these traditions.

But this does not prevent the retention in principle of a limited interest prohibition. What is remarkable, is the shift in reasoning.

Aristotelian reasoning had an ontological basis. The interest prohibition was intended as a means towards aiming the economy at its actual target: the realisation of the natural priority of needs and values, the stabilising of the household and the polity. The Jewish and Islamic interest prohibition has a very different social origin and reasoning. The Sacred Scriptures originated in the context of new communities, inspired by religion, which felt a strong tie with the poor, marginalised or oppressed sections of society. These communities did not aim to maintain an existing social order, but hoped – now or later – for new social and human relationships. The motive of social justice and the distribution of wealth to the poor became an important aim. There is no ontological basis for interest prohibition, but only social and ethical considerations. The basic text in the Book of Exodus reads: "If you lend money to one of your poor neighbours among my people, you shall not act like an extortioner toward him by demanding interest from him." (Ex. 22:24). Both the duty to provide interest-free loans and the prohibition of interest remind the Jew of his responsibility to the poor. The oldest passage in the Koran dealing with the prohibition of interest *(riba)* similarly refers to care for the needy and the close link with the legally instituted alms *(zakat)*: "So give to the kinsman his due, and to the needy, and to the wayfarer. That is best for those who seek Allah's Countenance. And such are they who are successful. That which ye give in usury in order that it may increase on (other) people's property hath no increase with Allah; but that which ye give in charity, seeking Allah's Countenance, hath increase manifold" (Koran, Sûrah XXX, 38-39).

The social-ethical motive alters the implications of interest prohibition. Capitalism is no longer condemned in essence, only in its consequences, particularly inequalities of wealth distribution. The application of the interest prohibition is thereby considerably limited. It applies only to the loan. In the Jewish, Islamic and Christian contexts a distinction is made in principle between investing one's own capital in an undertaking and lending money. This distinction between investment and credit provision is essential. In later scholasticism lending is defined as a temporary transfer of property, while investing capital in a productive company is not giving it up, but putting one's own property to use. To demand interest on a loan is usury, while yield from risk-bearing capital investment is a justified profit. In the various contexts, one sees the development of legislation which regulates the distinction between lending and investing capital in a company. Jewish law recognises the status of the *heter iska*, Islam recognises the *mudâraba*, and Christian scholasticism recognises the company.

In these religious traditions, lending is essentially different from profitable commercial activity. All sorts of arguments were developed in scholasticism to substantiate this idea. Firstly, money in itself does not create a surplus value, an argument going back to the Aristotelian view that money is only an instrument of measurement and circulation. But a more complex argument was developed by St. Thomas Aquinas to demonstrate that money cannot be rented like a house or land (Koslowski 1994, p.77f.). There are some things of which the use can be separated from the possession. This means that when letting a house we can demand a rent for use and still retain possession of the property. For Aquinas such an income is permissible. But this is not true of consumables such as money, bread or wine. In this case, ownership cannot be separated from use. Someone who lends money (or another consumable such as bread) cannot sell the use without the property because both coincide. In other words, it is a transfer of property which is used and then, after a space of time, given back in full. Whoever asks for more to be given back than was lent, according to Thomas, is selling a thing twice, for its ownership and for its use, even though the two cannot be separated. The principle of just exchange in trading is thus violated. Selling the use of money for a price is dishonest trading.

Behind the argument of Aquinas is a deeper concern to tie the loan of money to a religious-ethical function. A loan is an expression of the religious duty to help a needy fellow human being. This neediness need not be destitution, it could just as easily be a temporary cash-flow problem. For St. Thomas the interest prohibition applies to both consumption and investment credit. The essence of the interest prohibition can be summarised in a social-ethical way as the intuition that one should not profit by another's misfortune. Lending is thus essentially different from investment and commercial transaction. It is a mix of gift and exchange, a temporary transfer of what is mine to another, a *mutuum* (what is "mine" becomes "thine"). As a temporary gift, the loan cannot bear rent. There is also no creation of surplus value by labour. Commercial logic just does not apply.

As commercial activity became increasingly important to society, all sorts of subtle constructions were developed in both the Christian and the Arab world to present credit provision as a contract of sale rather than a loan (e.g. the so-called threefold contract, Beutels 1987, p.48). According to the principle "ubi non est mutuum, ibi non est usura" (where there is no loan, there is no usury) this hidden interest could no longer be described as usury. But besides the practice of interest evasion, the scholastics undertook an interesting theoretical attempt to justify limited interest. Through their theory concerning the extrinsic reasons for demanding interest on a loan it became possible to distinguish between permissible and impermissible interest, in other words between usury and (morally acceptable) interest on a loan.

Intrinsically interest, given the nature of a loan, is still forbidden. But the social logic of the loan does not demand that one must become the victim of a loan. There can, in other words, be *extrinsic* reasons to demand interest. They do not result from the nature of the loan, but from certain damaging side-effects. Reimbursement may be required for the losses and costs caused by lending, for instance if a time limit has not been met. This is different from usury. Interest as reimbursement for damages *(damnum emergens)* is permissible. St. Thomas of Aquinas, however, insisted that these must be real losses and expressly rejected the claim of losses of opportunity as a basis for requiring interest. According to him this would inflate the notion of costs so highly that the willingness to lend without interest, and thus the loan itself, would disappear.[3] In the later scholastics, however, the reasons for reimbursement for loss were defined more

---

[3] In a commentary on the passage (II 2ae q. 78 a. 1 ad 1) where Aquinas discusses losses as a basis for interest, Koslowski (1994, p.79) writes: "Thomas lehnt damit den Opportunitätskostengedanken beim Darlehen ab. Die Kosten des Darlehens können nicht in der höchstbewerteten, durch das Darlehen aufgegebenen Alternativverwendung ausgedrückt und dem Darlehensnehmer in Rechnung gestellt werden, weil diese Opportunitäten unsicher sind und stets als Argument *gegen* die Vergabe eines zinslosen Kredits angeführt werden können. Das Opportunitätskostenargument tötet die Bereitschaft, einen zinslosen Kredit zu geben und damit die Bereitschaft zur Hilfestellung. Der ordo caritatis, die Ordnung der Liebe, kennt nach Thomas keine Opportunitätskosten."

and more broadly. Initially only losses suffered were permissible, but the late scholastics broadened the concept to include loss of profit *(lucrum cessans)* and thus let in loss of opportunity as a basis for claiming interest. Lessius discusses a third basis for interest: loss of liquidity *(carentia pecuniae)*. This concession in effect further undermines the interest prohibition, because lending money always involves a loss of liquidity. In reaction to superficial readings of Lessius, Van Houdt (1995) has shown that Lessius discusses loss of liquidity, but only allows it very limited scope as grounds for interest. Only a merchant, for whom money is the tool of his trade, can plead loss of liquidity, but this in effect makes it loss of profits. Lessius, just like St. Thomas, wanted to keep a space for the interest-free loan. No doubt seeing that the purpose of the interest prohibition as a social duty was being lost in a society in which money had simply become potential commercial liquidity, he wanted to maintain the religious-ethical significance of money and credit provision. He was attempting to find a new balance between ethics and the economy of interest.[4]

The same attitude of maintaining the interest prohibition in principle, while in practice being open to a money and credit economy, can be found in Islam and Orthodox Judaism. Besides concern for the weak, another motive encouraged attachment to interest prohibition, namely group loyalty, the solidarity with the religious community.

3. Interest Prohibition and Group Loyalty

Reading the contributions concerning the origins of the interest prohibition one is struck by the fact that the prohibition usually applies to the particular community, and not to outsiders. The passage from the Koran quoted above refers not only to the needy, but also to relatives. The much older Deuteronomy, 23:20-21, is very clear on this point: "Unto a stranger thou mayest lend upon usury; but unto thy brother thou shalt not lend upon usury; that the Lord thy God may bless thee

---

[4]   Balancing the arguments of just exchange (interest for losses and costs) and solidarity (prohibition or limiting of interest) leads in Lessius's work to a realistic approach to credit provision with moderate interest. In this spirit Lessius, at the request of the Archdukes Albert and Isabella, defended the founding of *Montes Pietates* or Mounts of Mercy (low-interest public pawnshops) in the seventeenth-century Low Countries (Beutels 1987; Van Houdt / Golvers 1992).

in all that thou settest thine hand to in the land whither thou goest to possess it." The difference between "brothers" and "foreigners" is also found in the many other passages in the Pentateuch which deal with the repayment of debts and responsibility for the poor. Thus there was an obligation on relatives to buy back land which a member of the family had sold to repay debts (Lev. 25:23-28). Relatives should also purchase the freedom of someone sold into slavery as a debtor. If this was not possible, the Israelite and his family should be released in a jubilee year (Lev. 25: 35-43). All these rules applied to coreligionists but not to strangers. Concerning the ownership of slaves: "Slaves, male and female, you may indeed possess, provided you buy them from among the neighbouring nations" (Lev. 25: 44).

The attitude to one's own people differs from that to strangers. This dual structure is not only to be found among the Jews, but also in the Greek distinction between citizens and barbarians, and the Christian and Islamic distinction between the faithful and the infidel. This does not mean that there are no rules governing the treatment of strangers. The prohibitions against killing or committing injustice apply to the treatment of all people. But in the Old Testament the interest prohibition and the duty to redeem debts or slaves apply only to the Chosen People. They are expressions of group solidarity and are not universally applicable. Christian and Muslim theologians interpreted the interest prohibition more universally. Thomas of Aquinas does so very clearly (II 2ae q. 78a. 1 ad 2) but this does not prevent him from making an exception of the Jews elsewhere: Jews could, as was customary, lend to Christians at interest (Sen 1993). The exceptional position of the Jews explains their key position in the Western economy but also their vulnerability to persecution. The persecution of Jews became one way of violently reducing the burden of debt. Debeaussaert (1994) shows how Mohammed asked Jews for interest-free loans on the basis of a shared faith but was rejected, which may have been one source of friction between Mohammed and the Jews.

The interest prohibition as a sign of group loyalty and political independence now plays an important role in the Islamic revival. It functions as the ultimate symbol of an Islamic economy which will not be integrated into the Western system of global capitalism. The interest prohibition thus has a double meaning: resistance to Western capitalism and a symbolic reaffirmation of socio-cultural identity.

4. From Pre-modern to Modern Interest Theory

Jeremy Bentham's *Defence of Usury* (1787) can be regarded as a radical departure from the pre-modern view of interest. Bentham wrote the
book during a stay in Russia when he heard that Pitt wanted to reduce
the legal interest rate in England from 5% to 4%. Bentham was a fiery
proponent of free interest rates, even if they led to higher interest. He
defended so-called usury in so far as it had developed independently
and showed no obvious loss of social utility. Bentham saw no reason
to interfere in England. First he defended the principle of "the liberty
of making one's own terms in money-bargains" (Steintrager 1977,
p.63). Each individual knows better than the legislator where his own
interest lies. Bentham found the idea that there was a moral order
which precedes or surpasses individual preferences unconvincing. And
it was this idea which formed the basis of interest prohibition or regulation. But the weight of his argument lay in the utilitarian consideration that interest regulation had more drawbacks than benefits.
Bentham became involved in a polemic with Adam Smith, to whom
he had written a letter on the question (July 1790, see *The correspondence of Jeremy Bentham*, vol. 4, no. 702, pp. 132-134).

   According to Smith, the authorities should combat usury by fixing
a limit to the level of interest. If interest were too high, by which
Smith means 8-10%, then only "prodigals and projectors" (i.e. wastrels
and entrepreneurial adventurers) would dare borrowing money. The
thrifty and prudent, precisely those who would use money efficiently,
would be put off, while the adventures of "prodigals and projectors"
would easily lead to social loss. That is why legal regulation was
necessary. While Bentham understood Smith's view of "prodigals", he
completely disagreed about "projectors". In Bentham's view, their
adventurous risks revivify the economy: "For think, Sir, let me beg of
you, whether whatever is now the routine of trade was not, at its
commencement, project? Whether whatever is now establishment, was
not, at one time, innovation?" (Steintrager 1977, p.63).

   Although Smith and Bentham disagreed about the likelihood of
market failures and the necessity of government intervention in the
capital market, the logic of the market was basic to both of them. The
moral motive – both Aristotelian anticapitalism and the social-ethical
duty of redistribution – were no longer the measure of economic
thought and action. They were replaced by self-interest and the result-

ing improvement in social wealth. Although Smith and Bentham worked from very different moral premises (Smith was not a utilitarian), both of them saw the free market as the obvious foundation of the economic order. Any departure from market forces should be justified by rational motives and arguments. The attitude of scholastic treatises was the opposite: the interest prohibition in the name of duty to the community was the foundation, and any move towards free market forces had to be justified theoretically. With Smith and Bentham, the burden of proof is cast onto those who defend government intervention. Even though the practical conclusions may be parallel, the difference in the principles of social philosophy is clear.[5]

Following Bentham and Smith, the modern discourse of interest further neutralises moral reasoning. This occurs in two ways: through the theory of market equilibrium and through the subjective interest theory of the Austrian school. With regard to the former, Smith's "invisible hand" metaphor is developed in the general and partial equilibrium analyses of markets. Adam Smith held that in a competitive environment the market price (and thus also the level of interest) would automatically fall to its natural level, i.e. to the cost-covering level described by the scholastics in their just price theory (Cassel 1971). Moral or political concern is therefore unnecessary when free competition is assured. The Walrasian économie pure, which suggests a perfectly self-regulating system, has lost all theoretical link with ethics. Irrespective of the moral quality of the intentions, the "invisible" price mechanism ensures that wealth is equally distributed in relation to the functions of demand and supply. On the money and capital markets interest is completely determined by the mechanism of self-regulating equilibrium.

Besides the equilibrium theories which continue with the invisible hand metaphor, there are modern, subjective interest theories following v. Böhm-Bawerk and Fischer. In these subjective micro-economic theories, interest is explained by the motives of the person acting and not from the viewpoint of system functionality. This is an extension of

---

5   According to Sen (1993) Smith is an interventionist, in contrast to Bentham. This may be true where financial markets are concerned but in general Bentham's utilitarianism cannot be equated with laissez-faire liberalism. The principle of utility is the ultimate criterion for judging between intervention and laissez-faire in any given situation (Steintrager 1977).

the scholastic theory of interest as reimbursement for costs. But nevertheless there is a clear fault-line here too: the premise of the modern, subjective interest theory is the Benthamite sovereignty of the individual who has free disposal over his time and money: "the liberty of making one's own terms in money-bargains". In the modern Benthamite world in which individuals exchange time and money on a basis of mutual advancement no usury or exploitation can exist, since all decisions are based on freely made choices. A just society need only guarantee free choice, and by extension liquidate any monopoly position. Concepts such as solidarity and usury – which contain normative and religiously loaded concepts of community – do not fit this frame of reference. They disappear from the discourse or at the least lose their original meaning.

5. The Rediscovery of an Ethics of Interest

Is the scholastic philosophy of the *mutuum* as an economic transaction sui generis – a mixture of gift and exchange – still relevant today? Is there a link between the pre-modern ethics of interest and the post-modern reflection on "economics and ethics"? In our view there is indeed a link. We would like to draw attention to certain more recent tendencies to limit interest from the principle of solidarity, or attempts to balance just exchange against the duty of solidarity. Elsewhere we have discussed debt mitigation (Bouckaert 1994). Here we will look at interest on ethical investment and savings and the calculation of the discount rate in environmental reporting. In these two examples a *mutuum* transaction takes place, a combination of exchange and gift.

Ethical saving and investment is an investment strategy in which the saver aims at both social and financial surplus value. The social aspect is explicitly present in the selection of investments and usually (but not necessarily) also in the limiting of the interest. It is particularly in this last case that the ethical motive becomes apparent, since a partial renunciation of financial gain is made for social reasons. Yet ethical saving and investment is not about simple donation: reasonable reimbursement is expected for the "lost use" and the sacrifice of liquidity. In scholastic terms: the transaction combines an intrinsic ethical motive with extrinsic, economic considerations. The opposite case is of course also possible, for instance a bank setting up an ethical investment service for intrinsically economic motives, the ethical argument then being extrinsic. In principle the two are clearly different, but in practice it is not always easy to distinguish intrinsic and extrinsic motives. This ambivalence is not new. The existence of money and capital markets makes it unavoidable. In medieval practice the interest debate was often concerned with whether a transfer of money was a loan or a sale. To escape the heavy limitations on interest on loans, attempts were made to present the transfer as a sale on which profit could be made. Today, however, this ambivalence is not such a problem as there is no legal interest prohibition (except in some Islamic countries). Those who opt for ethical saving and investment do so of their own free will.

The second example is the calculation of discount rates in environmental reporting (Van Liedekerke 1994). When evaluating projects set up by national authorities or big companies an environmental report is required, evaluating the likely impact of these projects on the environment. What impact will a new nuclear power-station have on the environment in which future generations must live? What are the consequences of a policy of taxing carbon dioxide emissions to reduce the greenhouse effect? In the cost-benefit analysis in which welfare effects are weighed, a discount rate is used. This is an index which expresses the difference between current and future valuations of goods and services. An important element in the cost-benefit analysis is the necessity of comparing the current and future valuations of goods and services. The negative effects of nuclear waste and carbon dioxide emissions are only noticeable decades later. Less importance is attached to them than would be the case if their effects were immediately apparent. The same is true, for example, of the positive effects of investment in reducing the greenhouse effect. These will only be felt by coming generations. In general most economists assume we have a positive time preference: we attach greater value to what we have now than to what we will only get tomorrow. Costs and benefits which will only be due far in the future are considered even less. We will only give up benefit now for a future benefit if some surplus value is offered as compensation. Or put the other way: when we convert the future rewards into current values we will have to apply a deduction.

According to von Böhm-Bawerk this difference, the discount rate, is reflected in the interest rates on capital markets.[6]

The ethical problem arises when we have to decide the level of the discount rate. Usually one of the interest rates on the capital markets is taken. But these interest rates reflect the individual preferences and expectations of living generations who mostly have a relatively limited temporal horizon. They do not reflect the desires of future generations. At the most they reflect the extent to which current generations are concerned about their descendants. Whether they are at all and to what degree remains very uncertain and dependent on all sorts of coincidental circumstances. From the moral intuition that future generations have a right to the same opportunities as ourselves, we will tend to moderate the positive time preference of generations now living. The preference for the immediate must give way for a temporal horizon which transcends attachment to the present. This means that responsibility for future generations needs a *social or moral discount rate* which corrects individual time preferences. Such a moral discount rate must be anchored in the concept of *sustainable development*.

Sustainable development is a normative concept and cannot be deduced from the short-term horizon of individuals. It relies on a much longer-term perspective which takes into account our responsibility to future generations. Such a broadened temporal perspective presupposes the conviction that time is not simply the possession of the living but a public good which belongs to future generations. Such a concept of time is in fact a traditional view which has been weakened by market-oriented attitudes.

In traditional cultures a strong attachment to the dead is anchored in all sorts of rituals and customs which are mostly given a religious interpretation. A favourite argument in the medieval debate on interest was to stress that time had a dual structure: God's time and human time. Precisely because time could not be privatised, claiming interest as a reimbursement for relinquishing one's positive time preference was a limited possibility. In a modern and competitive society time is strongly privatised. But in an environmental crisis, time again appears as an intergenerational process, no longer with the emphasis on soli-

---

6   von Böhm-Bawerk (1921), p.318: "Present goods are in general worth more than future goods of a similar nature. This sentence is the heart and the centre of the theory of interest which I wish to propose."

darity with the dead, but on solidarity with future generations. Tradition is no longer the leitmotif, but our responsibility to the future. Thus the postmodern transcendence of the privatised concept of time differs from the traditional, pre-modern temporal horizon. An interest-limit based on our responsibility to future generations becomes necessary, especially on projects with long-term external effects. Such investments based on a moral discount rate can be regarded as a *mutuum* or a loan to future generations.

6. Conclusion

A theory of interest poses two questions: the reason for interest and the rate of interest. In an Aristotelian framework the second question is meaningless because interest has no right to existence. The interest prohibition is total. In a modern interest theory the first question is redundant. Only the second question matters – what is the interest rate: a question which needs no moral clarification, only market analysis. An ethics of interest moves between the two positions. Interest is both legitimate and limited. Legitimised by the logic of the market, limited by the logic of solidarity.

The historical outline of the interest debate furthermore teaches us that an ethics of interest is culturally determined. But according to the fault-lines of historical rather than national cultural differences. The historical transformations from pre-modern to modern and from modern to postmodern culture are the determining factors. The interest prohibition exists in various pre-modern cultures, but wanes as the transformation to modern society increases. The modern theory of interest, based on the autonomous time preferences of individuals and on the market as coordinating mechanism, destroys the last remnants of the interest prohibition. Time and money become private property. Future generations being excluded from consideration in the exchange of capital are placed outside the "economic". A postmodern theory of interest brings ethics back into economic play, as we have demonstrated with two examples. Environmental concerns force us to consider time from the perspective of our duties towards future generations. We express this in the concept of sustainable development, which moderates interest as a market price. The other example, ethical saving and investment, again introduces the philosophy of the *mutuum* into the world of market-economic credit management.

References

Baeck, L. (1994): *The Mediterranean Tradition in Economic Thought*, London.

Bentham, J. (1981): Letter to Adam Smith, in: Taylor Milne, A: (ed.): *The Correspondence of Jeremy Bentham*, Vol. 4, London: Athlone Press, pp. 132-134.

Bentham, J. (1952): Defence of Usury, in: Stark, W. (ed.): *Jeremy Bentham's Economic Writings*, Vol. I.

Beutels, R. (1987): *Leonardus Lessius 1554-1623*. Portret van een Zuidnederlandse laat-scholastieke econoom, Wommelgem: Den Gulden Engel.

Bouckaert, L. (1994): Van Intrestverbod tot schuldverlichting, in: Bouckaert, L. (red.): *Intrest en Cultuur. Een ethiek van het geld*, Leuven: Acco, pp. 11-35.

Cassel, G. (1971): *The nature and necessity of interest*, New York: A.M. Kelley, (1903).

Debeaussaert, D. (1994): Het intrestverbod in de Islam. Recht of ethiek? in: Bouckaert, L. (red.): *Intrest en Cultuur. Een ethiek van het geld*, Leuven: Acco, pp. 77-99.

Koslowski, P. (1994): *Die Ordnung der Wirtschaft*. Studien zur Praktischen Philosophie und Politischen Ökonomie, Tübingen: J.C.B. Mohr (Paul Siebeck).

Le Goff, J. (1987): *De woekeraar en de hel. Economie en religie in de middeleeuwen*, Amsterdam: Wereldbibliotheek. Translated from: La Bourse et la Vie, Machette 1986.

Sen, A. (1993): Money and value. On the Ethics and Economics of Finance (Baffi lecture 1991), in: *Economics and Philosophy*, 9, pp. 203-227.

Steintrager, J. (1977): *Bentham*, London: Allen & Unwin.

The Glorious Koran (1976), translated by Muhammed Marmaduke Pickthall, London: Allan & Unwin.

De Wit, T., & Terpstra, M. (1991): Het maatschappelijk geschenk. De verlossing van de schuld in Hobbes' Leviathan, in: Terpstra, M., *Schuld en Gemeenschap*, Baarn: Ambo, pp. 45-97.

Van Houdt, T., Golvers, N. en Soetaert, P. (1992): *Tussen Woeker en Weldadigheid. Leonardus Lessius over de Bergen van Barmhartigheid*, Leuven. Acco.

Van Houdt, T. (1995): Money, Time and Labour. Leonardo Lessius and the Ethics of Lending and Interest Taking, in: *Ethical Perspectives*, (2), no. 1, pp. 11-28.

Van Liedekerke, L. (1994): Tijd, preferentie, tijdspreferentie. De intrestvoet als beslissingsvariabele, in: Bouckaert, L. (red.): *Intrest en Cultuur. Een ethiek van het geld*, Leuven: Acco, pp. 127-143.

Von Böhm-Bawerk, E. (1921): *Kapital und Kapitalzins*. II. Positive Theorie des Kapitales, 4. Aufl., Jena: Gustav Fischer.

The Principles of the Advertising Self-regulation in Europe

Edoardo Brioschi

1. A Far-reaching Research

Businesses, while carrying out their communication activities –
especially those with commercial purposes such as advertising, sales
promotion, public relations, etc. – more and more frequently have to
confront, on the one hand, the users of their productions who are
becoming more and more alert and are increasingly less inclined to
receive huge quantities of advertisements; and, on the other hand, a
more and more sophisticated and world-wide competition.

This happens while an increasing number of markets – particularly
in the consumer goods field – are becoming mature.

All this has led businesses to develop communication strategies
which – both by exploiting their own productions and/or their own
basic features, and, even more than that, by treating non-commercial
themes (in particular social issues) – risk, in many cases, incurring the
non-observance of ethical principles. These principles should, on the
contrary, regulate the activities taken into consideration.

These important matters, though they have been commanding
attention since the 1910s in the United States and since the 1930s in
Europe (as referred in particular to the activity of the International
Chamber of Commerce), in the period after the second World War led
to the issuing – by advertisers and professionals belonging to different
contexts – of specific self-regulation codes which take into consideration, first of all, advertising, public relations and sales promotion.

The above problems interested experts on ethical questions – with
reference to businesses and/or mass communication media – and
scholars of various disciplines (economists, business management
experts, psychologists, sociologists, etc.).

H. Lange et al., Working Across Cultures, 321–339.
© 1998 *Kluwer Academic Publishers. Printed in the Netherlands.*

At first, this trend involved only English-speaking countries, where specialized publications have been flourishing for many years now. Later on, this same tendency has made its appearance both in continental Europe and, especially, in Italy, where a self-regulation code has been applied to advertising since 1966.

As far as the above issue – in its general rules – is concerned, I deemed it proper and suitable to propose an ambitious, far-reaching survey to the National Council for Scientific Research of my country in order to:

- *state the ethical principles* which should regulate business communication;
- *identify the basic directions* followed by the most reliable domestic and international literature on the analysis of said principles and of their application with reference to various economic and social contexts;
- *identify the problematic areas* which still appear susceptible to investigation.

As far as the methodology of the proposed survey is concerned, we have the following aspects:

a) *a comparative analysis of the main self-regulation codes* developed in the United States and Europe, and referring to the various fields of business communication;
b) *the analysis of the databanks* of the most important and significant universities in the above-mentioned geographic areas, with reference to the ethics of business communication;
c) *the identification of the works and periodical publications* which are most relevant for the determination of the research directions about the subject generally followed up till now, and the determination of the problematic areas still in need of investigation;
d) *the drawing up of a summary* in order to allow other teams of experts, if any, to investigate further and suggest solutions for the problems which have been discovered and duly highlighted.

It is an extremely complex, demanding research which started in the second half of 1995 and is to be developed during a period of five years. Today's presentation concerns only its first stage, which is necessarily restricted as follows:

- comparative analysis of self-regulation codes is referred only to Europe;
- said analysis refers only to businesses advertising activity, this being, as everybody knows, highly advanced as far as self-regulation is concerned, especially if compared to other activities of commercial communication.

2. The "Alliance" Codes

When restricting to Europe the initial compass of the above-mentioned first stage of our research, it appeared logical to refer to an extremely important body with connecting functions, the European Advertising Standards Alliance (EASA), founded in Bruxelles in 1991. In July 1995 the self-regulatory bodies of fifteen countries subscribed to EASA, two of them (Denmark and Switzerland) as associate members.

At any rate, by the above date a few East European countries had already submitted their applications for membership as corresponding members[1]: these (Czech Republic, Slovakian Republic, and Slovenia) would later be accepted as members by right, a designation also given to Finland and Turkey in 1996.

At any rate, at the beginning of the survey the sources used for the self-regulation rules were as indicated (Table 1).

As for the particular survey presented, the Slovenian Code of Self-Regulation in Advertising (approved of towards the end of 1994) has been taken into consideration. At the beginning of this survey, no other codes of East European countries were available.

The direct or indirect references to the International Code of Advertising Practice of the International Chamber of Commerce – sometimes references are actually linguistic translations – allow us to say that the Code examined (starting from the initial 1937 publication) has represented, and still represents, the common source of inspiration for self-regulation rules in Europe[2].

---

[1] Said designation had already been adopted by a non-European body, the Advertising Standards Authority of South Africa.

[2] See also the case of the self-regulation system in Turkey, subsequent to the beginning of our survey.

Table 1: *Sources*

COUNTRIES	SOURCES
Austria	Selbstbeschränkungsrichtlinien des Österreichischen Werbewirtschaft
Belgium	Reglementation de la publicité du Conseil de la Publicité ASBL
Denmark	no codes
France	Recommandations du Bureau de Verification de la Publicité
Germany	Das Deutsche System der Werbeselbstdisziplin (Deutscher Werberat)
United Kingdom	British Code of Advertising Practice (*)
	(The ITC Code of Advertising Standards and Practice)
Greece	Greek Code of Advertising Practice
Ireland	Code of Advertising Standards
Italy	Codice dell'Autodisciplina Pubblicitaria
Luxembourg	no codes
Netherlands	The Dutch Advertising Code
Portugal	Codigo de Conduta do ICAP
Spain	Codigo de Autocontrol de la Publicidad
Sweden	no codes
Switzerland	Régles de la Commission Suisse pour la Loyauté en Publicité

(*) Together with the «Notes of Guidance for Broadcast Advertising»

The above code – in its last 1986 version – has therefore created the basis for the comparative analysis carried out with reference to the various European Countries[3] .

---

[3]   I would like to thank Dr. Vincenzo Guggino of the Italian Institute for Self-Regulation in Advertising for his co-operation in the search of the sources for my survey.

3. Advertising and Its Identification

The scope of the already mentioned International Code of Advertising Practice is represented by advertising "for any goods, services and facilities, including corporate advertising".

The concept of "advertising" is typical theory in English-speaking countries; therefore it has or might have different characteristics compared to the other concepts described in the following table (Table 2). As a matter of fact, the concept of "advertising" is wider than the Italian corresponding term "pubblicità", a word which usually translates the English "advertising". The same could be stated for the concepts of "publicité commerciale" and "die Werbung der Wirtschaft".

Table 2: *Self-Regulation Scopes of the Various Codes*

COUNTRIES	EXCLUSIVE OR MAIN REFERENCE SCOPE	OTHER SCOPES INCLUDED	
		Promotion	Other activities
Austria	Die Werbung der Wirtschaft		
Belgium	Publicité		
France	Publicitè commerciale	X	
Germany	Die Werbung der Wirtschaft		
United Kingdom	Advertising in most media (Broadcast advertising)	X	Political advertising
Greece	"Advertising"		
Ireland	Advertising	X	
Italy	Pubblicità	X	"Pubblicità sociale"
Netherlands	Advertising		Idea advertising
Portugal	Publicidade		
Slovenia	Advertising		Political advertising
Spain	Publicidad comercial		
Switzerland	Publicité		Propagande politique

However, to go beyond *this instance of comparative analysis (which does not have only theoretical importance)*, it should be noted that *any exclusions or integrations of varying importance can exist* – with reference to the above concept of "commercial advertising" seen

as the lowest common denominator of the different concepts mentioned, and adopted by whichever code subjected to comparative
analysis – as referred both to the media used (for instance, point of
purchase advertising) and to specific material (packagings, tags, etc.).
All these aspects should be well known, especially to the advertisers.

Identification of advertisements (art. 11 - ICC Code)

Advertisements should be clearly distinguishable as such, whatever
their form and whatever the medium used; when an advertisement
appears in a medium which contains news or editorial matter, it should
be so presented that it will be readily recognized as an advertisement.
As for the need of a clear identification of advertising in the contexts
of the various communication media, it has led – in all the cases taken
into consideration – to the drawing up of the above-mentioned *ad hoc*
general rule, sometimes accompanied by a proper identification of the
advertisers. Definitely worth attention, as far as identification of
advertising is concerned, are:
– guidelines of ZAW as referred to printed advertisements (Germany);
– general rule n. 10 of Dutch Code (of which more will follow);
– general rule n. 3.14 recently introduced in the self-regulation code
   of Switzerland, and referring to the clear distinctions to be made
   between editorial matter and commercial communication; this rule
   has prohibited the use of disguised advertising and is accompanied
   by Rule n. 3.1 which states the obligation on the part of the advertisers to openly employ their business name.

The rule of the Dutch Code is also interesting for two reasons:
– it evokes (even if defined in a mitigated form[4]) the *discussed concept of "subliminal advertising"* which should, in fact, be treated
   and thoroughly examined, once and for all;
– it prohibits the employment of people in radio and television
   advertisements who, because of their participation in programmes
   in the media taken into consideration, can be considered – by cer-

---

4 "Subliminal techniques are techniques whereby inserted images and/or sounds of
   very brief duration are used in order to try to influence viewers or listeners –
   possibly without their being (or being able to be) aware of them." See also Rule
   n. 7 – *'Subliminal Advertising'*- of ITC Code.

tain segments of the audience – reliable and influential or who, in any case, can directly influence the audience. In this case also, it *is a very delicate matter which could involve journalists and presenters* who have acquired (in a specific field) sufficient influence and authority over the audience.

It is, however, to advertising – which should be clearly identified as such in all communication media[5], and the truthful presentation of which should be properly demonstrated – that the principles apply which are the subject of the following observations.

4. A Comparison Between Self-regulation Principles

The basic principles of self-regulation are contained in the International Code of the Chamber of Commerce and described
– analytically:
   Advertising should be legal, decent, honest and truthful.[6]
– and synthetically:
   Advertisements should be inspired by a sense of social responsibility and should conform to the principles of fair competition. Advertisements should also be such as not to impair public confidence in advertising.

Even before being translated into specific rules of conduct, these principles have been
– in a number of cases, openly mentioned in the foreword to various codes (Belgium, Greece, Slovenia, Spain);
– in some cases (France and Italy) they have been generically referred to and partially mentioned in the foreword.
In other cases, however: these principles have been
– directly referred to – totally or partially – within the rules of conduct which are sometimes named after said principles (for instance in the United Kingdom, Ireland, Netherlands and Portugal);
In one case (Switzerland) the principles examined have been mentioned in the contexts of the various rules.

---

5   Important as far as television is concerned is – by the way – Rule n. 5 of the above British ITC Code.
6   This principle is also quoted at the beginning of the above mentioned ITC Code.

Said principles have been presented with particular emphasis and have
been abundantly integrated in the case of the Slovenian Code where –
in the Introduction – it is declared as desirable that advertising should:
–   be boundless in the development of its creative possibilities;
–   conform to the ethics of democratic societies and to principles of
    conscience and honesty;
–   be responsible towards advertisers, consumers and the whole
    community;
–   be true to the fundamental principles of fair competition;
–   be aesthetically valid in its expression and compliant with the cul-
    tural context;
–   be related to the increase of business competition, of the develop-
    ment of the quality of life, of environment preservation and of the
    success of Slovenian society at an international level.

It shows emphasis and far-reaching intentions which could character-
ize not only Slovenia but other countries as well; countries which only
recently have opened to the market economy and, consequently, to
advertising as a tool, as interpreted by the so-called Western countries.
      The basic principles of self-regulation in advertising are directly
applied through the general rules of conduct which in the International
Code of the Chamber of Commerce correspond to the first 13 articles.
      As it appears at once, the basic principles – given the same foun-
dation of the codes here considered – are translated into corresponding
general rules in the most part of countries. Yet for some of these
(Austria and Germany in particular) the existing legislation should be
thoroughly examined to establish whether this makes any intervention
in the self-regulation unnecessary.
      Before trying to give any interpretation of the above data is, how-
ever, necessary to specify that:
a) the existence in various countries of rules regarding a specific
    basic principle does not necessarily mean that said principle has
    been extended and explained with corresponding thoroughness;
b) in some countries the same basic principle can generate two or
    more self-regulation rules;
c) sometimes a rule which specifically refers to a fundamental prin-
    ciple can be endorsed by the existence of a code, that is, of *ad hoc*
    rules.

Decency (art. 1)

Advertisements should not contain statements or visual presentations which offend against prevailing standards of decency.

As far as the general statement is concerned, the rules or guidelines proposed by the following countries are particularly detailed:
- in Austria about the subject of "Man and Woman in Advertising";
- in France about "The Image of Woman";
- in the United Kingdom about "Decency";
- in Ireland about "Taste and Decency", "Sexism and Sexual Stereotypes", and "Vulnerable Persons";
- in Slovenia about "Decency";
- in Switzerland about "Sexist Advertising", to be understood as advertisements debasing both sexes.

The fundamental concern highlighted by the above rules – within the already mentioned needs of not offending or debasing anybody with undue references to age, disabilities, race, religious creed, and sex – is the need to place man and woman on the same level of importance, to have regard for their dignity, to suggest the existence of real-life relationships between them and, in general, to contribute to the development of modern behaviour.

Incidentally, within the Irish Code there is a specific concern about advertising using terms – whenever proper and possible – belonging to both genders.

Honesty (art. 2 and 3)

Advertisements should be so framed as not to abuse the trust of the consumer or exploit his lack of experience or knowledge (art. 2).
1. Advertisements should not without justifiable reason play on fear.
2. Advertisements should not play on superstition.
3. Advertisements should not contain anything which might lead to or lend support to acts of violence.
4. Advertisements should avoid endorsing discrimination based upon race, religion or sex (art. 3).

These aspects have been taken into consideration by the self-regulation codes of all the countries examined.

Truthful Presentation (art. 4)

1. Advertisements should not contain any statement or visual presentation which directly or by implication, omission, ambiguity or exaggerated claim is likely to mislead the consumer, particularly regarding:
a) characteristics such as: nature, composition, method and date of manufacture, fitness for purpose, range of use, quantity, commercial or geographical origin;
b) the value of the product and the total price actually to be paid;
c) other terms of payment such as hire purchase, leasing, instalment sales and credit sales;
d) delivery, exchange, return, repair and maintenance;
e) terms of guarantee;
f) copyright and industrial property rights such as patents, trade marks, designs and models and trade names;
g) official recognition or approval, awards of medals, prizes and diplomas;
h) the extent of benefits for charitable causes.

2. Advertisements should not misuse research results or quotations from technical and scientific publications. Statistics should not be so presented as to imply a greater validity than they really have. Scientific terms should not be misused; scientific jargon and irrelevancies should not be used to make claims appear to have a scientific basis they do not possess.

This is a particularly complex subject where often the problems of validity and soundness of the guarantees offered and of a straight forward use of statistics and tests are expressed separately; only in some cases (United Kingdom and Ireland) the theme of *matters of opinion* is explicitly referred to.

Self-regulation in Switzerland is especially abundant in details and it specifies the possibilities and/or instructions for the use of words, phrases and characters (Swiss products, academic qualifications, etc.). Two issues have great relevance:
1. the problem of the use of "obvious aspects";
2. the acceptability of overstatements in advertising.
Let us start by examining the first of these issues, with specific reference to Swiss self-regulation, which prohibits "any advertisements which credit goods, works, products or services with special character-

istics" on the basis that it "is misleading and, therefore, unfair if said characteristics belong to the majority of the items produced or of the works of the same kind, or if said characteristics are intrinsic or pre-scribed" (Rule n. 3.7).

This is a particularly far-reaching and delicate question, given the manifold patterns (explicit and implicit, verbal and contextual, etc.) through which a characteristic – common to other products within the same market grade – can, in fact, be assigned (as if specific) to a par-ticular product, often being the first to do so in the market.

The issue of overstatements in advertising is also important. The question of its acceptability is strictly bound to the internal legislation and/or interpretation of existing laws prevailing in every country; therefore, we can find it only in four self-regulation codes (United Kingdom, Ireland, Italy and Slovenia).

It is natural to refer here to the concept of legality, that is, the conformity of advertising to the existing laws, a basic principle which, in many cases, is explicitly mentioned in the forewords to the various codes and, in other cases (Germany, United Kingdom, Ireland, Nether-lands and Slovenia), is considered a general rule of conduct. Concern-ing this, we would like to point out the relevant formulation adopted by the Italian code, which "[explicitly] defines the activities conflict-ing with the aims ... [pursued by the Code itself], even though com-pliant with the existing legislation ..." as a good example of the deli-cate relationship between self-regulation and domestic legislation.

The rules concerning the employment of testimonials and endorsements, and the protection of privacy are to be placed halfway between the concept of truthful presentation and responsibility.

Testimonials (art. 6)

Advertisements should not contain or refer to any testimonial or endorsement unless it is genuine and related to the experience of the person giving it. Testimonials or endorsements which are obsolete or otherwise no longer applicable should not be used.

Concerning this point, particularly relevant is the fact that, in the case of Spain, specific rules for advertising using testimonials have been defined, actually creating *ad hoc* rules with reference to a typological rating of said testimonials (expert, famous or popular testimonials and common testimonials).

Protection of privacy (art. 8)

Advertisements should not portray or refer to any persons, whether in a private or a public capacity, unless prior permission has been obtained; nor should advertisements without prior permission depict or refer to any person's property in a way likely to convey the impression of a personal endorsement.

Concerning the protection of the privacy of any person employed in advertising – directly through his/her name, presentation, and recognizable voice; or by implication through the use of his/her property (a use which should, therefore, be explicitly and duly authorized) – two are the issues to be taken into consideration:

- the first, of a general character, concerning the employment of doubles; in France, in this case, the person whose double is to be employed is asked specific permission, and sometimes advertisements have to explicitly mention the fact that a double is being employed;
- the second, of a specific character, relates to the prohibition, in the United Kingdom, of explicitly mentioning members of the Royal Family or of making use of royal emblems and/or coat of arms (Rule n. 13.5 of the relevant code).

As for the issue of the *social responsibility* of advertising, we should refer to the rules concerning regard for personal safety and those concerning advertisements addressed to children and young people.

Regard to safety (art. 12)

Advertisements should not without reason, justifiable on educational or social grounds, contain any visual presentation or any description of dangerous practices or of situations which show a disregard for safety. Special care should be taken in advertisements directed towards or depicting children or young people.

Concerning this point all codes taken into consideration refer to the need of indicating clearly any dangers resulting from the use of dangerous products – in particular when said products are not clearly indicated or recognizable as such – and of avoiding any description or visual presentation which could be dangerous because tending to reduce necessary care and vigilance.

Children and young people (art. 13)

1. Advertisements should not exploit the natural credulity of children or the lack of experience of young people and should not strain their sense of loyalty.
2. Advertisements addressed to or likely to influence children or young people should not contain any statement or visual presentation which might result in harming them mentally, morally or physically.

The above-mentioned rules, which refer to a particular segment of consumers, represent an introduction to sectorial rules or special codes, of which more will follow.

As far as the general rules are concerned, we are still to comment briefly on those which specifically refer to the practice of a fair competition among businesses: comparison and denigration, on the one hand; imitation and exploitation of goodwill on the other hand.

Comparisons (art. 5)

Advertisements containing comparisons should be so designed that the comparison itself is not likely to mislead, and should comply with the principles of fair competition. Points of comparison should be based on facts which can be substantiated and should not be unfairly selected.

The theme of comparison has a crucial importance, first of all as far as the acceptable forms (direct or by implication) of comparison with competitors are concerned, and also for the utmost care to be taken into consideration regarding this delicate matter (especially about the selection criteria which should regulate any comparisons, specific examples and points, and possibilities to demonstrate with facts the comparisons proposed).

It is true, as stated in the British code and in the greatly detailed Irish code, that comparison – even direct instances of it – with competitors is permitted as it is aimed at giving more and better information to consumers and at promoting strong competition, but it cannot be forgotten that comparison should not, in any case, be misleading or not compliant with the rules of fair competition.

These dangers are, of course, also present when the comparison is by implication, that is, when it generally involves all competitors of a particular corporation (by using, for instance, terms and expressions like "number one", "the leader", "the best" and so on).

Comparison is the object of self-regulation rules in the majority of the countries examined, while in the remaining countries (Austria, France, Germany and Slovenia) present legislation shall have to be further investigated – as previously noted for the two German-speaking countries – in order to determine if self-regulation rules[7] have been rendered unnecessary.

Common to all countries where comparison is the object of self-regulation rules are two conditions the compliance with which appears essential to the use of comparative advertising:
–   said advertising should not mislead consumers;
–   the principles of fair competition are to be complied with.
Moreover, the specific elements object of the comparisons should be selected clearly and be relevant and demonstrable.

Denigration (art. 7)

Advertisements should not denigrate any firm, industrial or commercial activity/profession or any product, directly or by implication, whether by bringing it into contempt or ridicule, or in any similar way.

The principle which forbids denigration of the competitors' trade name, activity, firm and products is general and generically stated.

Exploitation of goodwill (art. 9)

1. Advertisements should not make unjustifiable use of the name or initials of another firm, company or institution.
2. Advertisements should not take undue advantage of the goodwill attached to the name of a person, the trade name and symbol of another firm or product, or of the goodwill acquired by an advertising campaign.

---

[7]   Generally speaking, comparative advertising is, from the point of view of legislation:
   – accepted in France, United Kingdom, Ireland, Portugal and Spain;
   – forbidden in Belgium (with some exceptions) and Luxembourg;
   – lacking a specific legislation in Denmark, Germany, Italy and Netherlands.

Imitation (art. 10)

1. Advertisements should not imitate the general layout, text, slogan, visual presentation, music and sound effects, etc., of other advertisements in a way that is likely to mislead or confuse.

2. Where an international advertiser has established a distinctive advertising campaign in one or more countries, other advertisers should not unduly imitate this campaign in the other countries where he operates, thus preventing him from extending his campaign within a reasonable period of time to such countries.

As far as imitation or exploitation of goodwill are concerned, we should draw attention to the fact that imitation – or plagiarism, as it is sometimes called – is the object of an explicit prohibition (even if referred to elements which are isolated but essential to competitors' advertisements) in the majority of the countries examined, and the same can be said of the exploitation of competitors' goodwill (especially for trade marks, trade names, symbols or advertisements).

Concerning this point, particular relevance have all the elements referring to the advertising activity of international advertisers.

The sections, that is, the general rules of the codes taken into consideration, deal with – apart from the principles already examined – themes of more or less general nature:

- *themes linked to the product* (availability of the advertised product, guarantees, offer of products free of charge, etc.);
- *promotion* (discounts, gifts, coupons or vouchers free of charge and contests);
- *themes linked to particular approaches of advertising* (e.g., ecological advertising);
- *general subjects* as, for instance, in the case of the Netherlands (compliance of advertising with public interest, politics and morality [art. 3]; compliance of advertising with national physical or mental health [art. 4]) or of Slovenia (compliance of advertising with constitutional principles [art. 1], and responsibility of advertising towards society and consumers [art. 8])[8].

---

8 The Slovenian Code, due to its peculiar formulation, should be the object of a thorough and separate examination.

There are also the six special rules of the International Chamber of Commerce Code, which refer to:
- the guarantees, which are the object of specific rules – even if of general nature – in various countries (Belgium, United Kingdom, Ireland, Italy, Netherlands and Slovenia);
- advertising concerning the credit and finance sector in general (consumer credit, loans, savings and investments) which is the object of an *ad hoc* code in France, and of specific rules in six countries (United Kingdom, Ireland, Italy, Netherlands, Slovenia and Switzerland);
- unsolicited goods, which involve a very delicate sales method;
  - franchise schemes, which are the object of sectorial rules in France;
  - parallel imports;
  - poisonous and flammable goods, a theme which can be linked to the general rules regarding safety.

Of crucial relevance is then the issue of advertising addressed to children, the object of one of the general rules referring to children and young people, and subsequently taken once more into consideration by means of special rules of conduct, appendices and *ad hoc* codes (in Spain, for instance).

Significant for their extension and abundance of details are especially the special rules of the British Code of Advertising Practice (Rules n. 47.1 to 47.5) combined with the provisions contained in ITC Code, Appendix 1, the content of which has been operatively widened by points n. 3.1 to 3.6 of the Notes of Guidance of the Broadcast Advertising Clearance Centre.

The special section of the International Code represents – as foreseen, and unlike the general rules of the code itself – *a first, rudimentary draft* of the corresponding, extremely diversified structures of the various codes taken into consideration.

The high number and peculiarity of the fields disciplined either by sectorial rules or by special codes in the various countries can already be clearly seen in the synthesis outlined in the following table 3.

Table 3: *Fields disciplined by sectorial rules or special codes*

Sectors	Diciplined Fields	
	Number	Subtotals
Sectors of marketable goods		
- Widely-used consumer	11	
goods	7	
- Consumer durables	5	
- Investment goods	6	
- Services		29
Other sectors	7	
- Sales methods	5	
- Communication media	3	
- Advertising themes	9	
- Particular fields		24
Total		53

In this way, we have more than fifty fields of specific self-regulation intervention, as compared with the six fields of the ICC code.

Some sectors or fields are traditionally dealt with in the self-regulation systems of many countries (for example alcoholic drinks), while others have special characteristics (jewelry and precious metals) or refer to the development as far as the offer of services (remote teaching) is concerned, or highlight the refining of certain media (direct advertising) or the employment of particular themes (e.g., ecology).

What comes to immediate attention is the extremely diversified distribution of the above-mentioned fields among the various countries, ranging from a country like France, that presents more than thirty fields subjected to a specific advertising self-regulation, to a country like Portugal, that foresees no interventions of this kind.

With regard to this, it seems meaningful to classify the countries being examined into some large groups:

Table 4: *Intensity of the sectorial self-regulation presence*

- High-intensity countries (more than 15 disciplined fields)		France
- Medium-intensity countries (from 8 to 15 disciplined fields)		Belgium, United Kingdom, Ireland, Italy, Netherlands, Slovenia and Switzerland
- Low-intensity countries (from 0 to 7 disciplined fields)		Austria, Germany, Greece, Portugal and Spain

The situation appears directly linked to:
- *the legislations of the different countries;*
- *the fear of any interventions at this level* (within the individual countries or regarding the European Union);
- *the development of certain consumptions;*
- *the existence and importance of consumerist movements;*
- *the sensitivity of advertisers, professionals and communication media.*

All these are *immediately apparent factors.*

A *detailed and correct survey* of such a wide theme would obviously require a twofold analysis:
- *for each country,* in order to examine the totality of the fields which have been proposed at the level of self-regulation;
- *for each field* in all the countries taken into consideration.

With regard to the latter point, it is of no slight interest to observe how frequently the various fields of sectorial self-regulation intervention occur within the countries taken into consideration:

Table 5: *Frequency of self-regulation intervention in the specific fields*

Frequency of Regulation ------------------------------ Fields	The field appears disciplined in:				
	one country only	2-3 countries	4-6 countries	More than 6 countries	Total fields examined
- Fields referred to sectors of marketable goods	15	5	8	1	29
- Fields referred to sales methods, advertising themes and media, etc.	17	4	3	-	24
	32	9	11	1	53

As shown by table 5, the large majority of the fields taken into consideration, with reference to a specific regulation, appears to undergo the self-regulation intervention in one country only; on the other hand, one field only (that of the alcoholic drinks) results to be specifically disciplined in more than six countries[9].

In conclusion, something worthy to be mentioned is the fact that the analysis of the self-regulation system – to which the research promoted by my University is referred – involves other codes in addition to the Advertising Code (International Code of Sales Promotion, of Direct Mail and Mail Order, etc.). Said codes will therefore be the object of analysis in further papers.

---

[9] A more detailed analysis of such a situation is the object of my contribution on *"I principi dell'autodisciplina pubblicitaria in Europa"*, published in: Problemi di gestione dell'impresa, 23, 1997.

About the Authors

Luk Bouckaert *(Catholic University of Leuven, Belgium)*
is professor of „Ethics and Economics" at the Katholieke Universiteit
Leuven (Catholic University Leuven). He started with some of his
colleagues the „Centre for Economics and Ethics" in 1987 in the University's Faculty of Economics and Applied Economics. His recent
research and publications are in the field of social responsibility in
profit and non-profit organisations

Edoardo Teodoro Brioschi *(Catholic University of Milan, Italy)*
was born in 1941 in Milan. He studied at the Faculty of Economics
and Commerce of the Catholic University of the Sacred Heart, where
he graduated in 1963. In 1965 he began a collaboration with Professor
Mario Apollonio, the founder of the School of Specialization in Mass
Communications of the same University. In 1971 this school asked
him to teach the „Advertising Doctrine and Technique", and he
became the first Italian professor of „Advertising Economics and
Technique" in 1980, when this Chair was established at the Faculty of
Economics. In 1995 this Faculty approved his transfer to the newly
established Chair of „Business Communication Economics and Technique". He is author of about 70 works concerning business communication and marketing.

Björn Erik Dahlberg *(Hydro Aluminium, Norway)*
has a background from industry, first as an occupational health physi-
cian, later as a corporate medical doctor and the last nine years as head
of Personell, Organization and Competence and Environment, Health,
and Safety in Hydro Aluminium. Hydro Aluminium was founded in
1986 through a merger between the two largest aluminium groups in
Norway, ASV and the aluminium division of Norsk Hydro a.s., and
has been through a major transformation process since then.

Ugo Draetta *(General Electric, London & University of Milan, Italy)*
has been for more than 30 years with the General Electric Company
(USA), where he is presently Vice President and Senior International
Counsel, based in London. He has also been part time teacher of vari-

ous international law courses for more than thirty years at the Catholic University of Milan, where he is currently a Professor of European Union Law at the Faculty of Political Sciences. Ugo Draetta is author of many books on International and EC Law, and he is co-editor of the journal „Diritto del Commercio Internazionale". Further, he is Member of the International Advisory Council of Transparency International, and Member of the Scientific Committee if ISDACI (Institute for the Study of International Trade Law, Milan).

Peter Duncan *(Deutsche Shell AG, Germany)*
was born in Fulmer, Buckinghamshire, England. He received a degree in Chemical Engineering from Canterbury University (New Zealand) and a degree in Business Studies from the London School of Economics. Duncan began his association with Shell as a trainee for the Shell International Petroleum Co. (London). Since then, he has worked in a number of Shell locations, such as Venezuela, Curacao, Singapore, Switzerland, The Hague, and Australia. His special area of concentration has been in financial evaluations and publications. Duncan has been the CEO of Deutsche Shell AG since July 1992.

Peter Eigen *(Transparency International, Germany)*
is a lawyer by training. He has worked in economic development for 25 years, mainly as a World Bank manager of programs in Africa and Latin America. Under Ford Foundation sponsor-ship, he provided legal technical assistance to the governments of Botswana and Namibia, and he taught law at Frankfurt and Georgetown Universities. From 1988 to 1991 he was the Director of the Regional Mission for Eastern Africa of the World Bank. Mr. Eigen was one of the initiators of Transparency International (TI) and is Chairman of the Board of this global organization promoting transparency and accountability in international development.

Warren French *(University of Georgia, Athens/GA, USA)*
is a Professor of Marketing and I. W. Cousins Professor of Business Ethics at the University of Georgia. He earned a Ph.D. in Marketing from Penn State, an M.S. in Marketing from L.S.U. and an A.B. in Philosophy from St. Anselm's College. Professor French is involved in research which focuses on several areas: marketing strategy, relation-

ship marketing and conflict resolution. The co-author of two books, his work has appeared in the Journal of Marketing, European Journal of Marketing, Journal of Business, Journal of the Market Research Society, Journal of Advertising, and the Journal of Advertising Research, as well as in 20 other Journals.

Carl Friedrich Gethmann (*University of Essen, Germany*)
was born in 1944, studied Philosophy in Bonn, Innsbruck and Bochum. In 1968, he received his lic.phil. (Institutum Philosophicum Oenipontanum); in 1971, his PhD (Ruhr- University of Bochum); in 1978, his postdoctoral lecturing degree in Philosophy (University of Konstanz). In 1972, he was a lecturer of Philosophy at the University of Essen. Since 1979, he has been a professor of Philosophy at the University of Essen with further educational duties at the Universities of Düsseldorf and Göttingen. He has been employed as a full professor at the Universities of Oldenburg (1990), Essen (1991), Konstanz (1993), and Bonn (1995). Since 1996 he is Director of the European Academy for the study of Consequences of Scientific and Technological Advance, Bad Neuenahr-Ahrweiler GmbH. He is a member of the Academia Europaea (London). His areas of publication and research are language philosophy, logic of scientific theory, and responsibility as an ethical problem regarding the environment.

Frene Ginwala (*Speaker of the South African Parliament*).
Hon. Dr. Ginwala left South Africa as a student to arrange the escape of the late O.R. Tambo and completed her studies while in exile. Her academic achievements include an LL.B, PhD, and Barrister at Law. She is currently a member and the Speaker of the National Assembly in the Parliament of the Republic of South Africa and a member of the Constitutional Committee of the Constitutional Assembly. Among her many ANC duties, she is the Chair of the ANC Committee responsible for the retrieval and deposit of ANC archives. Her primary areas of research are South Africa, Conflict Research, Women's Issues, and Development and Technology Transfer.

Thomas Kieselbach (*University of Hannover, Germany*)
was born in Bielefeld (FRG), studied Psychology, Sociology and Education at the University of Münster, where he worked as a scientific

assistant in the Institute of Psychology from 1974-1977. He received his doctoral degree in Psychology at the University of Bremen in 1977 where he has worked since then as a researcher in the Department of Psychology. Habilitation on "Psychological Unemployment Research" in 1989. Since 1993 he has been Professor for Health Psychology at the Institute of Psychology of the University of Hannover and head of the Research Unit Work, Unemployment and Personality Develop-ment of the Department of Psychology at the University of Bremen. He has been temporary adviser to the WHO in the program "Social Equity and Health." Since 1990 editor of the book series "Psychology of Social Inequality". His special areas of research are psychosocial consequences of unemployment, health psychology and community psychology, where he focuses on the development of outplacement/ replacement concepts for a social guidance of occupational trasitions.

Peter Koslowski *(Hannover Institute of Phil. Research, Germany)*
is Director of the Centre for Ethical Economy and Business Culture, The Hannover Institute of Philosophical Research, Hannover, Ger-many. He is a member of the Kuratorium of the DNWE and editor of the Springer book series "Studies in Economic Ethics and Philoso-phy," „Ethische Ökonomie" (in German), „Eticheskaya Ekonomia" (in Russian, together with V. Avtonomov, St. Petersburg), .and „Ethical Economy" (in Chinese, together with Y. Chen, Beijing).

Heiko Lange *(Deutsche Lufthansa AG, Frankfurt/M. Germany)*
was born in Breslau on April 28, 1938. After studying in Bonn, Cologne and Graz and finishing with a PhD, he began his professional career as research assistant at the Employer's Association in Cologne. In 1966, he moved to ITT, where he held various positions in human resources and organisation functions in Germany, latterly as Director Personnel and Administration of the Private Communications Division Europe in Brussels from 1979-1981. In 1981, Lange was appointed member of the Executive Board of Porsche AG in Stuttgart. In 1986, the Lufthansa Supervisory Board appointed Lange Member of the Executive Board and Chief Executive Human Resources. He is currently also President of the (world-wide) Airline Personnel Direc-tors Conference, and Chairman of the Board of the German Associa-tion of Personnel Management (DGFP).

Klaus M. Leisinger *(Novartis Foundation, Basel, Switzerland)*
studied economics and social sciences at the University of Basel,
Switzerland. His post-graduate work focused among others on sustainable development issues as well as different aspects of private
investment in Developing Countries. His Business assignments
include a four year term as manager of Ciba Pharmaceuticals in East
Africa. Since 1990, Klaus Leisinger has been Executive Director and
Delegate of the Board of Trustees of the Ciba-Geigy Foundation for
Cooperation with Developing Countries (now: Novartis Foundation).
In addition to his current position at Novartis, he is Professor of
development sociology at the University of Basel and serves on different national and international organizations dealing with sustainable
development as adviser (e.g. the Committee for International Devel-
opment Cooperation of the Swiss Federal Council and the Expert
Group of the Swiss National Science Foundation). In 1994 he was
elected ordinary member of the European Academy of Science and
Arts; in 1996 he became a founding board member of UNDP's "Global
Development Fund".

Albert Löhr *(University of Erlangen-Nürnberg, Germany)*
born in 1955, is a senior lecturer at the Chair for Business Administration and Management, University of Erlangen-Nürnberg. He is a
member of both the Executive Committee of the European Business
Ethics Network (EBEN) and the Deutsches Netzwerk Wirtschaftsethik
(DNWE), and he chaired the Programme Committee of the 9th annual
conference of EBEN in 1996. He is also a member of the editorial
board of Blackwell's „Business Ethics: A European Review". Many of
his publications are on business ethics, including his dissertation, for
which he was awarded the first "Max-Weber-Preis für Wirtschaftsethik 1992".

Thomas Maak *(University of St. Gallen, Switzerland)*
was born in Bielefeld. He studied business administration in Bielefeld
and Bayreuth, where he graduated in 1992. In 1993 he was a lecturer
at the University of Dresden. In that same year he started with his
doctoral studies at the University of St. Gallen. He has been a research
assistant at the Institute of Business Ethics since 1995. His areas of
research are political philosophy & economics, and business ethics.

Bernd Mühlfriedel *(University of Erlangen-Nürnberg, Germany)*
has been studying for nearly four years at the University of Erlangen-Nuremberg with emphasis on Management and Controlling. After receiving an MBA from the University of Georgia in June 1996, he returned to Nuremberg to complete his studies before his anticipated graduation as a Diplom-Kaufmann in October 1997. At both universities, he also studied Business Ethics at the faculties of Prof. Dr. Horst Steinmann and Prof. Warren French. Bernd Mühlfriedel has freelancing and internship experience with Procter & Gamble, Roland Berger & Partner, F&S International, Inc., Fergusson Wild & Co. Ltd., GfK AG and Bayerische Vereinsbank.

Karl Theodor Paschke *(United Nations, New York)*
a native of Germany, assumed his duties as Under-Secretary-General for Internal Oversight Services on 15 Nov 1994. His office is composed of the Audit and Management Consulting Division, the Central Evaluation Unit, the Central Monitoring and Inspection Unit and the Investigations Section. Prior to this five-year fixed-term appointment with the United Nations, Mr. Paschke served as Director General for Personnel and Management of the German Foreign Office until July 1990. In this capacity, he was responsible for the entire staff of the German Foreign Service (more than 8000 persons), for the management of the central office in Bonn and the more than 200 missions abroad. Before that, he was Deputy Chief of Mission of Germany's largest bilateral mission, the Embassy in Washington, D.C. for three years. He has also served as German Ambassador to the UN and other international organizations in Vienna and Austria, and as a Press Spokesman of the German Foreign Office (1980-1984).

Mark Pieth *(University of Basel, Switzerland)*
is a professor of Criminal Law, Criminal Procedure and Criminology at the University of Basel. He is the former head of the Section on Economic and Organized Crime in the Swiss Federal Office of Justice (responsible for legislation on money laundering and organized crime from 1989-1993). He was a member of the Financial Action Task Force from 1989 - 1993 and a member of the Chemical Action Task Force from 1990 - 1993. In 1990, he was Chairman of the UN Inter-governmental Expert Group to Study the Economic and Social Conse-

quences of the Illicit Traffic in Drugs. He is currently the Chairman of the OECD-Expert Group on Bribery in International Commercial Transactions and Chairman of the Expert Council of the National Research Program on Violence and Organized Crime of the Swiss National Fund.

Nicola Pless *(University of St. Gallen, Switzerland)*
was born in Osnabrück. She studied business administration in Bielefeld and Bayreuth, where she graduated in 1992. In 1993 she worked in Dresden teaching accounting and marketing to former East-German judges and public prosecutors. Since 1994 she has been a doctoral student at the University of St. Gallen and research assistant at the Department of Organizational Psychology. Her special areas of research are: intercultural and environmental management, dual career couples and theory of leadership.

Gerrit Popkes *(Institut f. Wirtschafts und Sozialethik, Rostock, Germany)*
born in 1965 in Weidenau/Germany, studied business administration in Göttingen with main emphasis on management and marketing. From 1990 until 1993 he started his professional career first as a business analyst then as a consultant at Roland Berger & Partner in Berlin. During that time, for 1 1/2 years, he worked in the "Treuhandanstalt " Berlin where he prepared valuations of East-German companies. In 1993 he decided to get his doctorate and started studying philosophy in Berlin. Since 1994 he has been working as an academic assistant for the "Institut für Wirtschafts- und Sozialethik" (IWS) in Rostock – mainly on studies refering the transformation-process in East-German companies and on business ethics training.

Kati Rieger *(Inst. f. Wirtschafts- und Sozialethik, Rostock, Germany)*
was born in 1967 in Wismar/Germany. She finished her studies in economy and management at the Technical University of Wismar and the Noordelijke Hogeschool in Leeuwarden/Netherlands in 1992. Subquently she obtained a one-year practical course grant within the EU-COMETT-Programm and worked in tourism management at the hotel business of Chania/Greece. Returned to Germany in 1994, she studied European Business in Rostock. Since 1995 she has worked as

an academic assistant at the Institute of Business- and Social Ethics in Rostock. Her fields of activity are management education and research in the East-German transformation-process.

Hans-Jörg Schlierer *(ESC Lyon, France)*
was born in Stuttgart, Germany, and received his MA in French and German Literature from the university there in 1991. From 1989 onwards, he has been active as a trainer in German language and business culture in French companies, and in 1993 he became a full-time member of the department of Intercultural Communication and Linguistics at the Groupe ESC Lyon. He is presently preparing a thesis in the field of intercultural communication at the Uni. of Saarbrücken and, in particular, is carrying out research into comparative financial reporting.

Fred Seidel *(ESC Lyon, France)*
graduated in French, History and Political Science from the University of Marburg in Germany. He is Professor of Business History and Comparative Management at the Groupe ESC Lyon in France and has been head of the Department of Intercultural Communication & Linguistics since 1987. He has published a number of articles related to his main research interests: ethics in international business and history of business systems, and, in particular, co-ordinated and edited the *Guide pratique et théorique de l'Ethique des Affaires et de l'Entreprise* (Paris, ESKA, 1995).

Horst Steinmann *(University of Erlangen-Nürnberg, Germany)*
born 1934, holds a Chair in Business Administration and Management at the University of Erlangen-Nürnberg. For more than 25 years his research has centred on the philosophical foundation of management theory. He is Chairman of the "Deutsches Netzwerk Wirtschaftsethik", established in 1993, a national branch of the European Business Ethics Network, where he served on the Executive Committee for 8 years. He is also a member of several editorial and advisory boards of business ethics journals (Journal of Business Ethics, Revue Ethique des Affairs, Business Ethics: A European Review) and of a book series (Kluwer Issues in Business Ethics). His numerous publications focus on issues in Strategic Management, Corporate Governance, and Business Ethics.

Recent book publications as author or co-author include: Grundlagen der Unternehmensethik; Unternehmensethik; Lexikon der Wirtschaftsethik; European Casebook on Business Ethics.

Ian Tovey *(ESC Lyon, France)*
was born in Birmingham, GB, and received his first degree in Modern Languages from the University of Oxford in 1980. After holding a post as assistant at the University of Lyon II, he became a full-time member of the department of Intercultural Communication and Linguistics of the Groupe ESC Lyon in 1988 and was nominated Assistant Dean for International Relations the following year. His research into comparative management education systems led to a number of presentations and articles in international conference. During this period he took a DESS in Business Administration.

Jürgen Weber *(Deutsche Lufthansa AG, Frankfurt/M. Germany)*
was born in Lahr in 1941. He studied aeronautical engineering at Stuttgart's Technical University. After receiving his degree in 1965 he remained at the university, working on the statics and dynamics of aerospace design. Weber joined Lufthansa's Engineering Division at Hamburg in 1967. He moved to Frankfurt in 1974, where he was Director of the Line Maintenance Department. In 1978 he returned to Hamburg to take over the Aircraft Engineering Subdivision. In 1980 he graduated from the Massachusetts Institute of Technology's Senior Management Training pro-gramme, having specialized in Business Administration. Weber was appointed by the Lufthansa Executive Board as Chief Operating Officer/Technical in 1987. In this capacity he headed the Technical Division, answering directly to German's Federal Civil Aviation Administration on questions of aircraft maintenance and overhaul. He was also responsible for the division's profitability. With effect from April 1, 1989 Weber was Deputy Member of the Executive Board. He became Chief Executive/Technical on Jan. 1, 1990. Since Oct. 1990 Weber also has been Deputy Chairman of the Executive Board. On May 14, 1991 the Supervisory Board unanimously elected Weber Chaiman of the Executive Board. He assumed this responsibility officialy on Sept. 1, 1991.

Issues in Business Ethics

1. G. Enderle, B. Almond and A. Argandoña (eds.): *People in Corporations. Ethical Responsibilities and Corporate Effectiveness.* 1990
   ISBN 0-7923-0829-8
2. B. Harvey, H. van Luijk and G. Corbetta (eds.): *Market Morality and Company Size.* 1991   ISBN 0-7923-1342-9
3. J. Mahoney and E. Vallance (eds.): *Business Ethics in a New Europe.* 1992
   ISBN 0-7923-1931-1
4. P.M. Minus (ed.): *The Ethics of Business in a Global Economy.* 1993
   ISBN 0-7923-9334-1
5. T.W. Dunfee and Y. Nagayasu (eds.): *Business Ethics: Japan and the Global Economy.* 1993   ISBN 0-7923-2427-7
6. S. Prakash Sethi: *Multinational Corporations and the Impact of Public Advocacy on Corporate Strategy.* Nestle and the Infant Formula Controversy. 1993   ISBN 0-7923-9378-3
7. H. von Weltzien Hoivik and A. Føllesdal (eds.): *Ethics and Consultancy: European Perspectives.* 1995   ISBN Hb 0-7923-3377-2; Pb 0-7923-3378-0
8. P. Ulrich and C. Sarasin (eds.): *Facing Public Interest.* The Ethical Challenge to Business Policy and Corporate Communications. 1995
   ISBN 0-7923-3633-X; Pb 0-7923-3634-8
9. H. Lange, A. Löhr and H. Steinmann (eds.): *Working Across Cultures.* Ethical Perspectives for Intercultural Management. 1998
   ISBN 0-7923-4700-5

KLUWER ACADEMIC PUBLISHERS – DORDRECHT / BOSTON / LONDON